Hull, Hell and – Fire

Ron Sagar, MBE

Highgate of Beverley

Highgate Publications (Beverley) Limited
1999

Acknowledgements

It is impossible for me to express my appreciation to all those people who gave their professional support during the enquiry and its aftermath.

To the team of detectives who remained with the investigation from beginning to end I owe a special word of gratitude. No matter how demanding the days, weeks and months, they often gave me bright smiles, dedication and friendly support. No words can express the respect and admiration I have for them and I doubt that any senior detective could ever ask for more from any investigation team. They are Alan Young, Geoff Walker, Ray Harrod, Paul Bacon, Colin Moore, Mick Trafford, Ollie Barry, Dave Everingham, Mick Sothcott, Steve Harman, Janet Peterson, Dick Connelly, Mick Fieldhouse, Dave Lewis, John Richardson, Kevin Sutton, John Martin, Tony Stead, Graham Bocock, Peter Nesbitt, John Guy, Geoff Sygrove, Alan Holmes and Gordon Bird.

Special thanks go to Graham Davenport and Roy Cooke, the two forensic scientists, whose expertise I shall always admire.

To the members of the legal profession who took it upon themselves to offer me words of support and encouragement when I was fighting to maintain my good name, I express my deep gratitude.

I must also express my thanks to certain members of the criminal fraternity who, in their own way, with touches of humour, offered support when my credibility was at stake. I asked no favours of them but by their very nature they helped restore my belief in fair play and justice.

Finally I wish to record my gratitude to the Chairman of my Regional Crime Squad Committee, the late Charles Brady, who with Councillor Graham Stroud and all the members of the Humberside Police Authority backed me financially when I was facing bankruptcy and the loss of my career and home. Charles Brady put his head on the line when I was almost at my wit's end with mounting financial pressure before my libel case. His faith in my integrity saved my family and me from complete disaster. I shall forever be indebted to him. Bless you, Charles.

British Library Cataloguing in Publication Data.
A catalogue record for this book is available from the British Library.

© 1999 Ronald Sagar

ISBN 1 902645 06 5

Published by

Highgate of Beverley

Highgate Publications (Beverley) Limited
4 Newbegin, Beverley, HU17 8EG. Telephone (01482) 886017

Produced by

ba*print*

4 Newbegin, Beverley, HU17 8EG. Telephone (01482) 886017

To my wife, Phyllis

Claims of Fire
North Hull Estate.

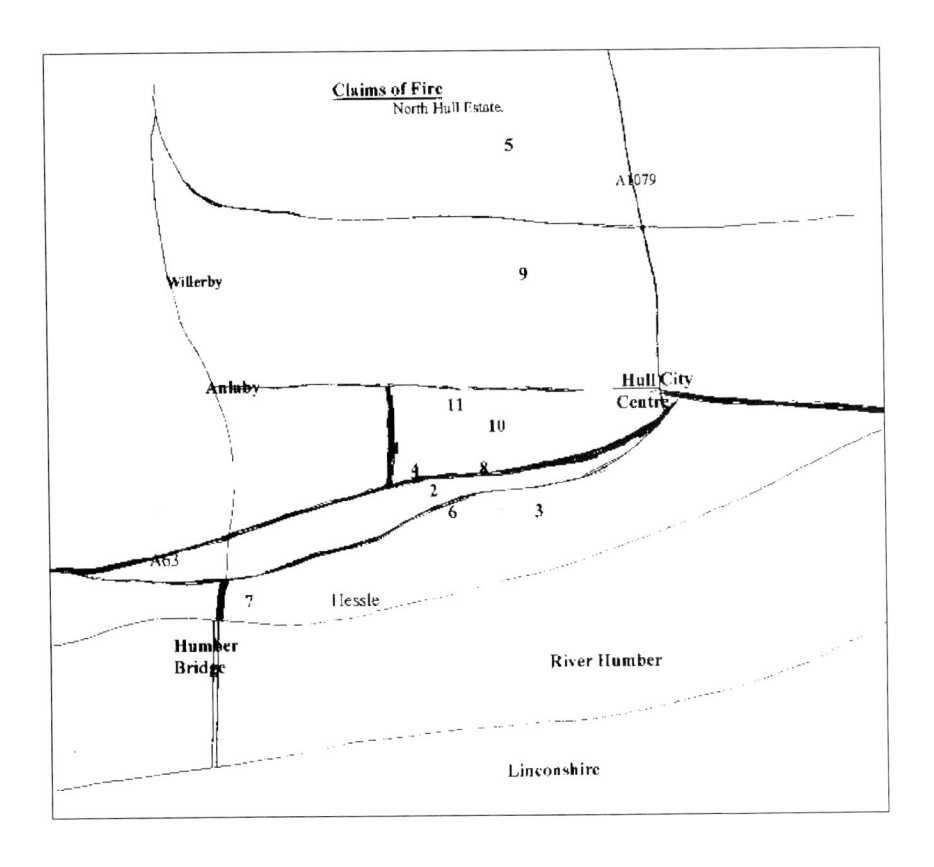

1. 23 June 1973, Askew Avenue, Richard Ellerington, 6.
2. 12 October 1973, Glasgow Street, Bernard Smythe, 72.
3. 27 October 1973, Humber Buildings, David Brewer, 34.
4. 23 December 1974, Minnies Terrace, Elizabeth Rokahr, 82.
5. 3 June 1976, Gorthorpe, Andrew Edwards, 12 months.
6. 2 January 1976, West Dock Avenue, Katrina Thacker, 6 months.
7. 5 January 1977, Wensley Lodge, 11 elderly men.
8. 27 April 1977, Rosamond Street, Mark Jordon, 7; Deborah Hooper, 13.
9. 6 January 1978, Reynoldson Street, Christine Dickson, 24; Mark Dickson, 5; Steven Dickson, 4; Michael Dickson, 16 months.
10. Troutbeck House, Rosabell Fenton, 27; Samantha Fenton, 8 (both survived after severe burns)
11. 4 December 1979, Selby Street, Charles Hastie, 15; Paul Hastie, 12; Peter Hastie, 8.

Contents

Map iv

Author's Preface vii

Foreword viii

Arson
Chapters 1-4 1

House Fires
Chapters 5-10 36

Inquests
Chapters 11-20 81

Trial
Chapter 21 125

Aftermath
Chapter 22-24 132

Appeal
Chapter 25-27 147

Libel
Chapter 28 180

Detective Superintendent Ronald Sagar at the time of the investigation.
(Picture by courtesy of *Hull Daily Mail*)

Author's Preface

Between June 1973 and December 1979, 26 people died in ten house fires in the Hull area. In the first nine fires 23 deaths were recorded by H.M. Coroner as misadventure, and the fires as accidental.

The tenth fire, in December 1979, was recorded as arson when it was discovered that paraffin had been poured through the letter-box and set alight at the front doorway of a house late at night. Three schoolboys died from their burns and police recorded their deaths as murder. The police had no witnesses and no suspects.

This book is about the investigation into the tragic deaths of the 26 people who lost their lives. It is also about the unhappy and lonely life of Bruce George Peter Lee and his claims to starting the fires, claims that echoed and rumbled about my head and underlined the dreadful reality of it all, and it bothered me tremendously.

I became involved in all this in December 1979 when I was called upon to investigate the deaths of Edith Hastie's three schoolboy sons. Her loss and the death of her husband in a road accident a few months later were so profound and her pain so deep that the thought of what she endured filled my mind with intense anguish. I remain full of admiration of her courage and strength at times of such adversity.

I am, of course, mindful of the sadness and suffering of all the victims and, for many years, was loathe to compound their agony by telling this story. Now, however, 20 years later, I feel that the time is right to explain, in some detail, and in the public interest, all that happened. I must add that this book is not a glory-seeking detective story, nor is it a story to damn Bruce Lee. That is not, and never has been, my intention. Also, it is not about money. In fact various charities will benefit from my royalties. I would never wish to make money from other people's sadness or Bruce Lee's pitiful life. All I am doing is telling an honest-to-goodness story.

My investigation did not discover all the answers, but then there is no such thing as a perfect investigation, just as there is no such thing as a perfect murder.

Ronald Sagar

Foreword

by
HIS HONOUR JACK WALKER, DL

Arson is one of the most wretched crimes in the criminal calendar. It is also one of the most difficult for the police to investigate, because, as in the case of Bruce Lee, there is often no obvious motive for burning down houses and killing children asleep in their beds.

It is only by the most thorough enquiries and meticulous attention to detail, coupled with an experienced detective's intuition and understanding of human frailty, that such crimes are solved.

I first met Ron Sagar when he was a young Detective Constable in the Hull Police Force and I was starting an uncertain career at the Bar. When I received a brief to appear at Assizes or Quarter Sessions I naturally turned to see who the important witnesses were and if the key witness was the author of this book I preferred to find myself prosecuting rather than defending. This was not just because of his fairness in giving evidence (in my experience nearly all policemen try to achieve that) but because of his ability to get into the mind of the men with whom he dealt.

There are many offenders who, like Bruce Lee, have suffered appalling disadvantages in life; no parents, a childhood spent in institutions and different homes, spastic disability and lack of education, but this book graphically illustrates Ron Sagar's initial disbelief that a young man, even with this background, could have developed into a serial arsonist who had caused the deaths of so many people in Hull. This is not just an account of a painstaking, and at times painful, investigation into an awesome series of crimes but also of the trust that can develop between a suspect and his accuser.

It also recounts an unexpected sequel to the story of Bruce Lee.

Chapter One

'I am going home, Ron. I've had enough for one Monday,' announced Bob Dixon, the Operations Detective Superintendent. 'Yes, that's a good idea,' I said. 'I've done enough for today too, but hold on a minute, Bob. I'll walk down to the car park with you'. I cleared my desk of some remaining papers, locked the door, and we left the C.I.D. Headquarters in Hull City centre. Bob Dixon and I were good friends and colleagues. We had both been promoted through the various ranks over the past 20 years and were now Detective Superintendents. I was then the Deputy Head of the C.I.D.

Bob had been on duty throughout the weekend and he had been out attending to a variety of matters. Being in something of a benevolent mood I said, 'You've had more than enough this weekend, Bob. I'll take the calls tonight. You'd best catch up with your sleep.' 'No, it's my job,' he replied. 'Never mind whose job it is. You deserve a rest, Bob. I'll contact the Operations Room and tell them to pass any important calls over to me. You get some sleep. After all, it's Monday night – there's never much trouble on Monday nights.' We chatted for a few more moments and then made our separate ways home.

Being the senior detective 'on call' was mostly a question of giving advice following contact by telephone. Only occasionally, in very serious cases, the 'on call detective' was required to actually attend the scene of crime. Should this happen it would sometimes mean taking over the investigation and continuing the enquiry.

I had recently moved into a rather large house on Holderness High Road and, in choosing to do much of the decorating myself, could ill afford to give up any precious off-duty time. In fact, our hallway was half decorated and my wife and I were naturally keen to complete the job before Christmas.

It was about 4 o'clock the following morning when the telephone rang beside my bed. 'We have a problem down in Selby Street,' said the Operations Room duty officer. 'There's has been a fire in the house where the Hastie family live. Five of the family have been taken to hospital suffering from burns. Three of them are very badly burned. The house has been gutted and arson is suspected. The Divisional Chief Inspector is asking for you to attend.'

As I took a quick shower I decided to be more cautious about volunteering to cover anyone's night duty in future. However, I drove to Selby Street as quickly as I could. It was still dark. I noted the time: 4.45 a.m., some 3½ hours before daylight on the first Tuesday of December 1979. Stepping from my car I saw Fire Brigade officers were damping down the smouldering council house at No. 12. It was brick-built and situated at the corner of an L-shaped block, set some 50 yards back from the road.

Scenes of Crime Officer, Detective Constable Frank Munns, who had arrived in Selby Street some time before me, told me he had found two spent matches on the concrete near to and just below the letter-box. He had preserved the scene for a full forensic examination later in the morning. Several uniformed police officers were there too. The weather was mild and a light rain was beginning to fall and glisten around the street lamps. A gentle breeze blew from time to time. I glanced around the adjacent rather drab houses and saw several neighbours peering from behind curtains. 'It looks as if it started just inside the front door,' said a fire officer, as I began to take stock of the situation. A police officer standing guard nearby told me that three young boys in the Hastie family had been found in the front bedroom and were so badly burned that their chances of survival were grim. They were now on their way to the Specialist Burns Unit in Wakefield, 60 miles away. 'They were little terrors around here but they didn't deserve to be burned alive,' called a woman neighbour.

Standing alone a few feet away from the front door of No. 12 I could smell paraffin. I sniffed the air rather loudly. A passing fireman said, 'Yes, that's paraffin you can smell.' How could I smell paraffin after such a fire? Surely, if paraffin had been used to start the fire it would have been swallowed up in the fire. I took a careful look about me and along the path leading to the door. Bits of rubbish were occasionally blowing about nearby. In the light of the street lamps I could also see what appeared to be a damp circle about four inches in diameter on the concrete path several feet back from the front doorway. I took a closer look and realised by the smell that the circle was of paraffin, as if a container of some sort had been put down there, I guessed it had been put down there after the contents had been used; otherwise there would not have been the drains of paraffin from the can on the concrete. The smell of paraffin was unmistakeable; but where was the paraffin can?

With Constable Munns I examined the scene around the door further. The letter-box was fitted in the wooden frame at the centre of two frosted panes of glass at the side of the door. The whole of the framework was badly charred, and we could also see the burned fragments of net curtains hanging limply near the ceiling inside. The fire left us with no chance of seeking any fingerprint evidence about the letter-box. Nevertheless, after careful examination, we came to the conclusion that someone had poured some paraffin through the letter-box and set it alight. We could see by the extent of the burning that the seat of the fire appeared to be just below the letter-box, inside the house in the hall, and directly at the bottom of the stairs. But our examination was merely a preliminary look. I needed expert evidence as to the cause and quickly arranged for a scientist to attend from the Home Office Forensic Laboratory at Wetherby as soon as possible. There was no doubt in my mind. This was a serious case of arson.

What a sad burnt-out home it was now: a home which only a few hours earlier was bubbling with children's voices, no doubt looking forward to Christmas, just three weeks away. Who would pour paraffin into the house in the middle of the night and set it alight, knowing that people were sleeping upstairs? Edith Hastie and four of her children had been asleep in the house and were now badly burned and receiving hospital treatment.

Edith's husband, Tommy, had several convictions and had recently been imprisoned for burglary. Was Tommy still in prison? I knew him as one of the most likeable petty criminals I was ever likely to meet. And where were the other children in the family? I knew that Edith and Tommy had more than four children. Most of the detectives in the City knew of Tommy Hastie and his family. My first question was soon answered. Tommy was still serving a 12-month prison sentence for burglary. He had been arrested with his schoolboy son, Charlie, just a few months earlier after they had cheekily burgled Hull Rugby League Club just a few 100 yards from their home. It was said at the court hearing that Charlie had been led on by his father, so in their wisdom the magistrates simply imposed a £5 fine on the unemployed schoolboy!

Now, however, the injured party was the Hastie family. We had to know the circumstances when Edith went to bed earlier that night – and where were the other members of the family? We soon discovered that at bedtime Edith, aged 34, was at home with her four sons. Charlie, who had just had his fifteenth birthday, went to bed in the top bunk in the front bedroom upstairs. Paul, 12-years-old, and his brother Peter, who was just eight-years-old, shared the bottom bunk, where every night they were joined by their faithful crossbred Alsatian dog, Rinny. Edith slept in the back bedroom with her son, Thomas, aged nine. He suffered from muscular dystrophy and had great difficulty in walking.

Fortunately Edith's three daughters, Angeleena (16), Nicola (11), and Sonia (8), were staying overnight with friends and relatives. It must have been one hell of a nightmare being caught up in that uncontrolled blaze in the confined space of the small council house bedroom. In trying to cover all possibilities, it did cross my mind that perhaps, just perhaps, one of the girls could have returned to set the house on fire. But, no, they would never do it. After all, I knew that all Edith's children thought the world of their mother and the family simply lived for each other.

I saw Edith in Hull Royal Infirmary later in the day. She was suffering from an injured ankle and various burns to her face and right arm and hands, and was still in a state of shock. Looking sad and dejected, she told me that when she went to bed all her sons joined her in her bedroom where they chatted away for a while before Charlie, Paul and Peter went to their own bedroom. Edith read a paperback until Thomas fell asleep beside her. About midnight she switched the light off, leaving the house in darkness. She soon fell asleep.

Suddenly something woke her up. Was she trapped in a terrible dream? Unexpectedly Edith found herself sitting 'bolt upright' in bed. She sensed something was wrong, but didn't know what it was. In a state of sleepy confusion she stumbled out of bed. The bedroom door was slightly ajar as it never did close properly. She went to the small landing and switched on the light. The wooden bannister was already so hot her naked hands could not keep hold. In disbelief she looked down the stairs. 'I couldn't believe it,' she said later. 'The front door was a mass of flames, and flames and smoke were shooting up the stairs. My hands burned on the bannister. It was so hot.' She dashed into the front bedroom and pulled the sleepy Charlie from the top bunk. In a state of dreadful fear and panic she went back to the landing. Charlie followed. His two brothers and their dog were still asleep in the lower bunk. Knowing that Thomas was unable to walk, Edith and Charlie first attempted to get to the back bedroom to rescue him but the heat drove them back. The smoke was now becoming unbearable, too, but the flames had not quite reached them yet.

Even now Paul and Peter were still asleep in the bunk. Seeking an escape,

Charlie grabbed at the bedroom window and wrenched at the handle, pushing the window wide open. Standing beside him, Edith shouted, 'Jump Charlie, jump.' He ignored his mother. Instead, he pulled her across the room and then shoved her to the open window. 'Oh God! Somebody help us!' she shouted. But before she fully realised what was happening, Charlie had managed to get his mother on to the window ledge and then pushed her out of the window. As she fell forward her night clothes caught on the window catch. Charlie saw what had happened and yanked her free. Dressed only in pants and a top, she fell 15 feet to the ground, her hands already burnt, and she injured her ankle in the fall. Struggling to her feet, she looked up to the open window and saw the bedroom light go out. Charlie had not realised that by opening the front bedroom door and window a great draught had been created which intensified the flames.

Neighbours were awakened as Edith kept shouting to Charlie telling him to jump. 'Jump, Charlie, jump!' the terrified mother kept shouting. But with total disregard for his own safety, and despite the heat, smoke and flames now entering the room, Charlie was doing what he could to save Paul and Peter, still there with their dog. Sadly Edith's escape route did not last long enough for her sons to follow her. Being the protective mother she is, Edith would have been the last out, not the first and only one, if she had had the time to make the decision.

Barbara Newell, on a visit from Thetford, in Norfolk, was staying with her sister next door at No. 11, and was awaked by 'a flash of really bright light' outside her sister's home. She dashed to her bedroom window and saw flames leaping out of window from which Edith had just jumped, and dialled 999. Within minutes the Hull Fire Brigade and ambulances were on the scene. Standing directly below the open flame-filled window, Edith was hysterical and kept shouting that her boys were still in the house. 'And Thomas is in the back bedroom!' she bellowed. Efficient as ever, the Hull firemen quickly got to work attacking the blaze. Within a few minutes they had it under control and quickly set about their rescue work.

Thomas was still in bed when they found him, and within seconds of their arrival Edith was relieved to see the firemen carrying him outside. Shortly afterwards she was also comforted to see them carrying Charlie, and Paul and Peter away from the now smoke-filled building. 'Charlie saw me and gave me a nice little wave when they carried him away,' Edith told me later. The boys were immediately taken by ambulance the short distance to Hull Royal Infirmary. Edith followed in another ambulance, little knowing that she was never to see her boys Charlie, Paul and Peter, alive again. Firemen had found Charlie lying on the front bedroom floor by the side of Paul and Peter. Nearby, but already dead, lay their ever faithful mongrel, Rinny.

Hospital consultant, John Gosnold, found that Charlie was gravely ill with burns over 80% of his body surface. Paul had gross burning to over 70% of his body surface, and Peter had deep burning to almost 85% of his skin. Paul and Peter were desperately ill. After initial treatment John Gosnold decided that, if there was any hope at all, the three boys needed treatment at the Specialist Burns Unit at Pinderfields Hospital, Wakefield. During their short lives the boys had often been excited by the sound of sirens as the ambulances regularly went dashing in and out of the Infirmary just a few hundred yards across the main road from their Selby Street home. They had no idea that one day they would actually be travelling in one of the ambulances themselves. But it was not necessary for the driver to sound the siren on this occasion, for the streets were quiet. It was in the early hours of the morning and the people of Hull were still asleep.

Apart from her injured ankle, Edith was found to have badly burned hands and thighs, and also had some superficial burning on her face. She had inhaled quite a lot of smoke too and was admitted to the Infirmary for continuing care. 'I am not concerned about myself,' she kept saying. 'Are my boys alright?'

Little Thomas was suffering from burns on his legs and left hand as well as some minor burns on his face, but his burns were not too severe; and there was no need for him to join his brothers in Wakefield, West Yorkshire.

Whilst it was my concern and responsibility to find the arsonist, I could not help but think about the boys' father locked up in prison, miles away in North Yorkshire. He was going to hear the horrifying news about his family when he awoke that morning. Regardless of what he had done to be imprisoned, I felt deeply concerned about his plight. I had to get him out of prison as soon as possible.

BBC Radio Humberside would soon alert the three daughters and they would no doubt go direct to the Infirmary to see their mother, so, knowing others would take care of them, their welfare was of no real concern to me. But I was concerned about Tommy, who had now been in prison for five months. I decided I would ensure that the Home Office Prison Department arranged for his release on compassionate grounds as soon as possible.

Meanwhile, dawn would soon be breaking over the City. In very little time the people would be hearing about the fire in Selby Street. And whoever was responsible for it would surely be anxious to know the outcome of his wickedness. Who was it, and why, in the name of God, could he, or she, actually set such a fire directly beneath a peacefully sleeping family? From my initial appraisal of the situation it appeared that we were not going to be presented with a simple matter to resolve and, if we were going to be successful, I needed all the resourcefulness I could muster. I wanted as many experienced detectives and uniformed officers as I could get. I also wanted a forensic scientist so that I could have real evidence of the seat of the fire as well as the actual cause. I was fortunate that morning when a telephone call to the Home Office Forensic Science Laboratory, Wetherby, soon brought to the scene, Roy Cooke, a Principal Scientific Officer with special responsibility for fire investigation with the Forensic Science Service, and a very experienced forensic expert in arson cases. In his examination of the entrance of No. 12 he found an area of one and a half to two square yards of burnt carpeting which had been soaked in paraffin. This was the seat of the fire, directly beneath the letter-box. He also found fragments of burnt newspaper beneath the letter-box inside the building. Later he carried out experiments which supported his view that up to three pints of paraffin had been poured through the letter-box. The paraffin had then been ignited by lighted paper – in fact the *Sun* – being pushed through the letter-box.

Edith, born and bred in Hull, was only 15 when she met Tommy, who was born in Italy but was brought to Yorkshire as a baby. His father came from Leeds and his mother was Italian. Tommy's mother had died when he was only eight and his Aunt Julie then looked after him. Tommy and Edith married when they were both 16 and their first home was a typical old two-up and two-down Hull terrace house near a dockland timber yard. Edith soon became pregnant. Tommy went to sea on Hull trawlers but this work was interspersed with labouring jobs, unemployment and imprisonment. 'It's only when I'm not working all hours God sends that I get into trouble. It wouldn't be so bad if I was a good thief, but I'm not, am I?' he said to me a few years previously. 'But don't worry about me. My family look after each other when I'm inside, and when I'm in the nick I don't get into more trouble, do I?' Tommy and Edie, as Tommy called his wife, thought the world of each other. He was always a friendly rascal, even when he had perhaps drunk a little too much of his favourite Hull Brewery ale.

As the family had increased they moved from the little terrace to Selby Street. Their new house was in a corner and part of a crescent of 17 council houses, facing a flyover on a main road into Hull City centre from the west. To the front there was also the main Hull to London railway line, which formed a local community boundary. At the rear were Victorian houses with rooms rented out cheaply, and generally, apart from the Selby Street council houses, the housing was old and rather dilapidated as in many inner city areas, and only a stone's throw away from Hull fish docks and Hull Rugby League Club. The nearest operational police station was over a mile away at Humberside Police Headquarters in Queens Gardens. That was too far away for my needs in Selby Street and, in any case, the Headquarters building had no vacant space for a murder enquiry. It had been a grand building for the once proud but now defunct Hull City Police, but, following the 1974 creation of the County of Humberside and the amalgamation of the Police in the East Riding, parts of Lincolnshire, and a part of West Yorkshire, Hull City was now at the hub of the new county's policing and the building was crammed full.

No one had been killed in the fire, but, as sure as daylight was breaking through that morning, I knew that with body surface burns of about 80%, at least one – if not two, or even three of the boys was to die before many days passed. I also suspected that whoever was responsible had some kind of connection with the close vicinity and the Hastie family, and I did not want my officers wasting precious time travelling to and from Headquarters just to attend to their clerical work. We needed to be there near the scene, and be seen to be there 24 hours a day enquiring, analysing, listening, watching and asking more and more questions.

Just a few hundred yards from Selby Street was the old Victorian Gordon Street Police Station which had not been used for its original purpose for many years. It was now a police store with a small back room used by police radio mechanics to repair radios. Although a little cramped, it had a certain workability about it and was ideally placed to base a Major Incident Room. It had two rooms up some well-worn and rickety stairs on the first floor. One was ideal for use as my office; the other became a tea room. It did not have a room large enough to brief the approximately 100 officers I now required to help with the enquiry, but, nevertheless, I arranged for the use of a nearby church hall later. Selfishly, I also made sure that I had some of the best detectives in Humberside drafted to the enquiry, for I sensed that this could not only be a lengthy enquiry but one which would require officers who were thoroughly dedicated and as inquisitive as hell.

My intention was to seek out the movements of everyone who had been in the Selby Street district that night. We all knew the only way was to knock on doors and, if necessary, return time and time again until every man, woman and child was accounted for. Our purpose was not only to discover who caused the arson, but to find anyone who might have seen anything at all about the crucial time that fateful night in Selby Street.

My initial briefing was simply to provide the assembled officers with the facts as I knew them, and arrange for the allocation of tasks. To begin with, I wanted officers working in pairs to visit every one of the thousands of houses in the locality. The occupants would need to answer a carefully drawn-up questionnaire with the usual why, where and when questions if we were to stand any chance of discovering the whereabouts of everyone in the neighbourhood at the time of the fire. 'Assume that each person you speak to is likely to be lying or is likely to conceal the truth from you every time you knock on a door,' I said. 'Be fair to everyone and don't rush. We have a massive task ahead of us and we might as well not do it at all unless we do it properly.'

'What about people complaining about us, the types mixing with prostitutes or just having affairs who don't want anyone to know their whereabouts?' asked one young officer.

'Just ask them how they would feel if one of their relatives was fighting for life after being burned alive,' I answered. 'And if they are so damned awkward, refuse to answer your questions and insist on complaining, consider that they are obstructing you in the course of your duty. Provided you are fair, you all know me well enough to know you have my backing.' No one ever persisted with a complaint.

The 'House to House' team leader and his staff would ensure that addresses shown on master sheets included lists of every known member of the household, with cross-checks for visitors and lodgers. The cross-checks would be even more important in the lodging places in West Hull. I believed if we placed everyone where they really were on the night and at the time of the fire, then, provided they lived within the neighbourhood and people were honest, we should stand a reasonable chance of identifying the arsonist. But no one was rushing forward to tell us about any sighting of the culprit.

And we still had not found the paraffin can. The arsonist had obviously taken it away with him. A thorough search of the vicinity, including a search of numerous dustbins, revealed nothing. We also arranged for a small mobile police station to be parked in Selby Street near to No. 12 to facilitate the work of the House to House enquiry teams. It was handy for anyone able, and willing, to pass on to us any useful information about the problem confronting us.

The *Hull Daily Mail* quickly learned about the fire and I held a brief news conference midway through the morning. I hadn't a lot to tell the newsmen. Knowing how well the *Hull Daily Mail* is read, I pleaded for anyone who knew anything at all to come forward. That lunchtime first edition carried the bold black banner headline, 'FIRE HORROR: CHILDREN BADLY HURT'.

Meanwhile the old Gordon Street Police Station was alive with activity as detectives set up the major enquiry administrative systems, and prepared questionnaires for the House to House teams. Hull City Council, with its own unique telephone company, installed extra telephone lines in preparation for the anticipated calls from the public. We all believed that the newspaper headline would motivate the public to contact us with any knowledge they had about the arson.

Motivating the public was only a small part of our efforts. Apart from the residents, absolutely everyone who had been in the Selby Street locality at the material time had to be traced. And no matter how tedious, everyone known to frequent the vicinity, willing to be helpful or not, had to be seen, questioned and their whereabouts that night verified. We had no eye witnesses, descriptions, fingerprints, footprints, tyre marks, motive, blood, or likely suspect generated from criminal intelligence.

I had been responsible for many major investigations and was well pleased to have a good number of highly motivated, experienced and conscientious men and women join me on this occasion. I was going to need them, like never before!

Chapter Two

Domestic violence was a common occurrence in the City, especially among the fishing community, who would fight at night and shake hands the next morning. However, in 1979 the fishing industry in Hull was in the doldrums and most of the hitherto hard-working fishing community were unemployed. Hundreds of families had also moved away from the fish dock area and were living on the City outskirts in the sprawling council housing estates a few miles north of Selby Street. Being creatures of habit many people regularly returned to their old haunts to visit the numerous pubs and visit those who had chosen to remain in the old part of the City. Had one of them had an old grudge to settle with the Hastie's? One thing I did know from experience was that the people of Hull were always very keen to cooperate with the police when a child had been harmed.

The heroic Charlie died of his burns at 3 a.m. on 5 December. He would surely have lived had he not chosen to stay in the house to try to rescue his young brothers. With no father at home, Charlie had obviously decided to ignore his mother's pleas for him to jump, but tried instead to do whatever he could to save his young brothers. Just half an hour after BBC Radio Humberside announced his death a man was seen by a member of the public standing on the railway flyover walkway overlooking Selby Street. He was drumming his fingers against the railings and was overheard speaking to himself, 'One down and four to go.' We couldn't believe it. Who could possibly wish death upon these young lads? We only had a very brief description and, try as we might, we were unable to trace him.

Following our appeals for information on television, in the *Hull Daily Mail* and on BBC Radio Humberside, a great many telephone calls were made to our enquiry room. None of them was particularly helpful, but it was with increasing concern I saw there were dozens of messages coming in, not with the help we were seeking, but with complaints about the Hastie boys' behaviour during the twelve months or more before the fateful night. Officers making routine house to house enquiries were also receiving similar complaints.

It was not long before we found there was a disturbing feeling of animosity directed at the Hastie family and had been so for a number of years. And it quickly became clear that the ill feeling was in no small part due to the boys' behaviour. Enquiries in the neighbourhood also revealed there was a considerable feeling of unpleasantness and squabbling among neighbours. Anonymous letter writing and 'Peeping Tom' activity were also part and parcel of daily life in that unhappy corner of the City. However, this state of affairs obviously presented us with several interesting lines of enquiry.

On the second day of the enquiry, I was delighted to receive a message from the Home Office agreeing to Tommy's immediate release from Rudgate Open Prison under a Royal Prerogative of Mercy. Grief-stricken after being told about Charlie's death, Tommy went straight from prison to Hull Royal Infirmary to see his wife. I saw him soon afterwards, but there was little I could say or do to ease his sadness. I knew him as a chirpy and likeable rogue, but now he was a saddened and pathetic character, utterly stunned and deeply depressed by what had happened to his family. I chose not to compound his agony by telling him just how poorly his sons, Paul and Peter, really were. Tommy could offer no help in identifying the arsonist. 'They might have been little devils at times, but they didn't deserve this, did they, boss?' he muttered quietly. As practically everyone in the district knew Tommy was in prison at the time of the attack, the arsonist could hardly have been after him when the house was set alight. But we had no evidence that any particular family member was the arsonist's objective.

Complaints about the boys' behaviour were still coming in during the days which followed. Was the blaze and Charlie's death sparked off by a neighbourhood feud which became a vendetta attack? I told Tommy about the complaints we were receiving about his boys once when he called at my office. He just shrugged his shoulders. 'They was just boys, but they shouldn't have been burned,' he said. 'Sometimes I think of taking revenge myself,' he added, 'but it's no good doing all the neighbours in and maybe not getting the right one, is it, Mr. Sagar? I reckon I'll just have to let you get on with it. I'd kill the bastard I would. Then I would go down for good, wouldn't I?' As he was leaving, he gave me a quick glance and then in something of an outburst, as if to release some pent-up feelings, he raised his voice and said, 'If you lot hadn't got us for doing Rugby Club, I wouldn't have gone to prison and our house wouldn't have got burned down.'

I answered, 'Tommy, my old friend, I join you in your sorrow, but let's be more to the point. If you and Charlie hadn't committed the burglary at the Rugby Club, the house might not have been burned.'

Rumour soon had it that perhaps Edith was responsible for the fire. One neighbour suggested that she had been careless with a paraffin heater which she kept on the top of the landing. Forensic examination, however, at the time of the fire revealed that it had not been alight. Believing what Edith told me, I knew that no one in that house that night could possibly have started the fire.

Three days after the attack Peter Hastie died of his burns. His brother, Paul, remained 'very critical'. Meantime Edith and little Thomas were 'comfortable' at Hull Royal Infirmary where Tommy, often wearing a red tartan cap, was now a regular and well-known visitor.

Few people tend to walk through Selby Street late at night and, apart from the odd taxi taking a short cut, the occasional police patrol car coasting by, the stray dogs barking, and the odd ginger tomcat clattering a dustbin lid while searching for a mate, little is heard after midnight. But during the night of the arson attack someone had surreptitiously made his way into the corner of the crescent where devoted mother, Edith, and four of her offspring were peacefully sleeping. What did he (or she) feel like as he hurried away when the flames began to leap up the stairs towards the sleeping victims? A police patrol car had cruised along about the time the arsonist must have been there, but the ever-observant driver had not seen anything unusual. No. 12 was well set back from the street making it quite easy not to be well noticed from the road. A young couple made their way along the pavement too, but they had not seen anything suspicious either. Had the culprit been watching and waiting in the shadows or hiding under the nearby railway flyover bridge, just waiting until all was clear before making his move. And carrying several pints of paraffin too?

Paul fought for his life for ten agonizing days before he too died of his burns at Pinderfields Hospital. The *Hull Daily Mail* was now describing Selby Street as a 'Street of Hate'. That's a little harsh, I thought. But perhaps the media was right, maybe there was so much hatred down there that someone had been aggravated by the boys to such an extent that he, or she, could not take it any more.

Meanwhile we were exploring everything we were being told concerning the neighbourhood's complaints about the boys' behaviour. All we were finding was a great many people did not like the Hasties. 'It could be a neighbourhood conspiracy to get rid of them,' one young policeman suggested. The idea was unthinkable, but we could not be absolutely sure.

One day, shortly after Paul died, Edith and I were once again discussing the fire. After some time and in a very quiet matter-of-fact way, she told me that a year earlier, two or three weeks before Christmas, 'a real nasty' poison-pen letter, written on the back of part of a cornflakes packet the size of a postcard, had been posted to her just like a postcard and delivered through the same letter-box as the paraffin. The letter said 'something about bombing us out', Edith alleged. She didn't know why, but she had kept the card. She shrugged her shoulders as she muttered, 'It's probably been burned to ashes now.' She had last seen it when she was rummaging through a drawer in the living room some weeks ago. I could not bring myself to question her too much but it was clear she hadn't the slightest notion who the poison-pen writer was.

I returned to Gordon Street Police Station feeling rather optimistic as I knew the room had not been completely gutted and the forensic examination had been properly concentrated on the seat of the fire and the resultant damage. The living room was more smoke-damaged than anything else and what burning there was had been soon put out by the firemen. There was maybe just a chance that with careful handling of the charred remains we might just find the cornflakes postcard.

Several officers were soon on their way to sift through the remains of the fire. The house was now boarded up as a safety measure and to prevent looting. 'Let's turn the place inside out, lads, then maybe we'll see a smile on the boss's face for a change,' was just one of many cheery comments I overheard. We needed some good luck. Picking their way piece by piece through the remains of the living room the rummage crew quickly found what they were looking for and then returned to the Enquiry Room delighted with the find which they had carefully preserved in a sealed plastic bag. I couldn't believe my eyes when I saw it. 'Bless you Edith,' I thought. 'Little did you know that by keeping this "postcard" you were probably going to give us the lead to the killer of those boys of yours.' But here it was, hardly burned, the cut-out piece of a cornflakes packet, with a stamp on it, addressed to Mrs. Hastie, 12 Selby Street, Hull, and postmarked December 1978.

Written in a scrawling hand it read:

> *'A family of fucking rubbish. We all hate you, you should all live on an island. (Devils Island) but I'm not kidding but I promised you a bomb and by hell I'm not kidding. Why don't you flit while you've got the chance. We can't get you out normally then we'll bastard well bomb you and that's too good for you.'*

I went through every word with Edith and Tommy. They knew nothing of any previous 'promise to bomb them' and did not know of any action being taken to get them out of the house 'normally'. They could only guess that the letter was from one of their neighbours but they had no idea who that person could be. They said they had not told anyone they had received the threat and Tommy told me that he thought the writer 'must be some mad bastard who didn't like us and wasn't worth bothering about'. Obviously if Edith had told us about it without being able to show us the actual card, our task in seeking the author would have been a daunting task indeed.

Now at last we appeared to have something really worthwhile to follow up. The general tone of the letter tended to indicate that it must have come from someone living in the close neighbourhood. Each word had been printed in ink and spelt correctly but long-hand writing would have been much more helpful to us for identification purposes.

At our next morning conference I told everyone about the cut-out cornflakes packet postcard. 'Good grief,' uttered one young detective with a smile, 'I hope you're not going to ask us to search bloody bins for the remains of the cornflakes packet!' 'No,' I answered, 'not a year after the cut-out.' There was now only one way to find the author. We had to obtain handwriting samples from everyone in the Selby Street area and maybe beyond. We were also going to have to check the anonymous writing against any neighbours' signatures we had already obtained on the 'negative' statements we had so far taken from them which simply covered their whereabouts during the night of the fire (practically everyone stated they were in bed asleep). There was just a chance that some kind of similarity of style could prove helpful and – a bit of a long shot knowing that we were hunting for the author – the writer might panic and do something to reveal himself.

We studied the complaints against them. One elderly neighbour told us that whenever she was preparing to go out and saw the Hastie boys in the street she would wait at home, peeping from behind her curtains until they had gone. Another woman said that she was sick and tired of the boys climbing up on to her roof and dropping bricks down her chimney. Urinating through letter-boxes; throwing stones at the elderly; shoplifting; leaving their excreta on front doorsteps; smashing garden fences; smashing windows and robbing boy scouts attending a nearby scout meeting: these were only a sample of the allegations now being made against the boys. Neighbours living alongside the family also complained about their drinking habits and the noise from their stereo, which was forever playing Elvis Presley's *Wooden Stool*. Speaking to Tommy one day, I said I thought their favourite record was called *Wooden Heart*, but all Tommy said was, 'Yes, I just guessed you was an Elvis fan but, see, it's called Wooden Stool. You will have to listen to it with Edie and me with a beer some time.'

About one week before Christmas, as if to show that not everyone hated the family, an anonymous gift of £30 was sent to Edith. 'We will use it to buy another alsatian puppy for little Thomas when he gets out of hospital,' one of Edith's relatives announced.

Thomas was getting along fine but he was not well enough to be discharged and would be in hospital for Christmas. Edith was determined to leave hospital as soon as she could and decided to discharge herself so she could join her husband and three daughters. The Hull City Housing Department had gone to great lengths to provide the family with another house and one was available on the Orchard Park estate, four and a half miles away from Selby Street.

On Christmas Eve, 1979, Tommy and Edith visited Thomas in Hull Royal Infirmary. After the visit, and being so near to their old home, they could not resist 'paying a visit' to their old neighbours. They also believed it was the place where their son's killer was living. Tommy told me later that as they crossed the main road outside the Infirmary, they decided to knock on every door in Selby Street to see if there was 'anything in people's faces' which would assist in catching the killer. However, full of grief, the couple made their way to their old neighbourhood. Naturally overwhelmed with a mixture of emotion, anger and self-pity they let forth many obscenities and expressions of anger as they approached their former neighbours' houses. One resident said he was sitting back all ready (about 9 p.m.) for his 'first quiet Christmas in ages', when he heard voices which he recognised. Peering through his curtains he saw Tommy kick out at one of the windows and heard him say, 'I'll get you for killing my kids.' At another house a former neighbour was watching television when she recognised Edith's voice shouting outside, 'Come outside, you burned my kids. I'll do the same to you.' Windows were broken at the two houses before the police arrived and arrested the pair. 'We had to let them know we were still around,' Tommy told me rather gleefully a few days later. With a broad smile on his face he said, 'And you know, there was a summons out for us not having a dog licence for Rinny. He saved us that problem when he died in the fire two days before we was due in court.' Both were released on bail for Christmas. It was to be their last Christmas together.

By Christmas Eve everyone on the enquiry had been working very long hours, day in day out, for three weeks and were ready for some relaxation. I decided a complete break from all enquiries would do much more good than harm. I told everyone to take a couple of days off and then, with refreshed minds, we could begin again with renewed vigour after Christmas. One high-ranking officer at Police HQ told me that it was quite wrong to break off from such an enquiry just because it was Christmas. In a disrespectful tone I told my superior that regardless of whether he thought it right or wrong we were all having Christmas Day off. And we did.

Tommy and Edith failed to answer police bail to appear at the Hull Magistrates Court on 27 December and consequently arrest warrants were issued. The couple had not run away, and were soon found in their new home, still full of grief. Appearing before the magistrates the following morning they were told the court would release them on bail until after their three sons were buried. Bail was on condition that they did not frequent Selby Street, with one exception. They would be allowed there on 4 January to attend the Selby Street Methodist Mission for their sons, Charlie, Peter and Paul's funeral service. In any case, I thought, there was no way anyone, magistrate or police, was going to stop them.

In view of all that had happened I was not at all happy about having the funeral anywhere near Selby Street, but during my discussions with them, Edith and Tommy were adamant. 'We will show them bastards,' said Tommy. And Edith insisted, 'We are all going down Selby Street and I am going to take the boys right down the length of the street so as everybody can see what has been done to them. Somebody down there murdered them and one day they will pay for it. It is somebody down there, I just know it.'

I had spoken to the two of them on many occasions during those sad and dark December days. We got along very well together and, despite his criminal record, Tommy was always courteous, polite and as helpful as he could be when I enquired about the boys' antics and possible suspects. I asked Edith if it would not be too much for her having the funeral cortège travel the length of Selby Street. There would be a certain amount of media attention too, I told her. 'I have already made my mind up, Mr. Sagar. I am going to take my boys right along Selby Street. It is where they have lived, played and died.' Tommy added that the boys enjoyed themselves in Selby Street and should be taken there for the last time. I had no good reason to disagree. In fact, eventually I thought it might help to reveal the boys' killer.

We all knew that alibis were notoriously difficult to break when suspects told us, quite properly, they were in bed asleep at the time. We did have the anonymous letter, though, and, although it had been received a year earlier, the writer did in fact threaten to do exactly what had happened on 4 December. But if the writer was also the arsonist, why wait a year to carry out the threat?

Whilst we did not exclude anyone in our search for the writer, we did find ourselves being rather apologetic towards a number of elderly ladies when we asked them to write their samples of handwriting in the exact (obscene) words written on the cornflakes packet postcard. Officers sifting through the hundreds of samples we were now getting gradually began to whittle down the handwriting similarities and for a while we believed, with perseverance, we could discover our poison-pen writer and arsonist all in one. However, we were all experienced enough to know that a threat is but a threat, and on its own insufficient to justify a charge of arson. Having been raised in the traditional beliefs of the police service, and at a time, long since gone, when the public really did think that the British bobby was the best in the world, we all knew the wisdom of accepting nothing on face value and that good sound corroboration was the lifeline to a complete and successful detection. This attitude always paid off when confronted by lawyers who always believed their clients innocent, no matter how sound the evidence was.

We were no nearer to finding the killer four weeks after the fire, when, on 3 January, Mr. Philip Gill, the Wakefield Coroner, in whose district was Pinderfields Hospital, opened the inquest on Charles, Paul and Peter. Edith and Tommy did not attend the hearing. Pathologist, Professor David Gee, told the inquest that Charles and Peter died from burns and the inhalation of smoke, and Paul from multiple burns. I told the Coroner that enquiries were proceeding actively to identify the person responsible, but to date no one had been charged with any offence in connection with the fire.

That afternoon the *Hull Daily Mail* duly reported the Coroner's appeal for the guilty to come forward with the banner headline, 'APPEAL TO A KILLER'S CONSCIENCE'. Practically everyone in Hull reads the local newspaper so we hoped we would get just a few calls from people with perhaps some suspicion about a possible suspect. Sadly, no one answered the appeal.

Chapter Three

Some indication of the attitude towards the Hastie family could be gathered from the fact that, although 18,000 people lived in the district and knew of the tragedy, only about 60 attended the funeral.

Just before noon and in bright but cold winter sunshine, the five-car funeral procession made its way into Selby Street. The first three cars carried the boys' coffins. First there was Charlie, then Peter, who was followed by Paul. Each coffin was covered by a cross of white and yellow chrysanthemums. I watched from the footpath near the Hull to Kings Cross railway line as the cars slowed down, almost to a stop, as they passed the boarded-up council house. It was a poignant moment and I am sure I was not the only one to feel a lump in my throat.

Edith and Tommy watched in silence as the undertakers carried the coffins into the small red-brick Methodist Church Mission about 150 yards from their former home. As the third coffin, carrying Paul's body, was carried through the Mission doorway Edith suddenly lunged forward to face the small crowd of onlookers. With tears flowing down her face she waved her burned and bandaged hands at the crowd and yelled, 'It was one of you bastards. One of you in this street is the murderer!' There were few tears among the watchers as many of them averted their eyes from Edith's wild anger. Some walked away, perhaps in horrified amazement. Thankfully, with considerable restraint, Tommy quickly managed to calm his wife down; then they turned their backs on the crowd and slowly made their way into the Mission. In turn, their three tearful and trembling daughters, Angeleena, Nicola and Sonia, followed. Thomas was still in hospital.

A sorrowful gloom filled the air as a small number of people remained in the street outside. Arsonists are sometimes known to be in the background watching when firemen tackle the fire they started. Was our arsonist there now, watching the final act of his, or her, maliciousness?

I had questioned arsonists in the past. To my knowledge an arsonist usually had a straightforward motive. There are those who set fires to remove evidence of other crimes, or for insurance or revenge. But there are the people who have no motives for setting fires, and one of the problems was to pick out those with a psychiatric disorder. From experience I knew most arsonists to be male and under the age of 30. I had learned that arsonists tend to be small, slightly built people who are unhappy and lonely but possess a fair amount of animal cunning which helps them to set fires and get away with it.

There was now an eerie silence about Selby Street but my thoughts were disturbed as a solitary train rumbled by. Standing outside the Mission, I began to hear constant outbursts of emotion from Edith as the Rev. Arthur Crozier conducted the funeral service. He could be heard asking the small congregation to pray for 'the one whose conscience bears the most of this tragedy. Pray for someone unknown to us, the person responsible.' Listening to those words did Edith and Tommy no good whatsoever, for 20 minutes later, as Edith followed her three sons' coffins out of the Mission she bellowed away at the onlookers once again. 'I am coming back for you lot of bastards. I'll never give up. I'll never give up!' she shouted. Tommy bundled her, sobbing

Mrs. Edith Hastie showing her distress.
(Picture by courtesy of *Hull Daily Mail*)

her heart out, into a funeral car. The cortège quietly made its way to the Hull Northern Cemetery three miles away where the boys were buried in one grave, watched by their mother, father, three sisters, several journalists and some of my officers. If such a thing was needed, the sad and emotional scenes that day in Selby Street certainly made everyone there realise just how horrifying the arson had been.

Meantime we had a lot of work to do and, thankfully, the old Gordon Street Police Station was now a fount of enthusiasm and inquisitiveness. I think we all had an unaccountable determination to find the killer. We were getting along well seeking handwriting samples. No one refused to cooperate and we had several other useful lines of enquiry to follow up. However, after the funeral I decided to give priority rating to finding the author of the cornflakes postcard.

Edith and Tommy answered their bail before Hull Magistrates Court on 18 January. They were both given conditional discharges after admitting breaking windows at the homes of former neighbours.

The following day Detective Constable Paul Bacon came into my cramped little office at Gordon Street. His eyes were bright with excitement. He had a bundle of papers in his hand. 'We've got a good suspect for the cornflakes postcard!' he exclaimed. 'It's a woman who is well over 60 years old. Her handwriting sample looks a really good possibility.' We had all studied the penned writing on the 'postcard' to such an extent that we knew the style of the writing in almost every detail. Paul Bacon placed the sample in front of me. We were left in little doubt that the two were from the same hand. I lost no time in arresting the woman and she was brought to my office. I realised from the moment I saw her that she was deeply concerned about her arrest but did not protest her innocence in any way. Confronted with the various similarities of writing, she seemed relieved and soon admitted writing the words and sending the cornflakes postcard to Edith. She said that she had been tormented, aggravated and stoned by the Hastie boys whenever she walked along the street and she went on to say she had been at her 'wits' end,' when she wrote to Edith. She did not, though, want to waste money on a real postcard. When she heard about the fire she had been 'terrified out of her mind'. After all, she had threatened to do precisely what had happened. She had no idea who had started the fire and, in any case, never believed she could have fired the house herself.

During the days immediately after the fire she thought Edith could not have kept the postcard, but, she reasoned, if she had, then it must have been destroyed in the fire. With those thoughts, she told us, 'I relaxed a little.' She said she also felt a certain amount of pleasure when she realised she would now be able to walk to her corner shop in peace. Her peaceful state of mind did not last long, though, and she became 'intensely' frightened when she heard the police had recovered the postcard. 'I couldn't believe that Edith had not only kept the postcard but that it had survived in the fire,' she said. I was certain this elderly, nervous, and unhappy woman was responsible for writing and posting the 'postcard' but was not the person who had set Edith's house on fire.

We didn't know what reaction we would get from Edith, but when I told her the author of the 'cornflakes postcard' was not, in my opinion, the fire raiser, she took the news quite calmly, saying, 'Never mind, Mr. Sagar, you are all doing your best, but whoever you find who did it won't bring my boys back, will it? Promise me you won't just give up, though.'

I often told officers doing the spade work that, in my view, there were many honest-to-goodness people in the vicinity, and surely there must be some connection between the arson, the deaths and someone living, or at least frequenting, the vicinity.

Unfortunately there were continuing rumours that Edith was responsible for her own misfortune. Following the discovery of the cornflakes postcard writer I held another press conference. It was an ideal way of keeping the people of Hull informed about the enquiry. BBC Radio Humberside and the *Hull Daily Mail* were always most helpful. Having expressed my views about the now identified anonymous letter writer, I told the media that those pointing accusing fingers at Edith were doing so without foundation and they would do themselves and everyone else much more good if only they would stick to reality and stop rumourmongering. What we actually knew was that on that awful Monday night three weeks before Christmas someone, apparently with a grudge, had quietly gone up to No. 12 Selby Street, poured at least a pint of paraffin through the letter-box and set it alight. The fire that followed killed three schoolboys, badly burned another, and burned their mother as well. No matter how mischievous the boys may have been, and no matter how many appeals were made, we still did not have a clue which might lead us to the arsonist.

Now we had another problem: an indifferent public. We felt the neighbourhood was full of fascination and a fair amount of enthusiasm for us when we were seeking the anonymous letter writer, but once the line of enquiry was complete, and following the annoyance I had expressed in an attempt to protect Edith from the rumourmongering, we were presented with nothing but indifference. Perhaps it was understandable. Maybe we were forever striking a blank wall because no one in the vicinity or anywhere else really did know who had killed the boys.

Nevertheless, we did have another avenue of enquiry. A man had made an anonymous telephone call to our office the day after the fire. He said he had seen two men running away from the direction of No. 12 Selby Street about the time of the fire. He had not seen any sign of the fire, but he had seen two men drive off in a car, probably an old Rover.

We quickly traced his call to a City centre call box. Then Detective Sergeant Mick Trafford, bubbling over with his usual enthusiasm, sped into the centre in his own car, found the caller just as he was leaving the telephone and invited him to Gordon Street Police Station. At first he refused the invitation but no doubt a glance at Mick Trafford's friendly but determined face soon changed his mind. And Mick was certainly not going to let him go. Speaking rather apprehensively shortly afterwards, the caller could not give a sensible reason for making his call anonymously. Although it was a bit like drawing teeth, he went on to say he had been driving along Selby Street about the time the fire must have started when he saw two men running from No. 12 and get into a waiting Rover car facing the nearby flyover. One of the men ran around the front door of the vehicle to the nearside passenger door, while the second man ran across the pavement around the back of the vehicle to the rear nearside passenger door. Both got into the Rover which was quickly driven away. He did not see the driver.

One of the men was about 5ft. 10ins, of broad build, with a clean-shaven long, fattish face and rounded chin. He had short dark hair and was wearing greyish trousers, a brown jacket, which may have been corduroy, and an open-necked white shirt like a tee-shirt with a few buttons down the front. He also described the second man as about 5ft. 10ins., but of thin build and with dark hair which was wavy and collar-length. He was dressed in a dark jacket and blue jeans. The man went on to tell us that the Rover was of the type made between 1963 and 1976, probably a 2000cc model, possibly mustard-coloured, and with reflective number plates, but he could not recall any of the letters or digits, not even one. But it was an old car kept in reasonably good condition.

Our anonymous caller was dubious and unknown to us so we used the old adage always in our minds: accept nothing that we cannot corroborate. But if he was right, we had a good witness. He had been driving at night, yet, in the shadows of the street lamps, he had not only seen two men running but had got a good look at their faces, their height and their clothing. He had also seen enough of their vehicle to decide on its condition, make and colour. If true, this was vital information, but the detail he gave was more than we would normally expect from a person who, at the time, was also driving a vehicle, and at night too. Why, with such 'good' information, had he not identified himself instead of making his telephone call anonymously. Was he responsible for the fire? We interviewed him at length. He denied that he was the arsonist, and satisfied us that he was not the man we were looking for. But despite the reservations we had about his story, he insisted that he had seen the men with the Rover. I don't recall speaking to any officer who believed the man. His anonymous call gave him little credibility and further doubts came to mind because a number things he said did not tie up with other information which came to light. An honest-to-goodness couple innocently walking along the street after visiting friends about the relevant time did not see anything at all which remotely coincided with the Rover story. The patrolling police car driver did not see it either. And no one we traced who had been verified as being in Selby Street at the time saw the man behind the Rover story. We formed the opinion he was a romancer, always too ready to elaborate on what he had seen, if indeed he had seen anything at all. His appearance was rather scruffy and unkempt, which is rare in a person able to observe the kind of detail this man gave us. From the outset the most likely avenue to investigate was that the arsonist was probably a neighbour or an associate of the family who had been driven to despair by the aggravation of one, or all, of the family.

Apart from the obvious feeling of sadness I had about the boys' deaths, I also felt it was a great shame that Charlie, at least, had not survived. If only he had jumped out of the open window he would have lived and could have told us about his activities. He might have even led us to the killer. Meanwhile, I had to keep the enquiry alive, for I sometimes had a dreadful feeling that somewhere in our midst we had an arsonist who, by now, must be thinking he had escaped detection. Feeling untouchable, he, or she, might do the same elsewhere, just to aggravate us perhaps!

In order to keep the people of Hull up-to-date and to seek as much help as we could I had called many news conferences since the night of the fire. The BBC and Yorkshire Television crews attended the first few conferences but did not realise just how much light relief and quiet amusement their appearances gave us, for, when it was known at Humberside Police HQ that TV cameras were coming along to Gordon Street, we were assured that certain senior officers would also attend. They never offered us any useful advice, but did their best to look important and left as soon as the cameras were switched off.

Whilst we had our doubts about the Rover we could not exclude it completely. We all talked it over in great detail at our morning conferences, expressing not only our doubts but looking at the story more positively. There was always just a chance the story was true. In a press conference a day or so later, I did not express any of our doubts, but, instead, gave all the details of the story as they were given to us. The media was as helpful as could be and gave it good coverage. It was now two months since the arson attack. We knew there were thousands of Rover cars registered in North Humberside alone, and a great many more elsewhere. We had now set ourselves the daunting task of not only finding all of those registered in Hull, but discovering exactly where they were when the arsonist struck.

By this time I had been forced to release about 75% of my manpower as other murders were presented to the Force. Several weeks went by as we found more and more 'innocent' Rovers. During the search we discovered a small-time drug pusher who admitted ripping some of his customers off. He was actually lodging near the Hastie family in Selby Street at the time of the fire. Was there a possibility of an aggrieved customer wanting to attack the pusher and, by mistake, attacking the wrong house? With these questions in mind we explored the Hull drugs world. Many drug-takers were helpful, but once again all our enquiries ended with negative results.

The weeks came and went as we continued to pursue the hundreds of Rover cars we still wanted to trace. Then, at the beginning of May, the Rover witness told us he had made a mistake in part of his statement. His 'mistake' was not particularly relevant but merely related to who he had, or had not, seen before being in Selby Street. Some weeks later after a good deal of hard work had been done knocking on doors, examining Rovers and filling in questionnaires, the wretched man made a further statement. This time he said that he now thought that he had mixed up the night of the fire with a previous occasion when he had driven along Selby Street and had then seen two men in a Rover. Now we knew that the doubts we had in the first place were correct after all.

As any experienced detective knows, to take on the task of successfully tracing a particular make of vehicle without, at least, having some indication of the registered number is practically impossible. We did not trace all the Rover cars registered in Humberside, we never expected to, but perhaps our endeavour to do so together with the local publicity may well have brought pressure on the witness to eventually speak more honestly.

The one benefit gained by it all was that our wild goose chase for Rovers kept the whole investigation alive. Quietly, though, those Rover cars also began to sow the seeds of thought about another avenue of enquiry we were to concentrate upon in the weeks to come. It had been noticeable from the start that we were not getting the usual leads from any of the local informants. Detectives in touch with their regular 'snouts' – as informers are known in Hull – were picking up nothing at all. One morning I saw an old 'snout' who, a few years earlier, had informed on his own newly married son who had committed a robbery with violence. The son was imprisoned and the 'snout' was paid the lowly sum of £25 for the information. My old and most reliable 'snout' would obviously shop anyone but he was now rather frustrated when he asked, 'How much longer are you lot going to be buzzing around this neck of the woods? None of us knows nothing and no good jobs are being done with you lot busying about this bloody place day and night. The lads ain't even nicking car radios so long as you lot's here. Nobody knows nowt about Tommy Hastie's kids getting burned and you must know it was nothing to do with Tommy being a bit of a toe rag that his house got fired. But I'll tell you something for nothing. We'd all grass on whoever done it just to get you lot away from here.'

Early one evening during the early spring I took a directionless walk through the Selby Street district. I wanted to get more of a feeling of the place and be away from the telephones for a while. Eventually I made my way to the top of a block of high-rise flats and looked over our enquiry area.

If I had been seen up there, some jerk might have said that I was contemplating suicide, but how wrong they would have been. Up there I was able to see across the flat landscape of Hull and the silver-green tidal water flowing along the north bank of the River Humber, and west towards the mighty and expensive Humber Bridge. Why I was up there I was not exactly sure, but I wanted to assess all we had done, and as I stood there quite alone I could see practically every house and every street we had visited. I was unhappy that so many people appeared to have forgotten the three Hastie brothers. Hull is not an easy place to become fond of, but being a rather isolated city, detectives had good reason to like it, for, crime committed there was nearly always the work of local villains, which made the business of crime detection that much easier. The fire raiser had to be there somewhere. The sun was glinting on the wet roof tops of the hundreds of terrace houses and flats below. To the east I saw the railway lines from the junction right in the centre of Hull sneaking their way from the City centre and on past Selby Street and then along the north bank of the Humber and away towards Goole and Doncaster and on to London. To the south was the Humber with its once booming, but now derelict, fish dock. The City centre lay down below my vantage point. I could scan over the square mile or so surrounding Selby Street. Surely down there, somewhere, was the person we were looking for. Did he frequent any of the now half-dead pubs along Hessle Road, where, in days gone by, Hull trawlermen lived it up for two or three days before going back to the icy waters of the North Sea. Although it was well after 6 pm quite a number of people were still making their way home from work. Children with skate boards were playing near the top end of Selby Street and a small group of boys were playing rugby on some waste land. There was a queue outside a fish and chip shop where many detectives on the enquiry became regular customers. Never mind Harry Ramsden's, we would say, Hull has the most delicious fish and chips in the world, provided, of course, they are wrapped in an old copy of the *Hull Daily Mail*. The majority of people in the Selby Street area were no doubt watching early evening TV but the BBC and Yorkshire Television had long since stopped reporting news about the Hastie boys' deaths. Life goes on, I thought, but does no one care about the tragedy of the three boys?

Walking back to my Gordon Street office that evening I noticed that a newly planted tree had been snapped off just a foot from the ground. I also saw a bicycle chained to a lamp post to prevent some thief taking it, but the front wheel and saddle were already missing. This time Charlie and his brothers weren't there to be blamed. But that was irrelevant. My thoughts were more concerned with what aspect, if any, we had not covered in our enquiries. There had to be an answer somewhere. It was now early in March, four months after the arson. What could the boys have been involved in which we and their parents did not know about? We were almost at a loss as to what further steps could be taken to trace the arsonist but he, or she, had to be somewhere. Every likely line of enquiry had been followed up. We had even checked the monthly lists of missing persons and suicides without gleaning anything useful.

Charlie was 15 when he died. Had we examined all activities 15-year-olds get up to? We had carefully examined all the allegations about the boys' mischief, or boyish pranks, as father Tommy described them. Was there a possible homosexual motive? The thought first cropped up when we learned that one of the Rover car owners was in the habit of picking up young teenage boys from the City centre

We had no evidence and nothing had come out to reveal even the slightest hint that any of the Hastie boys were so involved, but then neither did we have anything to prove otherwise. It was with the homosexuality aspect in mind later in the enquiry, and with nothing else to work on, that I chose to see the highly experienced and respected pathologist, Professor David Gee, in Leeds to discuss with him again his post-mortem examinations of the boys.

He agreed with our theory but he could offer no evidence. His post-mortem examinations were always so thorough that, had he found anything at all, he would certainly have made all he discovered known to me. But certain aspects of the sexual theory still suggested a possible connection. In the first place, the house where the boys lived was fairly near a public toilet frequented by homosexuals. We also knew that a homosexually-motivated murder had occurred within a few hundred yards of the Hastie's house and the public toilet about ten days after the fire. Unfortunately the officers enquiring into that murder had discovered nothing to help in solving the Selby Street killings.

I decided that we should carefully observe any likely homosexuals using the toilets in the vicinity and make enquiries among other such people known to us. We all appreciated that homosexuals would be naturally wary of us but they would also know that, as long as they were not breaking the law, like any other members of society, they would have nothing to worry about.

One day, during one of the early morning discussions in the cramped General Office with the twenty or so officers now remaining on the enquiry, I said, 'I am sure Edith and Tommy will not accept it, and are we being fair to them in even exploring just the chance that Charlie may have become involved in some kind of homosexuality?'

'We don't know, do we?' answered Detective Sergeant Mick Trafford. 'We have looked at everything else, haven't we?' he continued. 'We might find there is a connection. We shall upset both Tommy and Edith whatever way it goes and we might well upset a few homosexuals as well. But, knowing you, I sense you are going to tell me we won't bloody know at all if at least we don't try to find out. One thing, Boss, we know we can always rely on our honesty of purpose if complaints come flooding in.' It was surprising we had not had any complaints made against us so far, for we knew that people in the district were getting fed up with our questions, questions, and more questions and within the Police force we knew there was a feeling that we were now 'wasting time and money' getting nowhere.

Our discussions continued well into the morning. Fortunately, I was blessed with being able to hold on to the most experienced and tactful officers as others were drafted away to attend to other matters. We all agreed that we would talk to anyone who might be willing to help us. I decided that I would not publicise our new venture because I did not want to upset Edith and Tommy unless it became absolutely necessary.

About this time the ever-loquacious Tommy often called at my office once more. As always, he expressed his thoughts about one or other of his former neighbours being the arsonist and considered no one else as a possibility. He often wore a jaunty bright red tartan cap when he called to see us, and, viewing the mountains of paper and the total industry of the Incident Room one day, he announced that he knew we would eventually catch the person responsible for killing his boys and, when that day came, he would throw his cap in the Humber, and then get 'real good drunk'. Sadly, Tommy's days were numbered.

He called again a few days later. As usual he was most amiable and appeared to have plenty of time on his hands. We chatted generally about whatever seemed to come to mind and he even mentioned that the local criminal fraternity were fed up with us 'still asking bloody useless questions'. Always dwelling on his sons' deaths, Tommy said that, as he had been arrested each time he had committed a crime, he believed his sons' killer would be arrested too. 'You know I often lie in bed thinking who done it,' Tommy added. 'I think of this one and then another one. See, Edith and me just live for the day you come and tell us you have got the bastard. You will get him you know. We know you will, Mr. Sagar. But, bloody hell, it is taking a long time, isn't it.'

Tears filled his eyes as he went on, 'I sometimes think if I wasn't in prison the bastard wouldn't have dared to set our house alight. And my boys would still be with us and enjoying themselves, wouldn't they?'

'On the other hand,' I said, 'you could have been there, and you too might have been killed. We don't know, do we, so really there is no point in dwelling on if's, but's and maybe's. As it is, you are here, Tommy, and I'm glad you support Edith like you do. God knows, she needs you.' I continued, 'Tommy, did you ever discuss sex with Charlie?' 'Sex, no. Come on, Boss, he was only 14,' he replied. 'Only interested in Rugby League was our Charlie.' I said, 'He was 15, Tommy, just a year younger than you when you married Edith.' He replied, 'He was 14 when I last saw him a year ago. He knew nowt about sex did Charlie.'

A week or so later I saw Detective Sergeant Raymond Harrod talking to a young man in one of the offices in Gordon Street. Sergeant Harrod told me the young man called himself Bruce George Peter Lee. 'He used to be called Peter Dinsdale. I have not arrested him,' the sergeant said, 'but he says he has acted indecently with a number of men. You are not going to believe this, Boss, but he says, apart from others, he has been indecent with Charlie Hastie! You'll also be interested to know Lee also says Charlie Hastie took money from him!'

I looked across the room at Lee. He was undernourished, pale and rather inconspicuous, sitting quietly beside a small table drinking a cup of tea. He appeared to be just another person giving us details about the Hastie boys, but he seemed strangely self-assured. That peculiarity made me curious about him so I decided that, if we were to see him again I would interview him myself. Also, if he was being honest, we were at least getting some confirmation about our sexual theory. I had no idea then that the young man sitting there would somehow hold a lasting interest for me.

Lee agreed he would make a written statement relating to his sexual activities and I left Sergeant Harrod to obtain a statement. He was later allowed to leave the Police Station and Sergeant Harrod began to seek whatever corroboration he could. We noted that Lee did not reveal any kind of irritation or annoyance about his admitted relationship with Charlie. His statement simply reinforced the view, if true, that Charlie was indeed involved in sexual activities.

Enquiries and surveillance continued into the sexual theory, and during the first week in June, following consultation with everyone on the enquiry, I decided that by the end of that week we should invite a selected number of likely men for interview. I decided that this operation should take place, as far as possible, in one day, so that those we questioned would be available to us all at the same time for any possible cross-checking and so prevent any unnecessary delays or embarrassment for those interviewed. Meantime Detective Sergeant Harrod made more enquiries into Bruce George Peter Lee's statement so I included him among those for questioning. His admitted sexual relationship with Charlie was interesting but I realised that with Charlie dead we had no chance of proving it.

I was now being asked to release even more of my small group of investigators, but refused to do so, and fortunately the assiduity of those who remained with me was as strong as ever. The *Hull Daily Mail* too was always willing to help with whatever I needed the Hull public to know, but on the current line of enquiry we publicised nothing. Meantime, I could not help but feel that there were still certain senior officers at Humberside Police Headquarters who believed that we were now wasting time and money in continuing the enquiry.

These thoughts were reinforced when, without any consultation with me or any of my men, the powers-that-be at Humberside Police HQ decided that no further overtime payments would be paid in respect of the 'Hastie Arson'. However, I need not have been too concerned, as, to a man, everyone was willing to carry on, regardless of the long hours without overtime money.

Shortly after the overtime limitation, one senior officer telephoned me saying I really ought to bring the investigation to an end as we had already spent six months at it and must have covered every possibility in that time. I asked the officer if he was actually giving me an order to close down and he replied that I should perhaps take it that way. I answered, reluctantly, that I would close down but only if I was given the order in writing. No such order ever appeared.

It is not good policy to release all details of a crime being investigated to the press, as it is essential, in my view, in the interests of justice, that pertinent detail is withheld to be able to test the veracity of a person's admission during interview. In my view this practice is also essential for the examination of evidence before the courts. Matters I currently withheld from the press related to the actual details of the scene of the fire such as the spent matches, the mark where the paraffin can had stood, the amount of paraffin used, and, latterly, of course, the homosexual aspect.

As is the case with many experienced senior detectives I have mixed with good people and bad people, and with the rich, the dubious rich, and very often with the poor and inadequate. I have always believed in being honest and reasonable with everyone. Eventually that belief was to be put to the test in a manner I would never have expected.

Chapter Four

On Friday, 6 June 1980, the anniversary of D-Day and now six months after the Selby Street arson attack, various men we had kept an eye on were found and invited to different local police stations in the hope that we would have a breakthrough. One of these was Bruce George Peter Lee. I saw him that afternoon sitting in one of the small offices after he had arrived at Gordon Street with Detective Sergeant Harrod. I noticed by his appearance that he had been drinking. I did not speak to him then but saw he was provided with a cup of tea and toilet facilities. He had been living part of the time at the local Salvation Army hostel.

Lee, then 19-years-old, was still the only real sexual connection with Charlie that we had discovered, although we believed there might have been others. I did not feel it was right and proper to embark upon an interview with him when he was brought in. He was not drunk but there was certainly the smell of alcohol about him. It was several hours later when I saw Lee again. He was still sitting in the office with Detective Sergeant Alan Young. Detective Sergeant Ray Harrod, who now joined me, had given Lee yet another cup of tea and Lee was just finishing off a plateful of fish and chips. I said, 'Hello, Bruce, do you remember me?'

'Yes, sir,' he replied. 'I saw you here before when Sergeant Harrod saw me and I made a statement about what I knew with the Hastie's.'

'That's right,' I said. 'I am Detective Superintendent Sagar. I am responsible for the enquiry into the deaths – the murders – of the three members of the Hastie family following the arson attack on their home during the early hours of Tuesday, 4 December, last year. We are enquiring, in fact, into three murders, the arson and grievous bodily harm by burning on little Thomas Hastie and his mother, Edith Hastie.'

'I understand,' he said. 'You are the boss aren't you.'

He was relaxed, appeared quite amiable, and it was now clear that he was sober.

I took out my notebook and I began making a contemporaneous note since only notes made at the time can be referred to by a witness giving evidence. As I wrote I could not help but feel intense observation, on Lee's part, of all that was happening and all that was about him. As time went on Lee's observation became fairly normal as he followed my written words and hesitated in his utterances until my note-taking was almost at the same point as his spoken words. As any contemporaneous note-taker knows, his attitude was most helpful. However, I had no idea what his comments and amazing powers of observation were to reveal in the weeks to come.

I told him that we had mounted 'quite an operation' that day and that we had been looking for him earlier in the day as part of the operation. I went on to tell him that I was going to ask him some very important questions and informed him that he must first understand that he was not obliged to say anything unless he wished to do so, but, whatever he might say, might be put into writing and given in evidence.

'Yes,' he replied. 'You will be tired of writing soon.'

In my normal, rather quietly spoken manner, and in nothing but a gamble,

Bruce George Peter Lee.
(Picture by courtesy of *Hull Daily Mail*)

I said, 'Bruce, I'll be quite blunt with you. I think that you started that fire at the Hastie family's house and that indecency with you and Charlie is probably the cause of it all somehow.'

Looking rather solemn and in a voice devoid of emotion, he said, 'I didn't mean to kill them,'

Concentrating as much on his words as I was on my writing, I said, 'Let's start at the beginning. You must, in fairness to you, know that I am guessing when I say indecency could be the cause because we haven't anyone to tell us that was the cause.'

He replied, 'You might be guessing but you're right. It was Charlie. See, after mucking about he would always want my money. It used to make me angry, see.'

I said, 'Why did you set fire to the house?'

He replied, 'Charlie, he just kept wanting my money.'

'When did you decide to set the house on fire then?'

'About a week before I did it. See, this friend I know, he bought me some paraffin. I had a container, it was one that had orange juice in before, you know the big plastic ones.'

'Go on,' I said.

He continued, 'One night I am thinking I am going to go to Charlie's house and set it on fire, give him a real frightener. I had a drink and left our house late on. Mum and dad was snoring asleep. They'd been drinking in Alex pub that night. I had my container nearly full of paraffin and had some matches.'

'What were you wearing?' I asked.

'Black jumper, denim jacket and my dark trousers. I didn't want to stand out. All dark stuff.'

He continued, 'I walked along Selby Street. There was one or two people about so I went under the bridge, the flyover, and stood in the shadows. I was standing there a good time until it went real quiet.'

'What did you see?' I asked.

'Just before I did it a police car went by and I saw a couple, just a young couple, walk down Selby Street from Boulevard way a good bit before that.'

'Anyone else?'

'Yes, a man with a dog.'

'Go on,' I said.

He replied, 'Just after police car went by I thought, knickers, shall I do it? Then I thought knickers, and Charlie's voice kept on in my mind and I thought knickers, I'm sick of Charlie taking my money, I'll do it.'

'Hold on,' I said. 'Tell me about hearing Charlie's voice in your mind.'

'It was in my head, Charlie saying, "I want money," nag, nag, nag. "I'll tell the police."'

'Tell the police what?' I said.

'About us mucking about indecent, and I was frightened he would tell the police. I kept giving him money but I didn't have much. I couldn't keep giving it to him.'

'How much would you give him at a time?'

'A pound or fifty pence or more, what I had, but always having to give into him made me angry.'

28

'He was quite a powerful lad, was he?'
'Yes, I suppose he was. I couldn't keep giving it to him. I was only getting £16-odd Social Security and what I got working at meat market and that.'
I said, 'Let's get back to you standing in the dark shadows under the flyover.'
'Yes, I thought, fuck it, I'll do it, and went across the road, down the footpath to his house.'
'How did you know which was Charlie's house?'
He replied, 'I'd been to back door in summer time. It was the corner house. It was easy for me to work out from that which was his.'
'Think very carefully,' I said. 'I want you to tell me very slowly exactly what happened from the time you approached the front door of the house.'
He replied, 'Have I been going too fast for you. You must be flipping fed up and tired writing all this. You can go home and we'll do it tomorrow if you like. I don't mind.'
'We are doing it tonight, Bruce. Do you appreciate the seriousness of this?'
'I know I will get about 15 years for it, that's how serious it is. I didn't mean to kill them.'
'So you went to the house. Go on.'
'I just stood there a minute. No one could see me in the corner. I know I was going to put the paraffin inside and through the letter-box. I wasn't going to be able to open the front door, was I, but all houses have letter-boxes, don't they?'
'Go on,' I said. 'Tell me what you saw there.'
'The letter-box was in a wide piece of wood between two pieces of glass at the side of the door. Well, I just unscrewed the top off my container and poured the paraffin through the letter-box. It must have soaked the net curtain inside.'
'Go on. Didn't paraffin run on the outside?'
'Some did but not much. It was no good pouring it outside, was it?'
Knowing that he had a partly paralysed right hand, I asked him to tell me how he actually poured the paraffin. He replied, 'I just lifted the letter-box flap with this (right) hand and rested the container on me knee and rested the top onto the letter-box real steady and poured it in real slow.'
'What did you do immediately after pouring the paraffin?'
'I just stood back from the door a few seconds and put the container down behind me.'
'Just where?'
'On concrete down behind me.'
'Carry on,' I said.
'I got my matches, struck one, and it went out.'
'Did it go out before you could do anything with it?'
'Yes, I just chucked it down on ground. I don't see it matters.'
'It does. Go on,' I said.
'I struck another match, it went out and I threw it away and then I got some paper and lit that with another match and that was all right. I put it all through the letter-box. There was paper about there. It was breezy and a bit of drizzle, but bits of rubbish paper was blowing about a bit.'

'What newspaper do you read?'
'*Mail* sometimes, but not much. *Mirror* sometimes. I get *Sun* if I want to see if there is a film on telly.'
'What did you think it was like inside the house? Any lights on in there?'
'No, no chance. They was all asleep.'
'Who did you think was in there?'
'Their dad was in prison. I knew that, so all the family was asleep in bed, all of them.'
'Do you know all the family?'
'Yes, I met Charlie through his sister Angie at the rugby ground, and I know Paul, little Tommy, Peter and, well, their mum and sisters would be there. And Charlie and their dog. It used to protect little Tommy.'
'Did you know where they slept?'
'Bedrooms upstairs, that's all.'
'Did you believe they were asleep when you were pouring the paraffin through the letter-box?'
'Of course I did,' he replied.
'And having poured the paraffin in you set the house alight with a match and paper?'
'Yes, put the paper through the letter-box, that is what I went there for and then I saw it go up. The net curtain was in flames straight away and then the rest went in big flames, real well. I picked up my container and ran.'
'Why take the container with you?
'Fingerprints. You would find them.'
'Go on,' I said.
'I saw little Tommy at his school the other day. I just knew you were thinking about me. I was never going to tell you and I knew you had no clues. You guessed right with the mucking about. If there was no mucking about, no asking for money, they would be alive today, all of them.'
'So you ran away from the fire. Where to?'
He replied, 'Past the motor-bike shop. I was soon puffed so I walked down in the shadows past this fucking place (Gordon Street Police Station).'
'With your container?' I asked.
'Yes, under my jacket. See, when I got to bottom near docks I went round to West Dock Avenue on waste land and set fire to me container there. Plastic see. It burned easy after having paraffin inside. I held it in my hand until only handle was left, then threw it down and it burned there.'
I was impressed by his recall and steady flow of words. Little did I appreciate at that moment how incredible that recall would be.
'Did you hear any fire engines after you ran away from Selby Street?'
'Yes. I thought that was quick. I was a good way away and I could hear engine noise going. It was quiet in the distance.'
'Had Charlie lived would he have known it was you who set his house on fire?'
'No, nobody would ever know.'
'So, as you've said earlier, a frightener can hardly be right because he wouldn't know it was you he should fear.'
He made no comment.

I continued, 'It's an important point, Bruce.'

'I know,' he said, 'but I'm thinking of myself now.'

'When did you first hear of Charlie's death?'

'On ITN News.'

'What did you think then?'

'I was a bit upset, then I thought, go for a drink. He was dead. No more nag, nag from him for money.'

'What did you think when you heard the other two, Paul and Peter, were dead?'

With just a touch of emotion in his voice he answered, 'I didn't mean to kill them. Knickers, I didn't mean to kill those two.'

'But you did intend to kill Charlie?'

His face was expressionless as he stared at me for about half a minute but made no reply.

I asked, 'Have you been sleeping well since?'

'I was when Charlie died but I wasn't when I knew Paul and Peter was dead; but it was alright when I'd had a drink.'

'Where have you been all day today?'

'Drinking at different pubs, Hessle Road and town. I thought you lot was looking for me. How did you know about the mucking about, indecency you say. I like doing puzzles in puzzle books. You lot can help me with some if you are good at guessing. You didn't have a clue about this fire, did you? I covered my tracks well didn't I?'

I continued, 'I have told you before, in fairness to you we just speculated, guessed, that maybe indecency was a possible connection because, my goodness, we have explored every other possibility.'

'I'm telling you the truth now, aren't I? I bet you're sick of writing.'

'Are you gay?' I asked.

'No. See it started when I was in children's homes but I stopped after the fire and Charlie and that.'

I said, 'The paper you lit the fire with, could it have been a *Sun* newspaper?'

'Yes, it could be, it was just a newspaper but you wouldn't know that, 'cause it must have all got burned after I pushed it through letter-box.'

'Was it just one small piece of paper, just enough to light the paraffin maybe?'

'No, 'he replied. 'A good bit, see, there was plenty of paraffin so I put a good lot of crumpled up newspaper in so it would burn. My container was nearly full of paraffin, you know.'

I continued, 'I must tell you that until now you have been here without properly being arrested, but now I am telling you that you are under arrest.'

He replied, 'Yes, I know. I am under arrest if you take me and put me in a cell. You will be doing that soon, I suppose.'

'And of course I must remind you that you are still under caution.'

'I know I don't have to speak but I am feeling better now I'm telling you.'

He then chose to make a voluntary statement under caution which I wrote down at his dictation. In it he repeated his responsibility for setting the Hastie home on fire.

Later that night I said, 'Some time after the fire and deaths we received a number of telephone calls, and so did the Hastie family, from someone who seemed to know something about the fire. We traced some of the callers and eliminated them from the enquiry. Did you make any such calls?'

'I did. I rang Central (Police Station) and said, "I didn't mean it."'

'Yes, you see that caller emphasised the second "D" in the word "didn't", just the same as you did earlier in this interview.'

'It was me who rang and said that. Did I speak to you?'

'No, but your brief message was recorded in our Op's room and I have listened to it.'

Later I said to Lee, 'Even when we saw you in May when we were well into our guesswork on indecency, you chose to keep your mouth shut regarding your guilt.'

'Yes, I wasn't going to tell you nowt.'

My colleagues and I were motivated purely by a search for the truth. But was Lee telling the truth? I examined what he had told me and realised it all rang desperately true. But what of corroboration? And did we really have a motive? We needed to study the questions and answers we had from this person calling himself Bruce George Peter Lee.

Lee made it clear that his motive stemmed from the fact that every time he was involved in sexual activity with Charlie Hastie, Charlie demanded money from him. The letter-box at No. 12 Selby Street was, as described by Lee, located in a wide piece of wood between two pieces of glass at the side of the door. There was, as described by Lee, a net curtain draped on the inside of the front door of the house. Lee described dropping spent matches and Detective Constable Frank Munns had found the spent matches outside near the front door. Forensic examination revealed paper was, as described by Lee, used to ignite paraffin. A police car did drive along Selby Street just before the fire, as described by Lee. A young couple did, as described by Lee, walk down Selby Street during the relevant time. There was, as described by Lee, a man walking there with his dog a little while before the fire. Lee described hearing fire engines very soon after he started the fire. Firemen were on the scene very quickly. Was this insignificant looking young man the person we had been looking for day and night for the past six months?

Detective Sergeant Harrod had discovered that Lee was suffering from a congenital deformation of his right hand and leg. This caused him to limp slightly when he walked but did not appear to cause him much difficulty. Examining the questions and answers in my notebook later that night it all seemed so neat and tidy. There again the truth is quite often neat and tidy. Lee could hardly know the detail he was telling us unless he was there at the scene at the time.

I decided to detain him and took him to the cells at the Priory Road Police Station a few miles away, telling him he was being detained while we continued our enquiries. Our Gordon Street Police Station was suitable enough for us to work in but was not up to Home Office standard to keep prisoners in either of the two cells there.

The following morning, Saturday, 7 June 1980, I again saw Lee and, although he hadn't asked for a solicitor, I told him that I believed that he should have legal advice (This was before the introduction of the 1986 Police and Criminal

Evidence Act). At first he didn't seem interested in legal advice, but after further prompting he asked me to telephone for a solicitor. I told him I wasn't just going to ring anyone and that it was a matter for him to select a solicitor from the yellow pages of the telephone book. This he did after some deliberation, and nominated the Hull solicitors, Frankish Iveson. I did not know if he had been a client with the firm before or not. Being a Saturday morning, there was no reply at the solicitors' office but eventually I located the Managing Clerk of the firm, Mr. Eric Pearce, who told me that he would attend at Gordon Street Police Station at lunchtime that day. Meanwhile I asked Lee to show me where he had disposed of his plastic container, and where he had stood under the flyover before setting the fire. He agreed. We then went in a C.I.D. car and on his direction went to waste land off West Dock Avenue, near Hull fish dock and about half a mile from Selby Street. I saw that this area was littered with rubbish and that there were numerous places where rubbish had been burned. I realised that the possibility of finding any remains of the plastic container was out of the question.

We left West Dock Avenue and shortly afterwards Lee indicated a spot under the flyover near to the railway lines: 'That's where I was standing that night till it was all quiet.' We returned to Gordon Street Police Station.

Shortly afterwards Mr. Eric Pearce called at my office. I had a conversation with him and saw Lee with Mr. Pearce a few moments later. I said, 'I have told Mr. Pearce what you are here for and have told him briefly what you have told me and what you have said in your written statement.'

Lee replied, 'Yes, I have told the truth, haven't I.'

'Yes, you have, just about,' I replied.

I then showed Lee a two-litre soft drink plastic container and said, 'Is this like the one you used to carry the paraffin?'

He replied, 'Yes, like that but I don't think it had those rings around it (indicating rings in the mould of the plastic around the container).' Mr. Pearce then had a private conversation with Lee which lasted about half an hour and then left the Police Station.

Later I asked Lee when he had decided to set fire to the Hastie house. He replied that he had thought about it a week or more beforehand. I also asked him if he thought that he would start the fire at night when all the family were asleep in their beds and have a big fire.

'Yes,' he replied.

Pointing out to him that the fire appeared to be a calculated act, carried out with a great deal of thought, and, according to him, with the intention of stopping Charlie taking his money once and for all, he replied, 'Yes, that's right. It's true.'

I added, 'You were after Charlie's life that night, weren't you, Bruce, and as far as you were concerned it was Heaven help anyone else who suffered in the fire?'

He replied, 'Yes, maybe I was.'

Upon further examining all the evidence, I decided there was sufficient evidence to charge him with causing Charlie's death.

I read out the police charge sheet, that on 5 December 1979 he murdered Charles Hastie.

He looked directly into my face, but made no comment.

Lee appeared before the Hull Magistrates Court, on 10 June 1980, charged with the murder of Charles Hastie. He was represented by Mr. Robert Gunby of Frankish, Iveson & Son. Mr. Gunby made no application for bail and the magistrates remanded Lee in custody to H.M. Prison, Leeds. They also granted him legal aid.

Meantime our enquiries continued. Fortunately, the many points Lee had made were, to a great extent, already corroborated by what was discovered at the scene of the fire.

I visited Edith and Tommy the day after we detained Lee and told them he had been arrested. Tommy appeared pleased. 'I don't think I know him,' he said. Edith smiled a little but was rather subdued as she said, 'It won't bring my boys back, will it?'

By now I knew the couple well, and I could not help but feel very sad for them, for their state of grief was still evident. Pictures of the three boys were prominently displayed in the living room of their new council house for all to see.

Bidding them farewell, I said, 'Thank God you two have each other to lean on. Take care of her, Tommy.'

'Don't worry about us,' smiled Tommy. 'We're beginning to sort ourselves out now. It will be better now we know you've got somebody. But I am not going to chuck my hat in the Humber. I don't feel like doing it now. See, I should have known who Charlie was knocking about with, but I didn't.'

One afternoon shortly afterwards, I was busy at Gordon Street when I received a telephone call from Police Headquarters. My heart leaped with disbelief as the Operations Room officer said, 'Sorry to bother you, Boss, but I thought you should know that we think Tommy Hastie is dead. Looks like he's been killed in a road accident.'

'Oh no,' I exclaimed. 'He can't be.'

'Well, the officer at the accident thinks it's him, but to be sure, and, as you know him so well, we would like you to go to the mortuary and have a look at the body. He was driving a 125cc motor bike and it's thought he had his daughter, Nicola, on the back. He failed to take a bend, hit the kerb and crashed into a concrete lamp post. He was dead on arrival at Hull Royal Infirmary. Nicola is hurt, but not too badly. No one else was involved in the crash.'

'Does Edith Hastie know about it?' I enquired. 'No,' he replied. 'It only happened half an hour ago, but the main reason for ringing you is to ask you to view the body, and, if you see that it's him, go and break the news to his wife.'

I put down the telephone, my mind in a state of anguish and disbelief. The Operations Room officer appeared certain, but maybe there was a mistake and it wasn't Tommy after all. But then, Tommy did have a small motor bike and one of his daughters was called Nicola.

Full of feelings of foreboding I knew that there was only one thing to do. I had to go to the City Mortuary and find out. Shortly afterwards I was ushered into the cold grey mortuary. One glance at the lone body lying there on a trolley was enough. The amiable and talkative Tommy was in an endless sleep, his life silent, cold and still. If I had not asked for his early release from prison Tommy would probably be still alive. Indirectly he too had become a victim of the fire and I felt responsible.

Thankfully, the ever-thoughtful Detective Policewoman Janet Peterson agreed to accompany me to see Edith. She had been engaged on the murder enquiry from the beginning and she had become quite friendly with Edith. As we drove the few miles to Edith's home we were both in a thoroughly unhappy state of mind.

'A policeman's lot really is not a happy one today, is it, Janet?' I muttered, as we drove along, foolishly trying to bring a smile to her face.

'No,' she replied, 'but then practically every avenue we've explored on this enquiry is touched with varying degrees of sadness, isn't it? But how are you going to tell Edith?'

Edith was tidying her small front garden when Janet and I arrived that afternoon. 'Can we go inside, Edith?' I asked.

'Yes, of course, we can,' she replied. 'But what's the matter. Why are you two together? You two don't usually work together.'

Once inside the living room I quietly told Edith about the accident and her husband's death. It was always my policy not to become personally or emotionally involved in matters involving my professional life, but on this occasion Janet and I were, to say the least, overcome with sadness. We did not have words to express our sorrow. 'Something's wrong,' Edith had said as the three of us sat down in the living room. 'What has happened? It's something bad. I can tell,' she said just before I broke the news.

The following day the press reported Tommy's death with items headed: 'Death jinx haunts Hasties again'; 'Tragedy family: now Dad is killed'; 'Fire-death father dies on road'. Edith also told the press that a few days previously a milk bottle had been thrown through her living room window, showering the family with glass. She also claimed that a few weeks before that she and Tommy had been insulted by their new neighbours. There appeared to be little sympathy for the couple, even now. It was impossible to imagine what Edith was going through, and, in my opinion, many a lesser woman would not have been able to handle the tragedy of it at all. 'I have to keep going for my surviving family, don't I, Mr. Sagar?'

Tommy's funeral was a particularly sad occasion, attended by some of us still working on the enquiry. Several members of the criminal fraternity attended too. Poor Tommy, a likeable rascal if ever there was one, his cheerful chatter whenever he called to see us would be missed. The sorrow of his passing permeated the whole group of us for days on end.

Chapter Five

Meanwhile our enquiries were focused on Lee. We had to know what kind of person he was. We knew that he had been known as Peter Dinsdale until he changed his name by deed poll to Bruce George Peter Lee in the summer of 1979, but the name change was of no real significance to us. He was born in Manchester in 1960 and since birth suffered with a congenital right spastic hemiplegia affecting the right hand and leg which caused him to limp with his right leg and often hold his right hand across his chest. The product of a broken home, he had spent a great deal of his life in the care of the local authority. Despite his handicap, he had, until recently, been employed as a labourer at the local cattle market. He sometimes lived in the local Salvation Army hostel and was described by many people as 'a bit of a loner'. I was prepared to dislike him, but I didn't. Significantly, no one, including social workers who knew him before his arrest, ever described him as dangerous or mentally ill and, apart from his disability, he appeared no different from the thousands of other people we dealt with during the enquiry.

Solicitor's Managing Clerk, Eric Pearce, and Defence Solicitor, Robert Gunby, did not voice any concern about Lee's mental state then either. But how could he apparently set fire to the Hastie family home, killing three boys, and seemingly go about his normal routine at the cattle market, in his favourite public houses and at Social Security offices as if nothing had happened? Why had he decided to make his admissions when he did? Just who was the amiable Bruce George Peter Lee, alias Dinsdale? He was now incarcerated on remand in Leeds Prison. And as is normal with prisoners on remand on murder charges, he would be examined by the prison medical officer.

It quickly became public knowledge that he had been charged before the Magistrates Court and several people called our incident room with information about him. None was of any evidential value, but Lee's arrest did cause plenty of gossip. The apathy we had encountered for so long had now come to an end, even the local villainy was friendly towards us. Maybe they thought we were, at long last, about to get out of their way.

Just as we felt we were getting nothing but tittle tattle from the public Mrs. Rosabelle (Ros) Fenton called our incident room. She had lived with her husband and daughter in a maisonette in a six-story building known as Troutbeck House, in Hull City centre. She was seen by Detective Sergeant John Martin. All along, unknown to any of us, ever since the arson enquiry began she had privately nursed a personal interest in our investigation.

Ros Fenton told Sergeant Martin that during the evening of Thursday, 21 June 1979, just one year earlier, she, her daughter, Samantha, then aged seven, and a neighbour, Mrs. Gail Lenny, were in the Fenton family maisonette. Mr. Fenton was working away from home. Samantha was put to bed shortly after 11.00 p.m. Ros and Gail then had coffee and a cigarette each before Gail left. Within a few minutes Ros went upstairs, checked that Samantha was asleep and went to bed.

Ros was about to settle down for the night when she heard some neighbours shouting. At first she thought they were arguing but then realised they were shouting, 'Fire!' She sat 'bolt upright' in bed (the same description as Edith Hastie used). Sitting there for a brief moment, Ros thought she could hear rain falling against a window but suddenly realised that what she could hear was the sound of fire crackling. She jumped from her bed, dashed to her bedroom door and switched on the landing light. As she did so, she heard a loud bang and saw a great ball of orange fire shoot up the stairs from the hall.

Ros immediately ran into Samantha's room and dragged her sleepy daughter from her bed. The heat was now so intense that she felt her skin peeling away. Samantha, now awakened by the commotion, found herself on the floor huddled against her mother. Ros tried desperately hard to protect her from the heat and smoke now leaping into the room from the open door at the top of the stairs. In fear of their lives, she opened the bedroom window and shouted for help. She didn't know if her cries were heard or not, but, with the open window creating a draught, the heat and flames became more intense and she collapsed to the floor. The next she could remember was being wrapped in a blanket and taken to Hull Royal Infirmary. Ros and Samantha suffered terrible burns to their bodies and Ros, who was seven months pregnant, also had a miscarriage and lost her baby.

Neighbours heard Ros screaming for help and saw smoke belching out of the windows. One male neighbour ran to Ros's house, where he saw other neighbours were now gathering, and shouting to Ros to throw Samantha out of the window. Ros did not hear. The man wrapped a wet towel around his mouth and bravely dashed through the flames to Samantha's bedroom. He found Ros unconscious on the bedroom floor. He dragged her across the landing to a balcony from where two other neighbours helped him carry her out of the house.

The rescuer thought somebody else might have gone in to find Samantha but no one did. Coughing and spluttering, he said to himself, 'In for a penny in for a pound,' and gave himself 30 seconds' breathing space before going back. Once again he went into the heat and darkness. Fighting against the now dense smoke he stumbled towards Samantha's bedroom from where he heard the sound of moaning. Groping his way along, he found Samantha lying on the floor. He carefully picked her up and carried her out and on to the balcony. The Fire Brigade arrived within minutes, quickly extinguished the fire and administered oxygen to Ros and Samantha until the arrival of an ambulance.

Like the three Hastie boys, Ros and Samantha were transferred to the Pinderfields Burns Unit, Wakefield. Ros was critically ill and told me later that, on her arrival in hospital, she was given just five hours to live. Medical examination showed Ros Fenton was suffering from 45% body burns to her face, neck, trunk, arms and legs. After two months' intensive care and many skin grafts at Pinderfields she was allowed home. Samantha suffered grievous burning to one of her arms, with patches of burning on the legs. She was discharged after six weeks and then referred to a burns specialist in Hull.

The police attended the scene of the fire that night but unfortunately did little to determine its real cause, wrongly thinking a discarded cigarette had been left in the entrance to the house. No one had been killed so there was no inquest. The police simply recorded the incident as a house fire caused by the careless disregard of a cigarette. No one gave any thought to the possibility of arson and the police did not see fit to arrange a forensic examination of the remains of the maisonette. When Ros was finally discharged the police had already decided the cause of the fire was accidental. And Ros was thoroughly occupied with continuing hospital treatment for herself and her daughter. In June 1979, Bruce George Peter Lee lived nearby.

Detective Sergeant Martin suggested I accompany him to see Ros when he saw her again as 'it appeared the police had not properly investigated the fire'. Ros told us she had never believed a discarded cigarette had caused the blaze in her home, but when she returned from hospital no one listened to her. And she said, being so badly burned fighting for her life and worrying about her pretty daughter, she was not in much of a position to argue with anyone. She told me she always suspected Lee was responsible. It was an instinctive feeling she had, but she had said little to anyone about her suspicions. Ros knew herself, and had since heard, that Lee had been seen in the vicinity during the night she and her daughter were burned. Now that he had been charged with killing the Hastie boys, she believed it was right for her to tell us of her suspicions and her intense dislike of him.

I instructed Sergeant Martin to investigate every aspect of her story as a matter of urgency. I did not want to interview Lee until I was satisfied that everything possible had been covered. Once I had read the statements Sergeant Martin had taken and listened to various items of information it was my duty to see Lee again. I contacted Eric Pearce to tell him of my proposed visit. Mr. Pearce thanked me, but did not wish to accompany me at the interview.

The following day, along with Detective Sergeant Martin, I went to Her Majesty's Prison, Leeds. At my request he was brought from his cell to the large open-plan visitors' room where several other prisoners were being seen by lawyers, police and probation officers. After cautioning him that he did not have to speak to me if he did not wish to do so and that whatever he did say would be taken down in writing and might be given in evidence, I continued, 'We have come to see you because we believe that the arson at the Hastie house, 12 Selby Street, was probably not the first fire you have started, Bruce.'

'I haven't done any more, honest.'

I said, 'Bruce I attended that fire during the early hours of 4 December last year and what I cannot get out of my head is the fact that to my mind the person responsible for that fire made a very good job of it.'

'Yes, I put plenty of paraffin in there. It was enough for three houses.'

I continued, 'The way it was done kind of tells me the culprit, who we now believe was you, surely wasn't doing it then for the first time'.

'I see,' he replied.

'Do you? I wonder if you do,' I said.

He replied, 'Do you know somat? You are the only bloke I know who shows any interest in me. You said before that in my life I've never had a chance. You are right.'

'Well, yes I did,' I said. 'You don't appear to have had much of a life. You haven't just been dragged up. You have been kicked from pillar to post, it seems to me.'

'That's what I think. You are right but you know you are the first to ever agree with what I think and be honest and say so.'

'Do you have a grudge against various people, Bruce?' I asked.

'I get sick and fed up with a lot of people. See, as you know I was brought up in children's homes. My mum never cared a shit about me. No one ever has. You know somat, Mr. Sagar, that's truth.'

'What of friends, Bruce? Do you have any?'

'No, not a real friend, no, no friends.'

I continued, 'What of fire, Bruce, fire in houses? Arson? Do you like fire?'

'What of it?' he muttered.

'I think you are responsible for quite a number of fires?'

'What makes you think that?'

'By the general circumstances of the fire at 12, Selby Street.'

What I was endeavouring to achieve by these questions and comments was to see if Lee would tell me about the fire at Ros Fenton's home in Troutbeck House without my first mentioning it.

'Maybe I have, 'he said.

'Like Troutbeck House, where Ros Fenton used to live?'

Lee stared into my eyes with intolerable directness for a long minute or more. Initially his stare and general demeanour made me feel just a little uneasy for he just stared hard but made no comment.

'Troutbeck House, Bruce.'

'What of it?'

'I think you caused that fire and so does Sergeant Martin here. Apart from burning the house badly, as I suspect you did, you caused dreadful burns to Mrs. Fenton and her daughter, Samantha. Mrs. Fenton was seven months pregnant at the time and lost her baby after being very badly burned.'

'I never did that,' he replied, but within a second or so he said, 'So if I tell you, then what happens?'

I replied, 'Well, I am going to be frank with you. I can't tell you. But really I am interested in knowing everything you have done. I mean everything.'

'But you will think I am a fire bug.'

'I'm not here to put a label on you, Bruce.'

'No, you are being all right, both of you are. I expected a good kicking or somat when you got me, but you didn't.'

'Troutbeck House,' I said.

He replied, 'Look, I did do that one but it wasn't through letter-box.'

'I know that.'

'It wasn't a paraffin job either. I just opened the door, see. It wasn't shut properly and I just got some paper, set it alight with my matches and then threw it well inside the door. It went up in no time.'

'What time of day was that?'

'It was night, you must know that. That woman was in there. She must have been in bed. She don't like me.'

'You knew her then?'

'Yes,' he replied.

'Why set her and her home on fire?'
'Just did it. Someone I knew didn't like her and, well, I just did it.'
'Why fire her house?'
'I like fires, I do. I like fires.'
'Do you like fires to such an extent that you will kill?'
'Don't know.'
'I understand Mrs. Fenton had about 50% of her body surface burned, and her young child was also subject to terrible burns.'
'Yes, I knew they was. I wasn't bothered.'

I said, 'Instinct or intuition tells me it wasn't the first fire you started either.'

He replied, 'Instinct, yes I know what you mean. What's going to happen to me?'

'That's a good question but you know perhaps the whole truth will, in due course, help to decide that.'

'I've never ever trusted anybody in my life. See, when I was young in children's homes I decided never to trust nobody, keep it all secret all to yourself, then you don't get caught. When I was real young in homes, if I told someone somat in secret, they'd tell somebody else, so years ago since then I thought, tell nobody nowt, that's best.'

'Is that your view now with me?'
'No, I don't think so, no.'
'Have you ever confided in your mum or stepfather?'
'No, no chance, never.'
'What of your drinking?
'I used to get home at weekends and they'd often have parties, boozing, and I'd drink from half-empty cans. I can drink plenty now.'

'Other fires, Bruce. Let's be perfectly honest. I want to know and I want you to tell me, but of course it's up to you. You don't have to tell me.'

'Yes, I know I can ask to go back to my cell if I like. I'm not going to, though, don't worry.'

'Weighing up how you contained yourself for over six months after the killing of the three Hastie boys, I just cannot help but think that you've killed before by fire, Bruce.'

Initially I could not think of any other fires and I certainly knew none where people had died that were recorded as undetected arson cases. I didn't have any planned questions in my mind and I found myself pondering over what I could say to him and what he might say to me. It was then that I suggested to him that he had committed even further fires and in fact went on to suggest he may even have caused further deaths in fire. These remarks were purely spontaneous and I honestly did not believe or expect any response.

At this point Lee stared hard into my face once more for several seconds, became very red-faced and then put his head on his hands, which were flat on the table between us. He remained so for about a minute. I did not interpret the 'head on his hands' situation as anything other than a deep thinking period. Then he looked up and said, 'Yes, you are right. I killed a little baby once.'

'In a fire?'

'Yes. West Dock Avenue.'
'Do you remember when that was?'
'Yes.'
I said, 'Maybe two years ago near where you lived in a terrace?'
'Yes, but we'd moved before the fire. Fire was in a front house on the left past the school. It was a little baby.'

When Lee made this admission I knew nothing of a fire at West Dock Avenue, but in the days after he was arrested there was plenty of gossip about him and I knew by this time that he had lived in West Dock Avenue about two years earlier. He had also told us he had destroyed the paraffin can used for the Hastie fire in the West Dock Avenue vicinity.

'How did you start that fire? Was it the letter-box?'
'No, not that one. I just went in through a window one evening. I sprinkled paraffin on some carpet and the couch. The living room, I think it was, and up it went. The little baby died in it and I killed her.'

He glanced at me, his sharp watchful eyes showing signs of tears but it was only for a moment. He did not lose his composure. He continued, 'I've done more, four killed, even more. I'm going to think and tell you. The three Hastie's was my last one, but there's four other fires with one dead in each one. There's more. You are bloody right.'

Simultaneously it occurred to me that he might have been fire raising for some considerable time. 'Perhaps the first one may have been quite a few years ago?' I said.

Again this comment was made without foundation and was aimed at inviting Lee to say whatever he chose.

He replied, 'Are you guessing again, 'cause if you are you are not bloody wrong?'

'You had to start some time, Bruce, and the feeling I get, although it frightens me, tells me you may have been causing fires for quite a long time.'

'Fucking hell, you are frightened! Well, I will tell you, but can we leave it and I'll think and then tell you all the truth. You know you will be the first I've ever told and spoke to like this. I won't tell you any lies. I will speak truth. There was a boy who went to school. I killed him in his house in a fire a few years ago. A good while ago it was. Honest, I'll tell you when I see you again, after I have had time to think about it. See, policemen and firemen don't know. They think they know when they go to fires but they haven't when I've done fires. They haven't known when I've done my fires. They think it's just a fire, they haven't know'd how they started. In house fires they don't think it's arson. I'm a arsonist I know. They think they know but they don't if you think about it. They've never known I've done them. Now because of the way you have been all right with me, I'm going to tell you.'

'Well, Bruce, I am going to give you time to think. Sergeant Martin and I are having to go now, but we shall come back tomorrow afternoon and see you then.' I stopped myself asking any more questions, despite the fact that many were lined up in my mind.

'All right, all right, thanks.'

I recorded the interview verbatim. I was impressed by his patience as I wrote on and on. I don't think I had ever tried to read 'upside down' in the

41

way Lee was doing as I wrote down all that was being said. He measured his words with apparent thought, and with obvious care he connected them with the speed of my hand writing. I had not known any suspect be so considerate in this way before.

Detective Sergeant John Martin and I each had just over 20 years' investigating experience behind us and were used to interviewing all kinds of people in and out of prison. Lee was different. Apart from the Fenton house fire, he was now admitting very serious crime about which we had no previous knowledge. Apart from what he was saying, Lee's apparent lack of emotion, cool composure, careful study of the handwriting in my notebook as he spoke, caused me considerable anxiety.

Sergeant Martin and I travelled away from Leeds prison and along the M62 motorway towards Hull with Lee's words bouncing about our minds. We had plenty to think about. As we neared the Humber Bridge, Sergeant Martin said, 'You give me the impression that you feel sorry for this lad, Boss.'

'That's interesting, John, I'm not sure that I do, but I do feel it a shame that he's been brought up in the way he has. If things had been different for him we wouldn't be seeing him as we are now,' I said.

'Yes, poor little bastard's never had a chance,' came the reply.

Later that day I telephoned Lee's solicitors clerk, Eric Pearce, and told him exactly what Lee had told us. I also told Pearce that I had arranged with the prison authorities to further interview him again the following day. Mr. Pearce answered that a further visit was alright by him, but he would probably be too busy to attend himself.

I returned to Leeds Prison with Sergeant Martin the following afternoon. Mr. Pearce did not join us. As I cautioned Lee I could see his intentions were clearly written on his face. 'That (caution) don't matter 'cause I'm going to tell you anyway. My solicitor told me not to speak to you if you came to see me but I've got it on my mind. It's on my mind, not his. He can go and get fucked 'cause I'm going to tell you in any case.'

Completing my contemporaneous note and not being sure of what to expect next, I said, 'Well, Bruce, go on.'

'There's quite a good few. I told you about some yesterday. Troutbeck, Askew Avenue and the baby down West Dock Avenue. See, I know more about fires than coppers who go to them. And firemen in some ways. I start 'em and I know police have not known until you started with your questions. You know somat, I've never told anybody. Anyway, I will tell truth 'cause that's what I want to do. I did that old blokes' home at Hessle.' He was earnest and unemotional. His words tumbled out and overwhelmed my wrist as my pen hurriedly recorded his comments.

I knew that some time ago several elderly men died in a fire in Hessle, just west of Hull. I didn't know the premises or how many men had died. I wanted to say, 'What the hell are you talking about?' But I was so engrossed in getting his exact words into my book that I simply carried on writing.

Lee continued, 'I don't think anybody will believe I did, but I did. I broke a window, up some stairs and set it on fire. Don't suppose they even knew it was arson. I'm a good arsonist so Fire Brigade don't find out 'cause the evidence goes in the fire and Fire Brigade start guessing how it happened and don't find the true cause. I've killed a good few people and I don't really want to talk about it too much but I know if I don't it will always be in my mind, and I don't want that so I'm going to tell you. See, I've lived with this being a fire bug for years.'

Watching me writing he added, 'Fucking writing. Do you always have to keep writing everything down? Must be fed up doing it.'

He now seemed to abandon the care he showed with his dictation earlier.

'Never mind, Bruce, I don't mind.'

'Know somat? Meths burns just as well as paraffin, but it's slower, see. If you wanted to do a fire in a big building you want to give yourself time to get out and don't want it flaring up around you. You need to know, see. I don't think I've used meths on a fire, mind, just paper and paraffin. I like smell of paraffin.'

'Go on,'

'Right, I was just thinking. Down Askew Avenue, in school bus once, they said this boy had been killed in a fire at night. I just sat on bus and said nowt when we was at his house. I killed him. It's been secret all the time since then. Now I'm telling you and you are first I've trusted.'

He continued, 'See, I'll give it you in a statement. You can write again. I mean, see, there was the three Hastie's and you know I've done at least eight more, and then there's an old blokes' home at Hessle, eleven blokes died there. But you can write it in a statement that I can sign. You'll want me to sign it, won't you?'

The fervent confidence with which he uttered his words disturbed me. Was he speaking the truth? Was he stretching the truth? Was he seeking some kind of perverted glory? His actual words were of paramount importance for, as most experienced detectives know, many a Queens Counsel has said, 'Never mind what witnesses there are, what has the accused said to the police?'

Still under caution, Lee repeated, 'See, I killed a baby once. I just set the house on fire. I've never had a friend and I've never ever told anyone anything. I keep myself to myself. See, do a fire by yourself, tell nobody, then only you knows and I just keep it a secret and tell nowt to nobody. I used to get sick and tired of people I was with and then I would just go out and set fire to a house somewhere. When I was about 12 I knew a lad who lived in Askew Avenue. It was about No. 70. It was in summer time and this young lad died. I like fires. I think I've done about 30 fires altogether. I used only a small amount of paraffin on most of them except the Hastie's. I made a mistake there using so much paraffin. I want time to think about my fires in the sort of detail I know from what you asked me about the Hastie's, so give me time to think. I'll tell you now I did a big house at Hessle about three years ago. I didn't know it was an old blokes' home at the time, believe me, but, see, I went up there to Hessle to this house not far from (Humber) Bridge. I had a real can, not a plastic one, and got in through a window. There was carpet everywhere and plenty of dry wood, really dry all on the stairs. See, pour paraffin, just sprinkle it, then put a bit of paper about, light it and then you make a good job of it. I was fed up that night. After I got it going, well I cleared off. Took my can with me and you will never find it. See, it went floating on the ocean waves. Yes, the river. I threw it in river and that was it. I'm feeling better now I'm getting this out of my mind. Not all fires I've done have killed people.'

A few moments after completing his written statement Lee's eyes locked into mine. As I recall it, I wanted to ask him why he chose to share his secrets (if that is what they were) with me. But I didn't. I wish I had but I was dealing with evidence and concentrating on note taking and I did not have the presence of mind. Then Lee said, 'Can I ask you somat, Mr. Sagar? Could I trouble you to try and get me a Bible? See, I can read a Bible in here. It's the only thing I think they can't stop you having in this dump.'

I promised I would provide him with a Bible.

Shortly afterwards Sergeant Martin and I left H.M. Prison Leeds. We were both feeling greatly troubled about all Lee had told us.

We travelled away from the prison and towards Hull with Sergeant Martin driving. I just sat beside him, assessing the veracity of what Lee had been telling us. From the outset I found the interview extremely alarming. There had been instances that afternoon when I just sat looking at Lee, lost for words.

I couldn't help but feel that perhaps someone, maybe in prison, had put Lee up to admitting things that had never happened, let alone his being responsible for them. This view troubled me because I thought maybe Lee was attempting to negate the statement he had made about the deaths of the Hastie boys. I knew nothing of a fire killing a boy in Askew Avenue. I did know there had been a fire at a residential home for elderly gentlemen which was known as Wensley Lodge, at Hessle, near the Humber Bridge. I also knew a public enquiry and a coroner's inquest jury had decided the cause of the fire was accidental. I was to learn, with great astonishment, just how accidental it had appeared. Arson had not been discovered or really suspected.

Has he really done all he claims, I kept asking myself. If he did, then it really is one hell of an accomplishment. I expressed these thoughts to Mr. Pearce on the telephone later. He answered, 'All I can say is that he seems to want to tell the truth and, although I have advised him, he just wants to tell you. I can't stop him.'

From experience I knew only too well that records of interviews are always open to attack in court. Such attacks, carried out by eminent barristers ,can be extremely damaging to the prosecution so I have always found it important to both prosecution and defence to be careful and absolutely accurate in all my contemporaneous note taking. This occasion was no exception but I had no idea how important the accuracy of my note-taking would prove to be in the years ahead.

Chapter Six

On Monday, 30 June, 1980, Lee appeared before Hull Magistrates Court on a pre-arranged remand hearing. There were no objections to my request for Lee to be remanded to the Hull Central Police Station. I discussed briefly with Eric Pearce and solicitor Robert Gunby the admissions Lee had made and gave them a copy of Lee's latest statement. I also told them that it was my intention to invite Lee out into the streets of Hull to see if he could point out any houses he said he had set on fire.

'We shall not need to join you. Let us know how you get on,' said Pearce.

Robert Gunby also saw Lee in private that morning.

Shortly afterwards, I asked Lee if he was willing to show us any of the places he had told us about when we saw him in Leeds Prison. 'Yes, I'll show you, Mr. Sagar. Let's go,' he replied.

Good grief, I thought. I'm not a gambler but I bet he can't show us. At that time I was desperately determined to see that he was wrong. I simply wanted to be able to prove that what he said in Leeds Prison was not true. I had spent the weekend thinking about Lee and his admissions and found that I did not really want to believe what he had said. How could he have been responsible for the fire at Wensley Lodge, let alone other fires, without anyone knowing about him, or at least suspecting arson at some of the fires?

Nevertheless, in company with Detective Sergeant Martin, and with Detective Constable Paul Bacon driving, we left Hull Guildhall in an unmarked police car. I reminded Lee he was still under caution and continued, 'Right, Bruce, where to?'

'Go down Hessle Road,' he replied. I noted that he took a rather long, thoughtful look at my open notebook after he spoke.

On the journey, Lee first took us to point out the old people's home, Wensley Lodge. There was no prompting whatsoever, and from the time the car engine was started our destiny was in his hands. I did not know the location of Wensley Lodge. We travelled west along the length of Hessle Road and into Hessle, on the outskirts of Hull. Lee then directed us along Woodfield Lane. 'Turn right down here. I remember all these trees. It's down here on left, a real big house.'

I caught a glimpse of Wensley Lodge, now partly demolished, standing in its own grounds and off the beaten track. Whatever else, Lee's ability to take us to Wensley Lodge convinced me that he had at least visited those premises on a previous occasion. He was quite clear in his directions and I got the impression he had been in the area more than once.

He continued, 'In its own grounds with a few seats outside I think, not many. I think there was two seats I saw in garden, a real big garden. Stop here. Yes, there it is.' He pointed to a now boarded-up entrance and said, 'I went in there, see. See, there's a sign, Wensley Lodge, there still, see it?'

As we pulled into the side of the road and came to a stop I had a clear view of what Lee was indicating: the badly burned and now boarded-up remains of Wensley Lodge standing in a wilderness of overgrown and neglected garden.

'See, it was real quiet that night. I came on bike down here. It were a fucking job with the can, see, I held it in me hand on handle bar of bike, it

The Fire at Wensley Lodge.

(Picture by courtesy of *Hull Daily Mail*)

marked me hand. It were real quiet. I like it quiet. I don't like people crowding me.'

Speaking from the back seat of the car and leaning over my shoulder to watch my note-taking, in order, it appeared, to keep in time with the writing, he continued, 'You speak quietly. I get sick and tired of people shouting, "Do this, do that." I'm all right with you, Mr. Sagar. You're still writing, never mind. You know somat, I just came along here to do a big house, just ride along, any house, just saw this one, it was dark, right. I got my paraffin from shop around town somewhere, can't remember where now. In through open gateway, no one about outside. Think maybe a man could have seen me as I rode down that road. Anyway, I smashed a decent-sized window with me foot I think and climbed in.'

'Go on.'

'Sprinkled paraffin about a bit in one room or more. You know I can remember it just like it was yesterday I can. It took me about three quarters of an hour to ride up here. I manage okay riding a bike, see. There were some stairs I saw when I got inside, sprinkle bit of paraffin then along passage into a room. I remember seeing a bed and a wardrobe. First floor it was. Put good bit paraffin there but lit it just with a little bit paraffin near to where I got in. See, I could get out easy, but, see, it were only a little fire there but I knew it would get bigger. Fairly slow at first, then quick, right, quick it would go up.'

'How long were you in there?'

'Oh, a few minutes.'

'Where did you ignite your fire?'

'Not far from where I got through window. See it would be just a small fire where I lit it but it would soon go into a big one. I'd call it like a puff of smoke, see all go up really quick. There was smoke going about small fire, then I was out before it went up. See, Mr. Sagar I'd just picked on that house 'cause it was so nice and quiet.'

'When was it?'

'Do you mean time?'

'Yes.'

'It was dark but not real late.'

'What time of year?'

'It was only days after Christmas, but maybe a week or a bit more. I saw in newspapers what I'd done. I knew there must be a lot of people in there when I did it but I didn't know it was an old blokes' home till I saw a newspaper. It was eleven I killed in there, wasn't it? I didn't mean to kill eleven. It just happened like that. I cleared off on the bike I pinched, I mean borrowed, as soon as I'd done it, threw my can in river and was off back down Hessle Road quick. See I was near the cop box (Hessle Police Station) when Fire Brigade passed me on way to my fire.'

'Go on,' I said, as I completed my notes.

'Well, I went back to Hull. No one knew owt about it. Can we go to somewhere else now?'

'Certainly Bruce, where to?'

He replied, 'Back along Hessle Road. Go down Askew Avenue.'

47

We travelled to Askew Avenue, still in the west of Hull. As we drove along, Lee pointed to 70 Askew Avenue and said, 'Yes, there's where I killed a boy. It was my first time I killed in a fire. He used to go to Frederick Holmes School. I knew his house 'cause we'd pick him up in school bus. He was about six. It was a good few years ago and when we stopped in bus next morning they said, somebody said, he'd died in a fire during night. I just sat on bus quiet looking out a window and said nowt. See, I'm telling you things now that I've kept secret from everybody for years. It was a paraffin job this one too.'

'Let's move on,' I said, not quite sure what to believe or where we were to go next.

Lee did not appear to miss a thing but took a few seconds to look at my notebook before saying, 'You've got it in your book, Mr. Sagar. That's all right.'

Shortly afterwards, as we were driving along Hessle Road again, Lee pointed out Rosamond Street, where all the old terrace houses had now been demolished in the Hull Council slum clearance programme. 'Down here. Rosamond Street, that's it. I did one or two down here. One where two kids died and another one. The one with kids was not long after I did the baby in West Dock Avenue. Can we go now? Bloody hell, all the houses are down now, aren't they.'

Lee then directed us back to the Central Police Station where he was again detained.

I telephoned Mr. Pearce and told him about the morning's events. That afternoon I invited Lee to make a written statement under caution. He said, 'Not more writing. Yes, I know by now, you've no need to keep telling me. I want to speak so that's all right. I trust you and I'm only speaking to you cause of that. Can I ask you a question?'

'Yes, of course.'

'Did you ever go to any of these fires at all, like Wensley Lodge or any others?'

'No Bruce, it may seem strange to you but no, I haven't attended any of the fires you have mentioned and I didn't even know just where Wensley Lodge was until you directed me there today.'

'Yes, I hadn't been back there since the time I set it on fire. I was surprised. It had all been flattened but, see, I knew they'd have to pull it down some time, what was left, but there's still some standing, isn't there? We saw some left up, didn't we?

Lee then made a written statement saying when he was living in children's homes he'd had enough of people pushing him around, treating him 'like an animal' and, if he'd had a decent home right at the beginning, there would not have been all the fires. 'You know, 'he went on, 'I am quite good doing fires. You see my fires have never let a scientist or police or firemen believe I've done them. See, I mean you haven't even known it was arson. They haven't known how I've started them until Hastie's when I made my mistake and used too much paraffin.'

'Sometimes firemen have thought it's been caused by the fire in the house over-burning or cigs, or electrical faults. One fire I did, all I can remember now is people shouting and screaming in the fire. People sleeping, then shouting help and screaming. Rosamond Street was one like that. I killed some down there. I'm trying, you know, but it's difficult remembering all of them.'

'There was one I did where I killed another baby. I set fire to this house and after it I saw it on television somewhere on news that the young baby was dead. And I'd done it. I was living down Melwood Grove one, maybe two, years ago. The foster mother's daughter's baby died. I didn't kill her. I think it was a girl, but it died from natural causes, but I went to the rest room on Beverley Road and saw the baby laying there. I asked the man there if I could see the baby and he said I could, long as I wasn't too long. He asked who I was and then I saw the baby lying there. Its eyes was open. It's just about that time that I did the baby I saw about on TV. news. I'm sure that one was before the West Dock Avenue dead baby. There's another I did near that pub up Orchard Park. It was not far from pub where they have got a big horse sign. I think it's a white horse. You know, I think they call it Gorthorpe. I think it was a baby died there.'

Appreciating his poor and undernourished appearance I thought he spoke with amazing clarity and care. Taking down those words, words of fire and horror and death, as they continued to tumble from him was an uncanny and bizarre experience. Normally I would be putting facts to a prisoner, but now the situation was in reverse. I glanced across at Sergeant Martin; he had a look of disbelief on his face. What we were being told seemed almost impossible to believe.

Later that evening I gave Lee the Bible I had promised him. A smile flickered about his face as he took it from me. He flicked through the pages and then muttered in a somewhat self-satisfied tone, 'There's a lot of comfort in this book, you know.'

That same evening I was asked by some of my officers if I was worried about what Lee was telling us. 'No, I'm not so much worried as I am anxious. I'm not worrying too much for I feel that the proof of it all is in the inquests which must have enquired into any deaths he refers to. But, as it stands, I have no alternative but to let him talk and write down every word he utters. I would be wrong to try to stop him speaking and equally I would be neglecting my duty if I didn't record his words.'

'Why not tell Sergeant Martin to do the writing?' asked one detective constable. 'I could do so, of course,' I answered, 'but I think it's better to keep the situation as it is. Lee seems to be able to time his words with my writing, and even the solicitor's managing clerk seems happy with the current practice.'

It was often my practice to take my own contemporaneous notes in criminal investigation interviews, and over the years several judges and Queens' Counsel had expressed their satisfaction at the practice. Eventually my interviews with Lee would be questioned and in some quarters doubt would be expressed about the authenticity of, not only my comments, but Lee's admissions. It is always good that man does not know what the future holds!

Chapter Seven

The following day I contacted the defence managing clerk, Mr. Pearce, again by telephone and then sent him, by hand, a copy of the latest voluntary statement Lee had made. I also informed him that I would be speaking to Lee again. Mr. Pearce told me that he had told Lee to say nothing to the police and not make any more statements, 'but he insists, so now it's up to him. We can't stop him.' Mr. Pearce did not attend the interview which followed later.

Many of the words Lee uttered in that latest statement were still in my mind, 'People sleeping, then shouting help and screaming. I killed a baby... Another one I did near a pub where they have got a big horse sign.' The tale Lee was telling seemed to come from an unusual but somehow crystal clear mind. My witnessing sergeant and I would dwell on those words and many more for a long time to come.

Lee was soon escorted into my office. Seeing him walk in at that time made me realise, maybe for the first time, that just as there is a way of making your presence felt, so there is a way, without knowing it, of making yourself inconspicuous. If he were telling the truth, is this the manner in which he had gone about his fire raising, being noticed by no one?

Under caution again, Lee dictated another statement saying his solicitor had told him to make a statement contradicting what he had already admitted. The managing clerk naturally did not tell me this when I spoke to him. He was not obliged to, but Lee made it clear, in writing, all he wanted to do was 'clear it all up'. He repeated, but in more detail, that he had caused the fire at 70 Askew Avenue. Turning his mind back to Rosamond Street, he went on to say he had once got into a house there, put paraffin on the floor, lit it with matches and 'up it went'. 'I think an old woman died there,' he said. 'I did one in Glasgow Street,' he continued. 'I know it was early in the morning and I had been out for the night. The house was dirty with some windows broken. I got in through a window, put some paraffin about room, there was flames and smoke. I think there was an old bloke, but I think only. I didn't see anybody. You know I used to carry paraffin around under my coat in a bottle.'

He continued, 'One after was a house up Gorthorpe, up Orchard Park. There was this house and I know there was little kids in the house because I think I remember kids' toys there. See, I opened front door to get in and with a bit of paraffin, not much, I set it alight. See, when I did a job, a fire like this, I shove everything out of my mind and concentrate hard on what I am doing. This was a quick in and out up Gorthorpe. From what I saw there was little kids in there but being in and out so quick I didn't see anybody. Maybe one of the kids was killed in it. I don't know. It was still daylight, near time to get dark. I know I stood a good few houses away from the house till it was well alight, then I panicked in my mind and cleared off. It was stairs up, or should be. I mean it was under stairs I started it. I didn't pick on that house for any particular reason. It was just a house. That's another one I've got off my mind.'

He went on, 'Next one and I mean the ones I'm telling you about in my order are the real big nasty ones where I think people got killed. Well, the next one is West Dock Avenue where the baby got killed that I've told you about, haven't I. It was the one where I got in through window and poured a fair bit of paraffin near a fire in living room and on couch and bit paraffin on chair. That bloody paraffin burns quick and when I dropped match on paraffin on floor it was one out quick but I didn't give any thought to people or kids in houses or owt but I wasn't going to get caught in it. It was West Dock and I mean it was about two or three days after West Dock that I did that old blokes' home. I got the bike somewhere about Rugby Street and off I went on the bike with my paraffin. The can made a mark on my hand by time I got there but, see, I didn't really know where I was going to set on fire. I knew I was going to set house on fire, but didn't know which one until I found it. I was just out to do a big house, a real big house if I could find one.'

His statement continued, 'I had an idea there would be some big houses up that way and, well, I found this place. I knew there was people in there. It wasn't middle of night but it was late when I did it. I got my foot up and smashed a window, a big, a bit big piece of glass and when I realised no one had heard me, the glass breaking, I just climbed in. I found some stairs, I think there was the odd light on, anyway I went up these stairs real quiet. I heard some different blokes barking, you would say coughing but they, wherever they was, didn't know I was in there with my paraffin and matches. I went along a passage, a bit of a passage, there was one or two doors here and there. I went into a room. I think it was on right. Opened a door, I think, and went in. There was this bed and maybe a wardrobe or cupboard in the room, yes there was. I put paraffin in this room, quite a lot of it, and some more in different places but only a little sprinkling in different places, then I went into another room, sprinkled little bits in there. I went downstairs and put what was left of my paraffin, not much, near to where I got in and set it alight with my matches. See, I did it in a way that I could get out alright but, see, I knew that up the stairs on that floor there was most paraffin so as it gradually went up in flames there would be a fire like a puff of smoke, you know, where it would all burn in flames and that all at once, you know, and that would be that, the bits of paraffin sprinkled would help it but, see, there was lots of dry wood in there so it would go in a good big fire. It was a nasty fire, a real rotten fire I did and I knew it was going to kill people in there. I realised by the size of the place that there was a lot of people in there and a good few would die. I just knew they would be people who would die. I didn't know they was old fellows though, as I told you, Mr. Sagar, I heard them barking as I went up stairs. There was lights on so I could see all right. I know nobody believed it was arson, 'cause fires don't leave good proof. It depends how good you do them. I know!'

He went on, 'After that one I did another one where two kids died down a terrace in Rosamond Street. See, it was about three months after Wensley Lodge or somat like three months. I know West Dock Avenue and old blokes' home was soon after Christmas, then there was a good few weeks before the two kids in Rosamond Street terrace. See, there was a window into a room where they'd maybe knocked a wall out to make a big room instead of two rooms and there was them polystyrene tiles and a couch. There was someone sleeping there, I think downstairs I mean, and there would be people and kids upstairs asleep. I put paraffin around, some near the door and about the floor and set it alight and out through the window. I smashed the glass to get in. I've told you that, have I? I have now. I think it was front. I remember there was a TV and some fish in a tank. I remember seeing them, just. See, you get used to being in a dark room after you've been in a place a few minutes and, although you can't see too clearly, you can see. Am I giving you too much to write, Mr. Sagar? It was a terrace, you know, where the fish tank was that I did the fire. Then, see, I went a good while before I did another where somebody was killed. Over a year, maybe more it was, then went out up somewhere near Askew Avenue early hours, it was well after midnight. Well, see, I'm getting tired now and with your notebook and this statement you must be fed up writing. You've been writing most of last five hours. Just one thing to tell you tomorrow.

'When I was maybe ten or eleven I put paraffin in Roebank Arcade (a small avenue of single-storey shops) and burned it all down. I can laugh about that one for the simple reason no one got hurt. I can remember the bloody smoke and flames coming from that one. It was a long time ago, years ago, and I can still remember real clear, maybe 'cause I've kept it in my mind secret and kept it there without telling anybody at all until I've been telling you.'

Shortly afterwards I said, 'You know, Bruce, there will be a lot of people who will doubt you are responsible for these fires.'

'Yes. See, I've been good. I bet nobody ever knew a thing about me doing any of them, but I have done them.'

'How have you been able to live with it on your mind?'

'Well, easy. I just never bothered. Then when I knew you was never going to give up I got bothered then, and the day you lot got me in your fucking queers' round-up I knew you were getting nearer and nearer. I never meant to kill them Hastie's. Fucking hell, I'll get 15 years, even 20, like Gunby says. He don't know anyway, does he?'

'No, Bruce, he doesn't.'

With hundreds of Lee's words continuing to swim around our minds, Sergeant Martin and I were pleased to get away from the office that night. I saw Lee again the following morning. After cautioning him once more I continued, 'Is there anything else you want to say, Bruce? You see I am sure we haven't touched on everything you've done in the past, have we?'

He replied, 'No, see, I remember a bridge and a street near a school, Reynoldson Street it was. I did one down a terrace down there. This was one I did in daytime before dinner. In through a letter-box. I'd been wandering about, see, and I just picked on this house, not thinking. See, my fingers tingle when I do one, sort of funny feeling, but I concentrate when I'm doing it. If you can take me out I will show you the house. I think I can take you to it, down terrace on right. It was a bad fire.'

'Very well then, Bruce, we can go out now. Do you want to show me any other places whilst we're out?'

He replied, 'No, this one is what I have on my mind now. So just this one if that's all right with you .'

Shortly afterwards we left the Central Police Station in a CID car. Totally at Lee's direction we travelled through Hull City centre, then headed north along Princes Avenue and into Newland Avenue. Then, as we drove under a railway bridge, Lee said, 'Right, we are at Reynoldson Street, that's it there, go down there.'

We drove into Reynoldson Street and past its junction with Marshall Street. Lee then pointed to the first terrace on the right, where I saw the sign, Brentwood Villas. At that moment Lee said, 'There is the one, number, I can't see number, but it's that one where the front is changed now. See, window is different now and it's all painted.' I could see that the house front of the second house on the right of the terrace had a different frontage from the others.

I said, 'Seems you mean the second one on the right, Bruce.'
'Yes, that's it, you can have a good look when you've done your writing.'
'How long ago is it that you did it?'
'Well, see, I'm thinking. It was when they had them old green fire engines when firemen was on strike.'

I then took him back to the Central Police Station. We travelled back there in silence with Lee looking about him as we drove through the traffic and seemingly enjoying the car ride. I had no knowledge of any kind of fire in Reynoldson Street and, as I sat in the car looking at Lee, I could not help but feel just a little unhappy for him. Despite what he had been telling us he'd done, I felt he had been living a dreadfully miserable existence with little, if any, friendship in his life.

When we returned to the Police Station I said, 'What can you tell me about the circumstances of that fire? You know, the one at the house you have just pointed out.'

'I've said it was morning, after I'd been wandering about. I suppose I was day dreaming. I was always walking around day dreaming. I ended up down Reynoldson Street. See, it could have been anywhere, any house. Don't ask me why I picked on that one 'cause I don't know. See, I remember it was a letter-box job, just an ordinary letter-box in door. I put paraffin through letter-box, bit of paper through and up it would go, but I was away quick, well before that. No one would know. You don't hang around after 'cause that's how you get caught, see.'

He went on, 'Get your paper out. I'll give you another statement. You must like writing.'

Lee once again made a statement under caution. I found myself more alarmed than ever as I wrote down word for word what Lee was now saying. He went on, 'This morning we went down Reynoldson Street and I showed you a house down there. Most of my fires have been night or late evening like, but this one was day time. I'd been wandering around town all morning from early on and I had paraffin with me in a bottle under me coat. I'd got it from a place during that morning and just was wandering about. I called at this hardware shop and bought paraffin. Don't ask which shop 'cause I don't remember but you concentrate on your job and just same I concentrate when I do a house and that. I just walked past the school, down side of school top of Reynoldson Street and into terrace, saw this door second one on left, no it wasn't, second on right, and quick as a flash poured paraffin into doorway, lit bit of paper put it through letter-box and as I say I was away before anybody would know. I didn't know who was in the house. I just got fed up, bit bored and that, and did it. A bit depressed I was. If you ask me about me bottle, I took it with me. I didn't know who might be killed but I knew if there was anybody in, the fire was going to be big enough to kill plenty. Fire was in my head and I had to do one that morning. It was just hard luck on it being that house and the people in it. Some must have died there I know. You know somat, it was when firemen was on strike. When them green fire engines, old uns, was being used. They never used to get to a fire very quick. See, my fingers used to tingle when I was doing a fire, just before I had the urge to do a fire it was. I am sorry about what happened to anybody in there. It was just a house I picked on. I didn't think. That's it for now.'

As with all the written statements and utterances from Lee, I simply fed them through to my Incident Room staff for checking. It was my belief, in the interest of the enquiry, let alone justice, that I should not know any kind of detail my staff were finding in respect of the fires. I insisted on this point so that there would be no chance, at that stage, of Lee perhaps being tempted to agree with anything I might have known and mentioned to him. I did not fully appreciate it then but my not knowing was indeed going to be highly beneficial to me as time went on.

Chapter Eight

I handed Lee's latest statement to my Incident Room manager, Detective Inspector Alan Holmes. As he took it from me he said, 'I reckon what Lee is telling you will haunt you for years to come. I don't know about you, but I find it all absolutely amazing. If true, how has he been getting away with it?'

'We don't know if he's really telling the truth do we? Let's see what corroboration we find,' I replied.

Sometime after lunch that day I became aware that members of my staff were able to identify the fires Lee had told us about. I realised too that in order to continue enquiries it would be necessary to see close relatives of some of the victims of fires up to that time identified from Lee's statements. There was no way I would have officers making enquiries about fires and subsequent deaths without telling the relatives, for, as far as the relatives were concerned, the matter was closed. I considered it my duty to see these people myself and inform them we were re-investigating what had occurred. Therefore I instructed my Incident Room staff to send officers to trace the close relatives. Late that afternoon I saw relatives concerning the fires at Belgrave Terrace, Rosamond Street, Askew Avenue, and Gorthorpe. I was not in a position to have relatives from Wensley Lodge contacted because relatives of those elderly gentlemen were not so easy to trace. My conversations with those I saw were very brief indeed, primarily because of the intensely depressing and emotionally upsetting nature of the visits. I did not discuss with any of the relatives details of their fires or of Lee's admissions in relation to them.

Later that same day I discovered that one of my officers had identified that there had been a fire at 2 Brentwood Villas, Reynoldson Street, and I saw one of the relatives the following day to tell her we would be re-investigating the fire. At this stage I only said that we were having another look at the cause of the fires and that was all. I was naturally mindful that eventually there would be terrible repercussions in the minds of close relatives. For all I knew then, some of the relatives might have been looked upon as being in some way responsible for the fires in the first place.

The next day I saw Lee again. Having cautioned him once more, I said, 'You have told me quite a lot of what you have been doing in the way of fires over the years, Bruce.'

The words came tumbling out again without any sign of emotion, 'I can honestly look at you and say you have got them all, the bad ones, but, see, a good few others I can't point out to you, but if you were to tell me then I'll say if I've done 'em or not. See, I don't want to tell you somat I haven't done. That would just waste everybody's time and be daft.'

'Do you consider yourself a good arsonist?'

'I suppose I am an expert in that area. Yes, I am.'

'What is your reason for causing all these fires?'

'Well, see, I just had to set fire to houses. It all started from being small when I liked hearing fire engines and police cars.'

He then went silent for several minutes and eventually said, 'I want to say, and you write it down if that's all right, that if there's no good people left anywhere, I know there is some good ones here in Police Station. I really did think I'd get a kicking. You know somat, thank God someone saw the flames at Troutbeck (Ros Fenton's home) or there'd be more killed and that. All them flats so close together. Wensley Lodge, not a letter-box job, that was a good one, a real big fire. I don't think anybody ever believed it was me doing it. I know there was a big fuss about it but, see, fire doesn't help police to know one way or other. You know I can't tell you just every one I've done 'cause I don't keep a diary. I don't write down, "fire at somewhere street, 3 July, a thousand and one," not like you have to keep writing in your book. I can't always remember. You know somat, the doctor in Leeds Prison who does all them tests to find your mental age, well, I'll tell you it's a lot of harba jarba, they think that they know all about you if you can do the tests but I know what's in my mind, if I don't want to do the tests I won't. See, I can do things they could never do.'

'Like setting houses on fire?'

'Yes, that's just one thing.'

The following day, after administering the caution again, I asked him how he was feeling after telling us about his activities.

He replied that he was feeling better but he wasn't sleeping much at night. Asked why, he replied, 'See I've never been one to sleep much at night, that's how its always been and that's why I was out wandering and doing fires with nobody really bothering much about me.'

I continued, 'How do you feel when you think of the horror of what you have done in various houses?'

'Well, see. I feel sorry for all the people that died. I don't feel sorry for myself. If I hadn't done it they wouldn't have died. I'll have to pay the consequences.'

'It appears you are quite an arsonist. However, three matters concern me above numerous others. Firstly, you have caused fires never suspected as arson. Secondly, you have never been suspected, over many years, of being an arsonist. Thirdly, you have never been checked by anyone at a scene of a fire, or, probably more important, when you have been wandering about with your paraffin under your jacket. What have you to say on these three points?'

'I've been lucky not to get caught. No one has ever seen me. I've never hung around after I've set a place on fire. I've always been away like a flash before fires got big and, see, I could hear engines going from hundreds of yards away. No one ever really thinks about arson much in house fires, they always think of somat else. Firemen, police, everybody.'

'Tell me about your obtaining paraffin, Bruce. Did you ever have difficulty buying it?'

'No one ever used to ask. If you buy a bar of chocolate no one ever asks why you want it.'

'Thinking about shops, you couldn't possibly go and buy just a drop in a bottle, could you?'

'Oh, no, but I could get a can full. I'd get it and keep it hidden but somebody found it once and pissed off with it. Thieving bastards.'

'Could you tell me where you bought paraffin?'

'Garages, where you just put money in machines, and some shops, anywhere. No particular one all the time I've been doing it.'
'Could you always get matches?'
'They was never a problem.'
'Does paraffin always light?'
'Yes, no trouble. I've never tried and left paraffin without lighting it. See, you don't stand over paraffin 'cause it goes whoosh.'
'Did you ever give any thought to children being burned in your fires?'
'No, I've never thought. I never thought of going round just killing like, just big fires in houses. No thought for anybody in there day or night.'
'You asked me to give you a Bible the other day, Bruce, and I gave you one. Why the Bible?'
'I like reading it.'
'Do you find some sort of support in the Bible?'
'Yes, I know which religion is best. Jehovah's Witnesses say one thing, others say different things.'
'Such as?'
'In the beginning was the word and the word was with God and the word was God. He was in the beginning with God. All things were made through him. That's John 1.'
'Did you refer to the Bible after any of your fires?'
'Yes, , I did after Wensley Lodge and especially after Hastie's.'
'Any others?'
'I got satisfaction from the Bible after Reynoldson Street. I needed support after that, I did. See Bible shows me way to go. I couldn't help that Reynoldson Street fire. I felt I had to do one that day.'
'Why the second house in the terrace in Reynoldson Street?'
'If you went for some goodies in the second shop why pass the first? Don't know, just any house.'
'Did you know at the time that you would kill someone in Reynoldson Street?'
'I heard it later but I know houses go up quick with just a bit of paraffin. It depressed me a lot when I heard four, I'd killed four. I needed the Bible after that one. I really did.'

Later that day one of my staff told me that all the fires we were about to re-investigate had been resolved by the Coroner, Dr. Philip Science. I could not help finding myself deeply concerned about the whole wretched situation and pondered over everything Lee was telling me. I felt I should have told him to go to hell when he first mentioned Wensley Lodge, but I didn't. It would have been foolish and irresponsible of me if I did.

About that time I recalled a few words from John Buchan's letter to his friend Thomas Arthur Nelson, in Buchan's, *Thirty Nine Steps:* 'The incidents defy the probabilities, and march just inside the borders of the possible.'

The following Monday, again in company with Detective Sergeant Martin, I again saw Lee. He said, 'You know, Mr. Sagar, I think I have told you about all the fires but I might have missed a few, even bad ones.'
'Do you mean bad ones where someone died?'
'I don't think so but maybe one or two. If you took me around, see, I know

the picture of the place I've done in my mind so if I see it again I can tell you. See, if I can help you I will.'

'Have you given any more thought to any of those bad fires you have already told us about?'

'Yes, Wensley Lodge. I've thought a lot about that. See, at night when I do a fire and get inside a house I've got me sannies on and, see, I cat-creep.'

'Was Wensley Lodge one where you cat-crept?'

'Yes, but I had shoes on then, not me sannies. I had me sannies on in the one in Rosamond Street where kids was killed.'

'You appear to have caused a dreadful fire at Wensley Lodge, Bruce. Can you tell me more about it?'

'Well, I did it. I can tell you a bit more. I remember a bloke shouting, "Help, God help me," as I was getting bike off grass before getting away quick. I didn't wait to see flames much but, as I went away, after throwing can in river, I could see blaze getting going then, not too big but getting going alright.'

'Do you remember much about the place you actually set alight?'

'I think, but I'm not sure, that the bed was on the left. There was a chair or somat and wardrobe or cupboard. I just sprinkled bit paraffin near end of bed and a big lot not far away from it with a gap between, see, so as to give me time to get away. See, little bit burns other stuff on floor, carpet and that, then it moves over to big lot and that's when it goes whoosh, but, see, I'm out before whoosh. Little bit was near window, see, and more was near bed.'

'Are you sure about this, Bruce?'

'Look, I wouldn't tell you somat I hadn't done and I will tell you about it if I have done it. I did it, Mr. Sagar.'

'I feel that in all the circumstances there may well be people who will not believe you, Bruce.'

'They'd better, Mr. Sagar, 'cause it's true, but bloody hell, you believe me, don't you?'

Spontaneously, I replied, 'Yes, Bruce, as a matter of fact I do.'

'That's alright then.'

Actually at that time I was not sure what to believe, but I knew that in due course the whole of the evidence would be presented to the Director of Public Prosecutions and would also be well ventilated in criminal trials in the Crown Court by Queen's Counsel.

I continued, 'Did you hear any movements at Wensley Lodge that night as you set about your fire raising?'

'No, but I heard old men barking as I have said, and as I was coming out of grounds I heard shouting, men shouting.'

By this time my investigating teams had commenced their enquiries into Lee's admissions in order to seek corroborating evidence. Files in relation to the fires had also been obtained from the Coroner and it is fair to say, if I wished, I could have examined them. In fairness, right or wrong, I still did not want to examine the files or even have sight of them. I felt that I had details provided by Lee in my mind and did not wish to confuse my thinking at this stage on Lee's comments with other matters. Additionally I wanted to learn as much information as possible from Lee without having actual knowledge of the fires. This way his words could be more easily re-inforced if true, or we could maybe catch him out with facts if untrue.

To continue my conversation with Lee, I said, 'Well, now you may if you wish make a statement in writing about anything else you wish to say about Wensley Lodge, but you must understand that if you do it will be taken down in writing, under caution, and may be given in evidence.'

He replied, 'Yes, I want to if you don't mind writing.'

After I had written the words of the caution at the top of the statement, Lee read and signed the caution caption. He continued, 'I think it's pathetic you having to write this bit at the top every time I give a statement. Why do you have to do it, but I suppose there's a good reason for it. After me making one statement I know I don't have to and it's obvious I want you to write it. Well, see, Wensley Lodge, I didn't know name of place till I heard how many bloody deaths, that's what it was. Bloody deaths. Bloody is not swearing you know, 'cause it's in the Bible, bloody is. I have been thinking about them eleven old blokes. It was in my mind that night to set fire to a place where it was all quiet but I didn't realise old blokes was in there.'

'Nobody heard window break. See, there was one or two bay windows and some flat ones in between and I broke one of the flat ones. I didn't try door or owt, just in through window. Can't remember what was inside once I'd got inside window but I know I came across these stairs, but before that I went through a door from room where I broke window. Actually I'm a bit mixed up with windows, see, there was windows all over and there was other buildings but anyway I broke a window, a flat one, and when I say bay windows I mean them you get in terraces like. Windows in Wensley Lodge was bigger like, anyway I've said enough about windows. Anyway, I wandered up stairs. I remember seeing real dry wood and carpets. I went through a few doors. I had me can right at me side in my left hand. I was all quiet but thinking back it's a wonder somebody didn't hear me. It's amazing no one heard me.'

'I sprinkled paraffin about, just a little bit. See, once upstairs I wandered about a bit and went into this bedroom with cupboard or wardrobe. There was this little bed and it was a little bit dark but I could see quite a bit in this room. There was probably somebody in this bed anyway but I didn't sort of have a real good look.'

He continued, 'See, I poured paraffin in there on floor, quite a good lot on floor in one place near bed, just a little bit paraffin somewhere between end of bed and I think a window, just a little bit on floor. See, a little bit, lit, takes a few minutes to reach big lot. See it slowly picks up from one small lot to another but if I'd left a trail of paraffin from one to the other it would go whoosh. See, if I left no gaps it would have all gone whoosh like a bomb but, see, I left gap at Wensley Lodge. I set fire to little bit and I was off downstairs like a cat. I cat-crept, see.'

'You know, Mr. Sagar, I told you a bit wrong in my statement before. I was a bit mixed-up. I was near window in that bedroom I lit little fire. I knew with my experience that paraffin in the little bit would take just a few minutes to reach big amount and then whoosh. See, after I'd lit it, I was off down stairs and out of window same way I got in. It was easy to make my way out same way as I went in 'cause I concentrate on what I do just like you, Mr.

Sagar. I could hear like old blokes shouting, don't ask me how I know'd they was old blokes, but they was not women or babies, see. I was out in that road where we stopped in police car the other day, and I was getting the bike from grass by them trees where I'd shoved it before doing the fire. All I was bothered about was bloody getting away from place.'

'I know as I was getting on bike I heard a man's voice shouting "God help me!" I didn't see much fire then but after I'd thrown my can in river I pedalled back up that road a few minutes after, not down to the place but on road and I could see flames then. It was bloody terrible. As I said, when I was riding past Hessle Police Station I saw Fire Brigade and ambulances on their way there. I knew, see, when I saw flames after throwing can in river that the fire was killing people. I knew then alright. It's hard to explain. I mean it's hard to explain, you know, but, see, there's a lot of tension builds up and there was that night.'

'After I'd put bike back where I'd borrowed it from I was walking and then I was calling myself all the twats under the sun. I knew as I walked along blokes was dying in the fire. I was frightened I would get caught but that's all. I'd killed people before in my fires, so I wasn't that bothered like.'

It all rang desperately true but the most important thing I ever learned in criminal detection was never to believe anything until it is well corroborated.

And why did he give more than one description of how he started the Wensley Lodge fire?

Chapter Nine

A few days later I spoke to Dr. Daphne Sasiene, the Medical Officer at Leeds Prison. I began to tell the doctor about Lee's admissions when she interrupted, saying, 'Yes, I know what he says. He has been telling me what he has been doing too.'

'Has he told you much in detail?' I asked.

'Oh, yes, he has. There's all sorts of detail in that mind of his. You know, it is as if he has leapt from the pages of the few textbooks there are on arson,' she answered.

Dr Sasiene continued, 'We humans all retain a massive store of memory, you know. I am sure you know we all have a much more clear memory of something exciting we have at some time experienced, even though the experience was long ago. Just think how many people can recall in detail their wedding day; a great goal in a cup final; an illness; a car accident; the list is endless. In the same way there are many people in prison who can recall every detail of the crimes they have committed. It's because the mind is so much more attentive when the adrenaline is pumping well.'

As I left her in the prison yard that day she said something odd which I shall always remember: 'A police officer who does not learn the Judges' Rules, syllable by syllable, is a fool. From what Bruce Lee tells me you know them well, but, you know, the police officer who carries out the rules day by day, syllable by syllable, is an even greater fool.'

I should have asked her what she was driving at, but did not have the time.

Shortly afterwards I saw Lee once again. By now he had been remanded in custody back to Leeds Prison. Speaking to him in the open plan visitors' room I cautioned him once more. Was Dr. Sasiene suggesting I shouldn't ? However, I continued, 'Can I mention the fire at 70 Askew Avenue.'

'Yes, go on.'

'You have said you got in the house through a window. Was it from the back or the front?'

'At the back.'

'Was the window open or did you force it perhaps?'

'It was open, I think. Yes it was open.'

'Did you know the lad who died there in that fire very well?'

'Yes I knew him. I told you that.'

'Were you very friendly with him?'

'Yes, sort of. I made bit fuss of him sometimes on bus.'

'Tell me again just what time of night it was when you say you caused that fire?'

'Oh, early morning, see. I'd been out most of the night.'

'Was it long before you caught the school bus?'

'No, no, see, it was next day, I was on bus. Not same day. It was next day, see.'

'Where were you living at that time?'

'I'm not real sure. I've been in different homes, see, can't remember.'

'Where did you get paraffin and matches for 70 Askew Avenue?'

'Always had matches and paraffin. Well, see, you know there's a green gravel box place on Hessle Road. If you could take me out I'd show you where, but, see, there was a paraffin canister there and I just got some paraffin from it in a bottle, that's it.'

'I'd like to mention the fire you have spoken about in West Dock Avenue where the baby died.'

'Yes.'

'Tell me again how you got into that house.'

'Well, I think I told you it was window but, know somat, I think it was back door. I know for sure it was back way.'

'Did you see the lady of the house at all?'

'No.'

'Did you see the baby in the house?'

'Honest, I didn't see the bambino. If I'd seen it in there I wouldn't have done it. I like kids I do. I was annoyed with myself when I heard I'd killed the baby.'

'Did you see the cot?'

'I do remember a cot in the room but I didn't look in the cot. Honest, if I'd seen bambino there I wouldn't have lit paraffin. I wouldn't, honest.'

'So you left the house as soon as you lit your fire.'

'Yes, out back door. I just fled. I know that. I didn't want to wait for Fire Brigade or owt.'

'Did you see a fire of any sort in the house before you lit your fire?'

'Yes, I saw a fire. It was in the room just near where I started the fire near couch and that.'

'Why pick that house?'

'It's just like any other, just pick on any house and that's it.'

'Of course, you could have read about this house fire in a newspaper perhaps.'

'If I'd read it in a newspaper I wouldn't remember it like I do. Anyway, I didn't ever read newspapers. I don't know what you mean, Mr. Sagar, "could have read about it in a newspaper". I didn't, though. I did it and I'm sorry about the baby.'

'What of the house up at Gorthorpe, Bruce? Can you tell me how you got in there?'

'See, Mr. Sagar, it's difficult to know, see, because them houses make it hard to know which is front and which is back door. I told you it was front door but I didn't stand around to have a good look but I know it was door near staircase if that's any help to you.'

'Do you remember the staircase?'

'Yes. I remember some footsteps up top of stairs as I went in, someone moving about.'

'Did you pick that house because perhaps you knew there was a spastic girl living there?'

'I might have done. I can't remember. I told you, didn't I, that it was still daylight but near time to getting dark when I did it.'

'Now I just want to mention one of the two you have spoken about in Rosamond Street. It's the one where you say you think an old woman died.'

'Yes. I know the one. It's where there was string on key inside letter-box but, see, I tried it but went in back way. I cat-crept about, see.'
'Did you get into the house by forcing the back door, or what?'
'No, see, back door was open.'
'Why not go in by the front door if as you say you found that the key was on a piece of string inside the letter-box?'
'Can't remember. Actually, I don't think I could get in when I tried, so I went around back.'
'If I remember correctly you mentioned polystyrene tiles in the other house you have talked about in Rosamond Street.'
'Well, see, polystyrene tiles, polyurethane and that, it burns easy see . . . I've thought about some more things.'

He went on to say, 'You know after that fire in Glasgow Street. I did a bad fire down Humber Buildings, Madeley Street. I crept into this house. I was twelve or thirteen at the time and, see, I remember it . I saw this bloke and he was sat down. I watched him get up and go to his toilet. I was hiding in his kitchen, see, and when he went to toilet I went into his living room. I can remember it like it was yesterday. You know somat, I like to let people think I'm thick sometimes. I've let people think that and they've thought it at times, but I've thought to myself if you knew what I've done, the bloody damage I've done being an arsonist they wouldn't think I was thick and call me chicken. Well in this house, 50 Humber Buildings, when this bloke was in toilet I sprinkled paraffin on floor right in the living room where he had some clothes drying and set it alight. I fled out and then I heard this bloke shouting and I was away like a flash. I was out of the house some distance away and I turned and saw him running out of the house burning. I don't think he had all his clothes on. He must have got up to fire and tried to put fire out 'cause I didn't set him alight. I don't believe the whole house would have burned down. When I was a good way away I heard Fire Brigade or ambulance going there. You know it's amazing I can remember all this. See, people may not believe it's possible for me to do fires like I have but it's quicker for me to get into a house and set it alight in the day or night than it is for a burglar to get in a house and pinch things. I can set a place on fire in a flash!'

I said, 'You have caused a great number of fires it appears and a frightening number of deaths in those fires, Bruce. How do you really feel about it now?'
'Well, now that I've been telling you and getting it out of my mind, I'm feeling a lot better. But before, see, it used to make me feel depressed when I thought about different people I'd killed.'
'You said that it used to make you depressed when you thought about different people you have killed. Tell me, did you really intend to kill any of those people?'
'Look, Mr. Sagar, it was doing fires. I intended the fires, even the bad ones, but I didn't mean to murder people.'

On Monday, 21 July 1980, along with Detective Sergeant Martin I saw Lee at the Hull Guildhall once again. He was appearing at a remand hearing. After the usual caution I said, 'I would like to go out into the City with you, Bruce. I would like you to point out the house you have spoken about at

Madeley Street; where you borrowed the bicycle from in Rugby Street; where you took the paraffin from for the fire in Askew Avenue, and whatever place you would like to indicate to me.'

'Yes. Alright.'

I then asked the solicitor's managing clerk if he wished to accompany us. He answered that he was happy for us to carry on, provided we continued to supply him with any further written statements Lee might make.

On this occasion, accompanied by Detective Sergeant Martin, and with Detective Constable John Richardson driving, we went out in a police car and, without any prompting, Lee directed us to and pointed out No. 50 Humber Buildings, saying, 'That's where I burned the bloke.'

He then directed us west along Hessle Road until we approached Rugby Street. We then turned into Rugby Street and, as we approached Percy's Avenue, Lee pointed to the yards at the rear and said, 'I borrowed bike from one of them back ways when I went to do that old blokes' home and I put it back there, see, so as nobody would know I'd borrowed it. Don't ask me which back way 'cause I can't remember.'

Following this ,we travelled further along Hessle Road for a mile or so. Lee then pointed to a green-coloured wooden box built on the roadside and said, 'That's where I got paraffin from for Askew Avenue. See, it says road grit on it.'

'Was it locked when, as you say, you got paraffin from there?'

'No, they're not often locked. Look, it's not locked now.'

There did not appear to be a lock there.

'Where do you want to point out next?' I asked.

'I know we've been to Wensley Lodge once. Can we go again?'

'Yes.'

We then continued along Hessle Road into Hessle, along Ferriby Road and into Woodfield Lane. We travelled into West Hill from where we could once again see the remains of Wensley Lodge.

Lee said, 'There it is again, what's left of it. That was a good fire there alright. It's a wonder nobody heard me break glass.'

I was still anxious about Lee and his admissions because I could not help but feel very dubious. Obviously I knew all the admissions had been volunteered by Lee without any prompting from the police. I also knew in nearly all the cases, the only exceptions being the Hastie's, Wensley Lodge and the Fenton's, that when Lee admitted a fire I had no knowledge that there had even been such a fire.

On this journey, I decided to test Lee's credibility by taking him to the scene of a fire involving a death which had occurred in Manor Way, Anlaby, just a short distance away from Hessle. With this test in mind for some time, I had established that there had been such a fire through Detective Chief Inspector Gordon Bird in the Humberside Police Photographic Department.

As we left Hessle I said, 'There was a bad house fire in Manor Way, Anlaby, some time ago, Bruce. I would like to go up there now.'

'Yes, alright, I don't think I did one up there.'

En route to this house it was obvious that Lee was unfamiliar with Anlaby, and when we drove into Manor Way there was a marked difference in his attitude and he appeared uncomfortable. He said, 'No Mr. Sagar, I haven't done one down here. I've never been down here before.'

At least this gave me some degree of confidence that Lee was not open to suggestion.

I continued, 'Very well, Bruce, where to now?'

'I haven't shown you Glasgow Street yet. Can we go there now?'

'Yes, we can.'

We then drove across West Hull from Anlaby, and, as we travelled along Askew Avenue in the direction of Glasgow Street, Lee pointed to No. 70 Askew Avenue and said, 'That's one I've told you about, where that boy died.'

We continued on our way at Lee's direction and into Glasgow Street. As we travelled along that street Lee pointed to No. 33 Glasgow Street, which I saw was now all boarded up and said, 'That's where I killed that old bloke. It was a dirty house.'

As we drove along Lee said, 'I'll take you and show you that one up North Hull, Orchard Park.'

We travelled to Orchard Park Estate where Lee pointed to the Rampant Horse public house and said, 'There, see. I told you there was a white horse – that's it.'

I saw there was a large white horse sign on the wall of the public house. As we passed it and travelled on along the road, Lee pointed to the avenue known as Gorthorpe and said, 'Hold on, down there, there it is at the end. I did one down there, the one I told you that I did the fire under the stairs. The end one of this block it is.' He then pointed to what I saw was No. 9 Gorthorpe.

My Incident Room staff, working on the confessions Lee had made, now gave me the brief details of the actual fires Lee had spoken about. About 3 p.m. the same day, I saw Lee again. After the usual words of the caution I said, 'Now, Bruce, I'm going to put to you brief facts relating to certain fires which it appear to me you have probably committed. Listen to what I say, make any comment you wish, or, of course, you know being under caution you can say nothing. 'About 7 a.m. on Sunday, 24 June 1973, a fire occurred in a house 70 Askew Avenue, Hull, where six-year-old Richard Anthony Ellerington died as a result of the fire.'

'Yes, I've told you about that one. I admit I did it and killed him.'

'Why do that particular house?'

'Just did it. I wasn't very old then, but after that I said to myself I wouldn't do any more 'cause it frightened me. But I did. I think I might have been at home on trial. I just can't remember for sure.'

'Did you see anyone in the house at 70 Askew Avenue?'

'No.'

'Do you remember a dog there?'

'I seem to remember a dog, yes, but all I was thinking about was doing the fire. It's a good while ago now. It's no good saying something if I can't remember.'

'About 6. 45 a.m. on Friday, 12 October 1973, a fire occurred at the house 33 Glasgow Street, Hull where 71-year-old Arthur Bernard Smythe died as a result of the fire.'

'Yes, I've told you about that one too. That was the old bloke. It's that mucky old house.'
'Can you describe the front room there?'
'No, it's a long time ago but I know it was all mucky.'
'How did you get in there?'
'I don't remember, a window I think, but I was out the front door.'
'Did you take your own paraffin there or did you use some from the house?'
'Everywhere I go I take my own paraffin.'
'Where were you living then?'
'West Dock Avenue I think. Yes, it was.'
'Did you see anyone in that house?'
'Yes, the old man was just sitting there asleep, yes, that's right, and there was boxes inside near the door. There was a paraffin heater there as well.'
'About 8. 45 p.m. on Monday, 23 December 1974, a fire occurred in the house, 7 Minnies Terrace, Rosamond Street, Hull, where 82-year-old Elizabeth Rokahr died as a result of the fire.'
'Yes, that's right. I've told you that one but can't show you house 'cause it's all knocked down.'
'You have told me that you set a house on fire down there. This one was in 1974. What did you see in the house?'
'Well, I did see someone lying in a bed but I didn't know if it was a man or a woman. I didn't wake 'em up to ask, did I?'
'Are you saying that you set a house on fire when you could see someone in bed there?'
'Yes, but, see, in that room I was so attracted to setting it on fire that I didn't bother about anything else.'
'At that very moment it appears then that you intended to kill whoever was in that bed.'
'Well, I was devoted to the fire and despised whoever was in there. That's in the Bible, being devoted to one thing and despising another.'
'About 8. 15 p.m. on Thursday, 3 June 1976, a fire occurred in the house, 9 Gorthorpe, Hull, where 13-months-old Andrew Edwards died as a result of the fire.'
'Yes, I showed you that one this morning.'
'Why that house?'
'I was just up there.'
'Did you see any children in that house?'
'No.'
'Did any of them see you?'
'To be honest I can't remember. I did it under stairs and that's it.'
'What was in the cupboard under the stairs?'
'Can't remember.'
'What can you tell me about that house?'
'Well somebody was walking about up top of stairs. See, I was in and out in a flash. It was summer time, wasn't it?'
'I seem to remember you saying in one of your statements that it was night time when you did this one. What do you mean by night time?'
'Well, when it's a good bit after tea time.'

'About 7.15 p.m. on Sunday, 2 January 1977, a fire occurred in the house, 43 West Dock Avenue, Hull, where Katrina Thacker, aged 6 months, died as a result of the fire.'

'That's the baby down West Dock Avenue. Yes.'

'In your statement you have told me that the woman was out. Did you see her go out?'

'No, but, see, I didn't see her in there so she must have been out, it's logical.'

'I understand you knew Peter Thacker who used to live there.'

'Yes I knew the Thacker's.'

'I understand the woman of the house, Karen Frazer, and her little daughter had only left the room for a short while.'

'Well, I was in and out in a flash.'

'Shortly after 9 p.m. on Wednesday, 5 January 1977, a fire occurred in the residential home known as Wensley Lodge, West Hill, Hessle, which resulted in a number of elderly men dying.'

'Yes, I've told you.'

'You said in one statement that you sprinkled paraffin about but didn't mention going into a room on the first floor. Why?'

'Don't know. When I was doing it I had no idea I was going to be telling you about it, like I have been now. But, see, I thought about it a good bit, got it right in my mind just what I did and now I've told you as best I can remember. What I said, after thinking about it well a just as I remember doing it. That's truth.'

'Very well then, tell me about the bed in the room where you say you poured quite a lot of paraffin?'

'There was this bloke in the bed. I didn't speak to him or owt. He must have been sleeping. I think he barked, see, the smoke would have made him cough.'

'Was there smoke in the room as you left?'

'Yes, see it was going round from me bit paraffin and what was burning there. It hadn't reached the big lot then. Remember I told you that across the gap it would take time to reach the big lot and that's when there would be smoke.'

'Between 3 and 4 a.m. on 27 April 1977, a fire occurred in the house 4 Belgrave Terrace, Rosamond Street, Hull, where Deborah Gold, also known as Hooper, aged 13 years and Mark Jordan, aged 7 years, died as a result of the fire. Other people in the house suffered from burns and smoke inhalation.'

'Yes, I've already told you about all these fires.'

'In this one you mentioned breaking glass to get in. Was it in the door or the window?'

'It was window near front door, a side window right at side of front door.'

'You said in your statement that the fire you started was near a doorway. Which door?'

'One inside the house, you know, where two rooms are made into one.'

'Actually right inside the house?'

'Yes.'

'Did you believe people were asleep in there?'

'Look, I got in through the window I broke. I picked some pieces of glass out after I broke it and climbed in.'
'Had you ever been in the house before?'
'No.'
'Was there someone asleep actually in the room that you set on fire?'
'Might have been someone on the couch, but I don't remember. I know there must have been more people asleep upstairs.'
'So there was someone on the couch asleep?'
'I think there was, yes.'
'How did you get out?'
'Same as I told you before.'
'Do you remember much about the front door there?'
'Glass in it, that's all.'
'Did you know the family there?'
'No.'
'Did you visit that street and hang about there either before or after the fire?'
'Yes, but how did you know that? I did hang about there a good bit before and after.'
'Do you remember anything else about that house?'
'I used paraffin and it was a bad fire. I've told you everything else.'
'Shortly before mid-day on Friday, 6 January 1978, a fire occurred at the house, 2 Brentwood Villas, Reynoldson Street, Hull, where Christine Viola Dickson, 24 years, Mark Christopher Dickson, 4 years, Steven Paul Dickson, 3 years and Michael Ian Dickson, aged 16 months, died as a result of the fire.'
'Yes, I had to go to the Bible after that one. I told you. I'd been wandering around all morning. See, I was living at Melwood Grove, not very far from Reynoldson Street. I realised I'd killed a mother and three young ones when I heard people's gossip.'
'Where did you hear the gossip?'
'Just different places.'
'I find it incredible that you went up to this terraced doorway in broad daylight and set the house on fire.'
'Well I did, see. I had a Fairy Liquid bottle, plastic you know, open letter-box, just pushed it in, and then I just squirted paraffin well in. You can squeeze a Fairy Liquid bottle and I just moved it about right to left squeezing it and then just a little drip back to letter-box, light bit of paper, push it in and away, only takes a second when you know what you are doing.'
'Did you see anyone standing about in the terrace?'
'No, but you know nobody takes much notice of anything anyway.'
'But someone could have been just inside that doorway and caught you.'
'But nobody did, did they? I never used to hang around much. Away like a flash, that's me.'
'The woman of the house was only next door. Did you see anyone in the next doorway?'
'I never saw nobody in the terrace and if she was next door.' He laughed and said, 'She never saw me. I shouldn't laugh now, should I? I'm sorry.'

I had now been acquainted with the nature of the fire at 50 Humber Buildings and had read statements about it. I recall that some time before seeing Lee that day I was greatly concerned because I believed that the police attention at the time of the fire had been lacking. There was clearly a situation here which had not been fully presented to the Coroner and I felt that there was something perhaps much more sinister involved. I just could not accept the 'burnt clothing' theory put to the coroner. There was no burning of anything other than a human being.

I continued: 'About 4 p.m., on 27 December 1973, a fire occurred in the house, 50 Humber Buildings, Madeley Street, Hull, where 34-year-old David Brewer died as a result of the fire.'

'That's another one I've told you about. I showed you the house, didn't I?'
'Did you know the Lister family who lived in Humber Buildings?'
'Yes.'
'Did they used to keep pigeons?'
'Yes?'
'Do you remember Mrs. Lister once complaining and accusing you of stealing pigeons?'
'How the bloody hell do you know that? I shouldn't ask. Yes, she came around in a raging temper but I didn't steal them.'
'Not long after that a fire occurred at her home. Did you do it?'
'Yes, I did it. It was in a bedroom, wasn't it. I did it but it was only a small fire.' (There was little damage and no one was harmed)
'Tell me about the man who died at 50 Humber Buildings?'
'It's ages ago, but I can remember. When I was sneaking about he went to the toilet. I got some clothes burning and was out quick. He must have tried to put it out and caught fire or something 'cause he came out burning. I remember there was one or two people about but, see, I was a good bit away, and once I saw him in doorway burning I was off. You know that Lister woman might have been with him but I'm not sure.'
'Did it ever occur to you that you might get caught at any one of these fires?'
'No, to put it straight, no. If you start worrying about getting caught you most likely will, so I didn't worry about it. I didn't do it, like so, I would get caught. I used to think and watch out for people so I wouldn't be seen.'

Giving him an easy opportunity to retract his admissions, I said, 'Many people will look upon your voluntary statements as incredible.'
'I don't know why, 'cause it's true.'
'Well, Bruce, this is perhaps enough for today. I shall see you again tomorrow.'
'Yes. You've been writing plenty but I want to make a statement, Mr. Sagar, and I'd like to read my other statements again first so as I've got it clear, see, because I want it all cleared up as I'm not going to do any more fires.'
'Very well,' I said. 'We shall do that tomorrow.'

Few people appreciate just how demanding it is writing in longhand word for word, contemporaneously in a notebook, or for that matter on A4 size statement paper. I must have written close on 2, 000 words verbatim that day and I had had enough writing. I decided I would get all his statements from the Incident Room and he could read them to his heart's content the following morning when both he and I had some sleep.

But before that I contacted Mr. Pearce and told him that Lee would be reading copies of all his statements in his cell the following morning. I also told him that Lee wanted to make yet another statement and that he would probably do so after reading his statements over. Mr. Pearce asked me to forward to him any new statement made.

Accompanied by Sergeant Martin, I saw Lee again next morning at 9. 45 a.m. Following the usual caution I said, 'You may if you wish read all your statements now.'

'Yes, thank you,' he replied.

He looked bright and I sensed an air of self-confident importance in him as he fixed his eyes on the bundle of papers I was carrying. I handed to him the copies of all his statements.

Then, for over an hour, in silence and without raising a query, he looked at all the typed copies of the statements he had made under caution, carefully putting each sheet of paper to one side as he finished looking at it.

I found that hour of considerable interest as I was able to study Lee closely without needing to speak or, for the present, write whatever was said in my notebook. Had he really set fire to those houses? Was he really responsible for burning people alive? He appeared such an insignificant and pleasant young man, yet here he was quietly reading to himself his own revelations of the absolute horror which he was claiming to have inflicted upon so many good citizens of Hull.

As he completed his reading of the last statement he looked up, handed the papers to me and said, 'Yes, that's all right, but, see here (indicating the statement he made on 30 June 1980), there was one I did where I killed another baby. Well, I've got a bit mixed up there 'cause I think it's the one maybe down Reynoldson Street.'

I told him that he could, if he wanted, make a further voluntary statement and I cautioned him in respect of doing so.

'Yes, I know that by now. I'll say about the bit where I was mixed up, in the statement if that's alright.'

'Yes certainly.' I said. 'I think you should do that. Is there anything else in particular you want to mention?'

'See Mr. Sagar, the Bible, Matthew 6-24, it says, "No man can serve two masters for either he will hate one and love the other or he will be devoted to the one and despise the other." Well, I loved fire and despised people in the houses I set fire to. See, I've never had a home and at the time I had a feeling about doing a house, setting it on fire, like, well, I despised people 'cause they had a home and I didn't. I was just devoted to my fires, see, and just didn't bother about people.'

'What do you mean by the word "despise", Bruce?'

'Well, it means hate and at that time I just hated people, and when I picked a house to set on fire it was 'cause I hated whoever was in there.'

'Even though it appears you did not know who, or how many people actually lived in a particular house?'

'Yes, but, see, it was just people, but now, see, I didn't mean to kill them. If

I felt as I do now, I've told you, it wouldn't have happened but at the time the fire sort of had power over me more than anything. I knew what I was doing, like, but it was the thought of doing a fire in the house that made me not bother about what happened to people in the house. Do you understand?'

'Yes, Bruce, you are making it quite clear but you know, surely, by setting a house on fire with paraffin, knowing people were in there you must have believed that people would be killed or very badly burned.'

'Yes, at the time, but after I felt like I didn't intend to kill. It was more to do with fires.'

'Very well, do you now wish to make another (written) statement?'

'Yes, I'm sorry about all this writing.'

'Never mind about that, Bruce.'

He then went on to say in the written statement, 'See, I've read through the statements I've made and I've got a bit mixed up 'cause where I've said there was one where I killed another baby and had set fire to this house and after that I saw it on TV, well that's one of the others I've told you about, maybe Reynoldson Street. Anyway I've told you about all the fires where I've killed people. It's at least 26 people I've killed and there's others where no one has been killed. I know from paper that 11 blokes was killed at that Wensley Lodge, but there might have been some die, later like weeks later. Fire makes it that sometimes people die weeks and weeks later. When I had it in my mind to do a house fire, any house, I was devoted to doing the fire and I despised the people in the houses, even if they was babies, children or older people, even real old people.'

'I often got sick and tired of people and when I was in mind to set a house on fire, I would think how the people were alright in the house and then think what state I was in with no home and they had homes. As you know very well, I've never had a home at all and that's what's cause of all this, but, see, when I say I despised the people in the houses I didn't know them except for Hastie's and Askew Avenue, the lad there. I hated people who were alright in the houses. I've never been alright in a house and, see, at the time I was devoted to doing a bad house fire. I knew when I was setting it alight that there would be death. I knew it might be a man or a woman or child dead once it got going, but being devoted to the fire had more control over my mind than, than people dying.'

'I wasn't bothered about the people dying but I knew they would. We are getting down to rock bottom at this now, Mr. Sagar. See, paraffin is very effective and, well, I've killed plenty in my fires as you know. See, after doing a fire I would hear bits of gossip and hear that people had been killed but I knew when I was doing a fire people was going to be killed anyway. Paraffin will always make a bad fire and in a house everything is dry and with plenty of stuff that goes up in flames easy. You know, I've been lucky getting away with it but see people don't think that a fire in a house is ever arson, especially when there's people in the house at the time.'

'If you lot hadn't kept on about Hastie's month after month you might never have known. You know Mr. Gunby and Mr. Pearce asked me again last week if I wanted to retract the statements I've made to you. Well, I want you to put this down. I don't want to retract my statements because they are true. I wouldn't tell you about this sort of thing unless it was true. I've had a long spell at it and I've killed far too many people. You know they will want to examine me to find out about my mind and find out about my mental age. I think they are pathetic because I've known what I've been up to and I can tell you I'm telling the truth. Now them forensic people. I think that in house fires they should have found some of my fires as arson, not anything else. It's easy, I suppose, to say accident in a house fire but I've done arson and they haven't discovered it. I have had enough of fires and I want you to know that I'll never do another.'

The statement took one hour and 22 minutes to complete. I got the impression that he felt he had now straightened out all he wanted to say and he had a self-satisfied look about him. But I was mistaken, my impression was not quite right.

Shortly afterwards I handed Lee's latest statement to Detective Inspector Holmes. Alan Holmes remained my Incident Room manager throughout the enquiry. I chose him to do this particular job in the first place because of his reputation for always being careful, conscientious and judicious. Now, in view of what Lee was saying, I was thankful that I still had an officer of Alan's ability in control of all the checking, analysing and reviewing of every scrap of information we had.

It was 1980, the computerised Incident Room only began to come into the police service three or four years later. The system we employed was as good as we could get but it took a massive amount of dedication and care by the Incident Room staff in storing information and retrieving it.

As it was, we were faced with an enquiry of great delicacy with revelations which many people, including police officers, would find very difficult to accept.

We had a tremendous amount of paper work to attend to, with every item of information being subject to record. 'Who is going to believe what we have got here?' asked Detective Constable Dave Lewis one morning. 'Who would believe or even think that someone had been wandering about Hull with intent to ravage, with fire, houses at random.'

Chapter Ten

Shortly after lunch on Wednesday, 23 July 1980, I saw Lee, again at the Hull Central Police Station. As always the quiet, unassuming man of brief word, Detective Sergeant Martin, accompanied me. I said, 'One or two general comments, Bruce. I've listened to you a great deal and I've written quite a number of statements which you have dictated to me. My reaction is that you are telling the truth, no matter how incredible your activities might appear.'

'You say incredible again, but it's true, Mr. Sagar.'

'You said in one of your statements that you didn't read newspapers to find out about what you had done, yet you say police, firemen and scientists have put the cause of your fires down to cigarettes and so on. How do you know this if you didn't read about it?'

'Through experience. I know they didn't do murder enquiries after, see, because when you do a murder enquiry everybody knows about it, but it was only when I did Hastie's and made my mistake with too much paraffin that you did a murder enquiry. Others there was no murder enquiry, see, so it was obvious.'

'Were you ever nearly caught perhaps, setting fire to anywhere?'

'No, but quite a few times I've been going to do a house but somebody has come walking along when I've been thinking about doing it and, well, I've just walked along before doing anything.'

'Have you ever burned yourself in any of your fires?'

'Just a little blister once, on me hand, but nothing serious.'

'Which fire was that?'

'Oh, can't remember.'

'Is the reason for setting fire to houses really because of your upbringing Bruce?'

'Yes, me mother was a prostitute. I've known it for years. There's many a time she's been out all night and I've wandered about streets all night. She never cared. Once she slung me out.'

'You appear to have accounted for the deaths of at least 26 people, Bruce. How do you feel now you seem to have got it off your chest?'

'Put it this way, I don't feel glad about it. I'm not boasting. My thoughts for fire were greatest but if anyone, anyone could be glad about it they should be put in a mental institution.'

'What of the tingling feeling you have mentioned. Does this always come on when you are about to light a fire?'

'Yes, not all the time, but most of the time. See, this morning in the cell, I had the feeling and if I'd had paraffin I'd have set fire to the cell then.'

'When setting a house on fire, did you ever have thoughts for anyone at all?'

'My mind has been on the job fire wise. Well I didn't worship it, but I were thinking more fires than owt else. Fair enough, I've killed a lot but it's as Matthew 6-24, devoted to fire. See, I couldn't stab a child to death but in a fire I was devoted to the fires and despised people in houses.'

'Did you ever consider the agonizing deaths you were causing?'

In a steady, matter of fact way, he replied, 'No, but I'm sorry now. There again, being sorry now doesn't help.'

'This will be over one day, Bruce. Will you then be happy and say thank God, perhaps?'

'No, not thank God, that would be taking his name in vain, but I will say thank heaven. I'll be glad when it's all over. I'm going to plead guilty to manslaughter and arson for each fire I've done.'

'That's a matter for you Bruce,' I said, but I knew that I would be far from happy with a plea of guilty from him because I believed in view of all the circumstances it would be in the interests of justice for him to plead not guilty so that all the evidence could be properly tested before the court. I was not in any way worried about his 'plead guilty' comment for I firmly believed that in due course his defence counsel would quite properly advise him to plead not guilty.

Lee continued, 'Did you know much about my fires, Mr. Sagar?'

'What do you mean?' I said.

'Well, before I told you, did you know about them?'

'Actually I knew that fire had occurred at Wensley Lodge but little more than that (I was working in London at the time the Wensley Lodge fire occurred) I'd heard that there had been a fire in West Dock Avenue, but that's all. You see, Sergeant Martin and I chose not to check any files on any of the fires you have spoken about until well after you told us you were responsible for them.'

'Why?'

'There's very good reason, Bruce. Let's leave it at that.'

'Can I sign your notebook, Mr. Sagar? I've signed my statements when I've made them. Can I sign your notebook 'cause what you write is what I'm saying, isn't it?'

'Yes, it is Bruce. You can write your signature if you wish.'

He then signed my notebook just below the last comment I had made and written there.

During the evening of the following day, Thursday, 24 July, I saw him again in his cell.

He said, 'Mr. Pearce has been to see me and he's gone through my statements and showed me where I've said seven times that I've intended to kill people. Well, I want to make a statement saying I didn't intend killing and I don't think I really said "intended to" on my statements. See, he's got bits underlined and he's shown me.'

'You can make a further statement if you wish. It's a matter for you. But at the moment Sergeant Martin is not available and I would want him to be here should you make any other statement.'

'Yes. Has he gone home? Well, as long as I can make it before I go to court in the morning I don't mind. See, Mr. Pearce says he's going to surprise you with bits he's got lined.'

'Very well, Bruce, I'll see you in the morning.'

I saw him again the following morning and took another written statement from him. In it he repeated that Mr. Pearce had been to see him and had pointed out that on seven occasions he had said he had intended to kill. He continued, 'I set fire to houses but my intention was fire and only fire. I just didn't bother about people who was in the houses. See, that's better. See, Mr. Pearce has picked out a few bits in my statements and told me in some of my sentences I have been digging my own grave. Well, I just want to say that my intention has been fire only. He has told me it would be best for me to say nothing. He told me that when he first saw me in Gordon Street and told me again yesterday. See, Mr. Pearce is only trying to help me, I know, but I am sick of people telling me what to do. I'm telling the truth in my statements so sooner it's all over the better.'

He attended at the Magistrates Court shortly afterwards when he was further remanded in custody and I saw him again later that day: 'There are a number of points which I would like to talk to you about, Bruce. I want you to think very carefully when I speak to you. Firstly, how do you feel about the publicity that will no doubt result from this enquiry?'

'I don't want no publicity but I know that I won't be able to do anything about it. I don't want me photograph in papers and I don't like publicity.'

'There are some people, I'm sure, who would thoroughly enjoy the sort of publicity you are likely to get, Bruce.'

'Well that's not me. I don't want any of it but I know there will be some. You can't stop it for me? I don't suppose, can you?'

'No Bruce, I'm afraid there is nothing we will be able to do about it.' I continued, 'What of newspapers? Do you read newspapers a lot?'

'Well I get *Sun* for telly sometimes. I've told you that. Then I read *Hull Daily Mail* when speedway's on.'

'When did you start reading newspapers?'

'Just last year when them hostages was on the go. I never bothered before that.'

'But surely you would have read newspapers after some of your fires. Wensley Lodge for instance?'

'I didn't have to read about it, did I? I knew all about it 'cause I'd done it.'

'But didn't you need to see what the newspaper was saying?'

'No, it didn't matter. See, when there's a murder enquiry everybody in town talks about it. I didn't hear anybody saying murder and arson and that so I knew it was same as others I'd done. Just a fire.'

'You know Sergeant Martin and I have talked about you and, you know, it is just possible we think that you could have read about these fires in the newspapers.'

'What do you mean?'

'That you've read about them and have possibly made up the fact that you are responsible for them.'

With an obvious expression of annoyance, he raised his voice for the first time since I had known him, saying, 'Oh, no! How the hell could I have remembered all that. I don't go around reading newspapers anyway.'

He then quietened down, hesitated for a few moments and continued, 'What's the matter with you? I couldn't do that. I'm not a mad cracker. How could I read it all years ago and tell you now? Bloody hell, man, I've told the truth and I've even shown you the bloody houses. Fucking hell, excuse the language. But here I am telling the truth and you come up with this fucking

daft idea. You do believe me, don't you? Maybe you've just got to ask these questions.'
'What do you really think our job is?'
'Well I think it's like Pearce says. He's defending me and you are the prosecutors.'
'And what do you think prosecutors are?'
'Well, you take me to court for what I've done. You are just getting the truth.'
'Yes, you are right, but really Sergeant Martin and I are just seeking the truth.'
'Yes, I know,' he said.
'Did you often see the fire engines at your fires?'
'No, most often I wasn't there. Alright, Wensley Lodge. I remember them going up past cop shop as I came down on the bike. But it's best to get out of the way.'
'Yes, and when you saw the Fire Brigade then, near Hessle Police Station, didn't you also see a police car or two?'
'Maybe one, but I don't think I noticed many.'
'How would you feel if we told you that we just don't believe anything you say?'
'Suggestions like this are just pathetic. Anyway, I would have thought you barmy. If I'd given you a load of lies you'd know about it. I'm fucking sure about it. Can I ask you a question, Mr. Sagar?'
'Yes, go on.'
'You do believe me, don't you?'
'Well, Bruce, Sergeant Martin and I have discussed your activities and what you have told us quite a lot and, although what you have been doing seems quite incredible, we do in fact believe you, in spite of the fact that initially we found it hard to accept.'
'Thank you.'
'Tell me, Bruce. Why have you chosen to tell us about all these fires?'
'If I'd never told you, I might have let it slip in the nick. Someone might have asked me if Hastie's was the first fire I'd done. I would probably have said no and then maybe let it slip. See there'd be nothing much else to talk about in nick and I wouldn't want you coming to take me back to court and then maybe I would never get out.'
'Of course, some people might suggest that you believe you have set fire to these houses when in fact you haven't. Do you understand?'
'That's what fucking psychiatrist would say. Look, I'm not that bloody daft.'
'Fair enough, Bruce. I trust you appreciate that I feel it necessary to make these points with you?'
'Yes, I understand that. I said about them psychiatrists in Leeds nick trying to get my mental age.'
'I have a blown-up plan here showing Wensley Lodge. Do you think you could perhaps indicate on the plan where you got into the building?'
He looked at it for several minutes, then said, 'See, when I did it I just walked around the building. I saw the garden and that but, see, it was just a

bay window. I kicked it and went in. I didn't think, like, that one day you would come along with a plan and say, "Bruce, where did you get in?" I can't fucking think like that. I just went around and saw the window. I could just guess and say that window, but that would be daft. It was just a big house and I saw the window, but I didn't sort of stand back to see exactly where I was. Why should I do that?'

'Thinking about this, Bruce, you did mention at one time that you had put paraffin inside the house near to the window where you got in. Did you light that paraffin just inside that window?'

'No, I don't think I did. No, it was just up in that room. But, see, as fires spread it would catch up with that and burn anyway. There wasn't a lot inside the window, you know, not downstairs where I got in.'

'When did you start reading the Bible?'

'About three years ago.'

'Why?'

'When I was at Mrs. Fox's and a good few weeks after Wensley Lodge. Things was getting me down. See, tension was building up somewhere inside me.'

'Did Wensley Lodge get you down?'

'Well, I knew people was killed after I did the fire there and it got me down. See, I used to go out from Mrs. Fox's and walk along them old railway lines where there was no people and just think. And then when I got back I would read the Bible if I could find somewhere quiet.'

'Did you read any particular passage of the Bible when you had Wensley Lodge in mind?'

'I wasn't at Mrs. Fox's when I did Wensley Lodge but it was a few weeks after that I went there, and Bible, yes, it was Matthew 6-33, "Seek ye first the Kingdom of God".'

'What of the Bible after any other fire?'

'Reynoldson Street. I was at Mrs. Fox's and I remember I went to bed early that night and read Matthew 6-24. "Man cannot serve two masters". I read it as soon as it was all quiet when I got a chance.'

'Did you shed a tear perhaps after any particular fire?'

'Yes. After Hastie's and West Dock Avenue, the baby. I sobbed but I didn't cry my heart out.'

'What of others?'

'Reynoldson Street. I sobbed a bit that night after that.'

'Tell me, how did you know Wensley Lodge was so called?'

'Don't know. I think it was when there was gossip about it. It was just a big house to me when I went there.'

'Didn't you see the name plate on the wall outside?'

'No, I didn't.'

'Of course, you could have picked up a lot of gossip about Wensley Lodge and have invented the fact that you were responsible.'

Raising his voice a little he replied, 'Oh, no, not that fucking holy polony again. We've just gone through all that.'

'Why have you found it necessary to light fires?'

'When I was small, I used to like watching flames in bonfires. And well, ever since I can remember I've always loved fire. I'll tell you something. I just didn't pick it up overnight. Ten years I've been doing them and I'll tell you it's bloody hard to stop when you get the urge. See, I don't care two apes of a monkey what the Judge says, six days, six weeks, six months, six years maybe sixty years. I won't do any more anyway. But it is bloody hard to stop. You know if I went to open nick they'd kill me in five minutes for what I've done. But I can't see me going to an open nick, can you?'

'We shall just have to wait and see.'

About 3 p.m. on Monday, 28 July 1980, I asked him if he remembered the room at Wensley Lodge where he had said he poured paraffin and whether the paraffin splashed on the floor.

'Of course, it splashed, and it run up the wall,' he replied.

'Did it, do you remember that?'

'Yes, where would you expect it to run?'

'Was that wall the same one where you said there was a window?'

'No, I don't think so, but I can't remember.'

'Do you remember anything about the floor?'

'No, it was just a floor. It's a long time ago. Do you remember what you did or saw three weeks last Friday?'

'Was the room a small room or a large one?'

'A bit big room for two beds maybe.'

'Were there two beds in the room then?'

'I don't know.'

'Was there a light on in that room?'

'Yes, there was some lights on in different places.'

'You mentioned the window. Remember, you said you broke a window to get in. Was it very high?'

'No, I could just lift me foot up a good bit and kicked it. It didn't make a big smash but I took some of the pieces out.'

'Why not get in through the door?'

'Don't know. I just went in through the window.'

The following day Tuesday, 29 July 1980, I saw him again. In spite of having no authority to do so, I demanded that Mr. Pearce be present on this occasion. He attended and Mr. Gunby, solicitor, came too.

Lee replied, 'Yes,' to each of the fires I listed and in conclusion said, 'Yes, I would like to say that I'll be glad when this lot's finished with and I get to Crown Court and get it done with. I just want to get it behind me and get settled down.'

One matter, above all else, begged further questions: the killing of David Brewer in Humber Buildings in October, 1973.

So it was on Thursday, 28 August 1980, that Sergeant Martin and I went to Leeds Prison once more. I had not seen Lee for four weeks and he smiled broadly as he came into the prison visiting room.

'We have been wondering about the situation in 50, Humber Buildings, Madeley Street. You see from enquiries that have now been made it appears you may not have told us exactly what happened there. I know it's a long time ago but I would like you to try and remember.'

He stared long and hard into my face for several seconds, coloured up and then said, 'You're right. I couldn't tell you but I will now. See, this bloke, I got his pigeons and, well, he was asleep in a chair.' His eyes burned into mine for several more seconds and then continued, 'I just poured paraffin over him quietly when he was asleep and set him alight. I fucking left him quick.'

'So you must have intended to kill him, sprinkling paraffin over him and setting him alight.'

'I didn't sprinkle, I fucking poured it.'

Lee's correction to my statement and the irritation in his voice made me just a little anxious about his acute need for correctness.

'So you intended to kill him?' I said.

'Yes. He clipped my ear. He shouldn't have done that.'

'What of the fact that you have said there were clothes drying in that house and you set them alight?' I asked.

'Well, Mr. Sagar, it's hard to have to speak and say that I killed a man like that. I did but it was easier to say it was clothes drying, but it wasn't, it was clothes on him.'

I said, 'For reasons I am not going to mention I find it strange that you should say you set fire to clothes that were drying.'

'See, that's what people round there thought. They was all saying about it and that pleased me 'cause I know they didn't suspect me.'

I continued, 'But you also mentioned the man going to the toilet.'

'Yes, well that was part of it, see. Just a cover-up that I'd set him on fire when he was asleep.'

'What of other people who have died in houses you have set on fire?'

'You mean my intentions?'

'Yes.'

'Well, get your paper out and I'll make a statement with that piece on the top (the words of the caution) what I know off by heart. There's one or two things I'm going to say but you write it in a proper statement I can sign. See, Gunby and Pearce was on about you writing a lot of "see's" in my statements and that I hadn't said things, but, fucking hell, I know I talk like that and you two know. I wish you would tell them 'cause it's true. They seem to think you was making it up.'

'You may if you wish make a statement . . .'

He interrupted saying, 'Yes, I know that, get it down in a statement. I know it's up to me what I say.'

Lee then made another written statement: 'It wasn't that I have known the people in the houses. It's just despising people and my fires would kill them. It's just the way I feel, Mr. Sagar, like that old bloke in Glasgow Street, and the old woman in the bed in Rosamond Street, and the old blokes in Wensley Lodge and all of them. I've just had the urge to set fire to the house. I've known that I was going to be killing people because of the nasty fire I was doing but the urge has been there and I've just gone on and done it. You must know it's been murder but it's the fire that's been most in my mind. You know the end result with all this is that I'll be pleading guilty to arson and murder. I've been thinking about it a lot and I've listened to my solicitor and he's said it's up to me. Well, I'm pleading guilty to murder and arson. We've got down to the bare bones of it so now you know. Some people might think I'm insane and I can act daft but I know I'm not. I've been going around killing people for ages and if I was bloody daft I couldn't have got away with it, could I? Tell you somat. I would set fire to my mother's house if I could. I'd love to burn her, I really would. She put us in homes, my sister and me. I've intentions to kill her in a fire 'cause she is responsible for not bringing us up properly, that's me and my sister, I mean. I'd better tell you 'cause this is the last statement I am going to give you.'

On completion of the statement I said, 'I just want to refer to the fire at Gorthorpe where you say you caused the fire under the stairs there. There was a child there, you know.'

'Look I've said all I'm going to say. I can't say anything else. Fucking hell, I don't want to say about setting a baby on fire. No, this is my last statement, Mr. Sagar.'

His words tumbled out often and long enough, and I was, I think, relieved that he appeared to have no more to say.

Chapter Eleven

As in all cases where death is not natural, the actual cause of death is usually revealed by post mortem examination. In the majority of fires the cause of death is given as asphyxia due to the inhalation of smoke. The cause of the fire is a different matter and is most often open to conjecture. In the first place, searching the scene of a fire for clues is extremely difficult, particularly when the building has been gutted. The fire itself often destroys some of the best evidence an investigator is looking for and that, coupled with the vital actions of the firemen to put out the fire, often leaves police and fire investigators with little more than guess work.

Following Lee's statements, a member of the Incident Room staff visited the Coroner's Office in the Old Town of Hull to seek any documents likely to help identify his claims to particular fires as his doing. Every word he had uttered was analysed, checked and cross checked in the Incident Room by Alan Holmes and his staff and examined alongside the Coroner's documents.

I don't believe any of us appreciated then how many house fires occur in a large city, but officers delving through the Coroner's files were left in no doubt that fire in the home are by no means a rarity. During Lee's claim to fire raising in the 1970s, a further 50 deaths were recorded resulting from domestic house fires in Hull. If what Lee was saying was true, then his claim as an arsonist would only account for a small number of house fires compared with the number which occurred annually.

In my initial glance through the files of documents I soon found that several fires Lee was claiming as his own had not had the benefit of any kind of forensic examination when first reported. Apparently no one had considered forensic examination necessary and, surprisingly, no one raised the point at the inquests.

Incident Room staff had positively identified nine fatal house fires which Lee claimed as his doing and officers listed the papers for me in chronological order.

Examination of the inquest documents revealed the following unnatural deaths:

1. Richard Anthony Ellerington, aged 6 years, of 70 Askew Avenue, Hull, who died on 24 June 1973.
2. Arthur Bernard Smythe, aged 73 years, of 33 Glasgow Street, Hull, who died on 12 October 1973.
3. David Brewer, aged 34 years, of 50 Humber Buildings, Madeley Street, Hull, who died on 27 October 1973.
4. Elizabeth Rokahr, aged 82 years, of 7 Minnies Terrace, Rosamond Street, Hull, who died on 23 December 1974.
5. Andrew Edwards, aged 1 years, of 9 Gorthorpe, Orchard Park, Hull who died on 3 June 1976.
6. Katrina Thacker, aged 6 months, of 43 West Dock Avenue, Hull, who died on 2 January 1977.
7. Harold Akester, aged 95 years,
   William Beales, aged 73 years,
   William Carter, aged 80 years,

Victor Consitt, aged 83 years,
Leonard Dennett, aged 73 years,
Arthur Ellwood, aged 82 years,
Arthur Hardy, aged 65 years,
William Hoult, aged 82 years,
Benjamin Phillips, aged 83 years,
John James Riby, aged 75 years,
Percy Sanderson, aged 77 years,
all of Wensley Lodge, Hessle, who died on 5 January, 1977.
8. Mark Andrew Jordon, aged 7 years, and
Deborah Pauline Gold/Hooper, aged 13 years, of 4 Belgrave Terrace, Rosamond Street, Hull, who died on 24 April 1977.
9. Christine Viola Dickson, aged 24 years,
Mark Christopher Dickson, aged 5 years,
Steven Paul Dickson, aged 4 years,
Michael Ian Dickson, aged 16 months, of 2 Brentwood Villas, Reynoldson Street, Hull, who died on 6 January 1978.

A total of 26 people, all killed in house fires, whose deaths were officially recorded as 'misadventure.'

Starting with the file on the death of six-year-old Richard Anthony Ellerington, I read that he lived with his parents, Samuel and Catherine Ellerington, and their other five children, at 70 Askew Avenue. Richard was the second youngest in the family. From being a few months old Richard suffered from a condition which partly paralysed his right hand side, and he had no use of his right arm. Coincidentally, Richard Ellerington and Bruce Lee suffered a similar physical handicap. Richard attended Frederick Holmes School for Handicapped Children. A special bus called at his home on school days about 8.30 a.m. and transported him and other handicapped children to school. Significantly, Lee attended this school and travelled on the same bus during this time.

On the night of Saturday, 23 June 1973, Samuel Ellerington and his wife spent the evening visiting relatives at the other side of the City and returned home about 11 p.m. Carol Dennett (who later married their eldest son, David) acted as baby sitter and put the children to bed during the evening. The Ellerington's returned home shortly before midnight and had supper with Carol Dennett. Samuel went to bed about 12.30 a.m. and Carol and Mrs. Ellerington followed about 2.30 a.m. Mrs. Ellerington recalled that it was a particularly warm night and she left the kitchen window open, especially as Carol had cooked the Sunday roast on the gas cooker during the evening. Significantly no one closed this window before going to bed; neither did anyone lock the front door.

Carol and her baby slept in the small front bedroom looking out onto Askew Avenue. Mr. and Mrs. Ellerington slept in the medium sized front bedroom also facing Askew Avenue, and the four Ellerington children at home that night all slept in the large bedroom overlooking the rear garden.

Sometime shortly before 7 a.m. the next morning Mr. and Mrs. Ellerington were awakened by smoke in their bedroom. About the same time Carol was awakened by what she described as a kind of thud. She glanced out of her bedroom window and saw smoke belching out of the Ellerington's bedroom window. All three went on to the landing and found impassable smoke everywhere. In fear of their lives, the Ellerington's opened the rear bedroom window where their children were sleeping and found relatively light smoke inside. Carol grabbed her baby and she too dashed across the landing and into the rear bedroom. Keeping his wits about him, Samuel Ellerington closed the rear bedroom door to the landing as soon as Carol and her baby were safely inside. The thick smoke was now being followed by flames leaping up the stairs.

As more smoke seeped under the closed door into the room, Mr. Ellerington told his wife to get the children close to the rear bedroom window ready to jump out. He then jumped out of the window into the rear garden and his wife threw each child out to him. This included Carol's baby and Carol herself. When it came to her turn to jump Mrs. Ellerington suddenly realised that Richard was missing. In an awful state of fear, she went back to the bedroom door, opened it and found her way blocked by smoke and flames which were now reaching into the bedrooms. She fled to the bedroom window and jumped out to her husband's arms.

All the survivors were taken to Hull Royal Infirmary and treated for smoke inhalation. In jumping from the window Samuel Ellerington incurred a back injury which persisted for several years. Mrs. Ellerington broke a bone in her right foot as she landed in the garden, terrified about the fate of her son, Richard.

Hull City Fire Brigade received a fire call from a neighbour in Askew Avenue at 7.14 on that otherwise pleasant summer Sunday morning. They promptly attended the scene and found severe fire burning on the ground floor. Fire officers soon realised that the seat of the fire was somewhere in the kitchen. As they got the fire under control, firemen found Richard's body lying on the bed in the small front bedroom which had been occupied for the night by Carol and her baby. Firemen also found Rusty, the family dog, which usually slept on the landing, alive in the rear bedroom from where the family had escaped. Members of the Brigade also found that the front door was unlocked.

Forensic scientists were not called to examine the scene. Police officers made enquiries into the cause of the fire and it became apparent to them that Richard had been downstairs in the house sometime before the fire was discovered. But had he really been downstairs that morning? The deduction was made from the word of Richard's four-year-old brother who was questioned by a police officer several hours after the family learned of Richard's death. It was also apparent that Richard entered the bedroom where he was found, after Carol and her baby had left it. How and when he got there no one knows. According to Carol and Richard's parents, it was impossible to get up or down the stairs when they discovered the fire; that's why they had to escape through the rear bedroom window. So was he upstairs all the time? No one will ever know.

Police surgeon, Dr. Percy Mitchell Scott made a post mortem examination on Richard's body. He found slight singeing of parts of the hair of the head and post mortem burns on the shoulders, hands and feet. He told the Coroner that in his opinion Richard's death was not natural and was due to asphyxia due to the inhalation of smoke.

Coroner Dr. Philip Science asked Dr. Scott, 'You mention that the burns Richard showed were post mortem burns?'

Dr Scott answered, 'Yes sir, post mortem burns.'

Coroner: 'He couldn't have felt any pain?'

Dr Scott: 'Not from the burning, sir.'

Coroner: 'He was overcome by the smoke, but he was saved the pain of any burns?'

Dr Scott, 'Yes, sir, I am sure of that.

Examining that piece of evidence I concluded that Richard could not possibly have made his way upstairs through the smoke and flames after Carol and the rest of the family left through the bedroom window. Looking further into the Coroner's documents I examined the evidence concerning the gas cooker which had been used to cook the Sunday roast during the evening before the fire. The fire had gutted the kitchen and other parts of the house and, once the fire had been brought under control, it was found that the governor on the gas cooker was leaking. A gas fitter from North Eastern Gas Board was quickly called to the scene. He found that all the gas taps were in the 'off' position and the cooker itself was badly burned. The fitter was unable to say whether the governor was leaking prior to the fire and he was therefore unable to give an opinion as to the cause of the fire. The cooker was only one-year-old and was, according to Mrs. Ellerington, in perfect working order. Furthermore, the gas supply and the cooker had been thoroughly examined and converted to North Sea Gas only three weeks earlier.

The gas fitter told the Coroner that he was unable to say if the gas escape was there before the fire or was caused by the intense heat of the fire.

The Coroner asked him, 'It is impossible to say?'

The fitter replied, 'Yes it is, sir,'

The Coroner also asked the senior fire officer who attended the fire for his opinion.

Coroner: 'After consideration, officer, have you come to any opinion?'

Fire officer: 'No, sir, I haven't.'

Coroner: 'Is it impossible to be sure?'

Fire officer: 'Yes, sir, it is impossible to be sure.'

Coroner: 'We are concerned, however, as to how this fire might have started. There is merely a presumption that there was a leak in the governor of the gas oven which allowed gas to escape and build up until it was exploded by the pilot light, but the exact cause cannot be established. The verdict is misadventure.'

No one knew how Richard came to be in the small front bedroom. And no one considered arson. Lee was 12-years-old at the time and Social Services Department records show he was living with his mother in West Dock Avenue, a mile or so away from Askew Avenue. He recalled that he sneaked out in the middle of the night and went walking. He filled a bottle with paraffin from a Highways Department grit box. He came upon 70 Askew Avenue, went to the rear of the house and found the kitchen window open. He climbed in, sprinkled paraffin in the kitchen, lit it and left.

He said he was a passenger on the school bus the following Monday morning, 25 June 1973, when he heard some talk that Richard had died in the fire, but he just kept quiet. He corroborated his story by directing us to the house but his ability to identify the house was of little evidential value as he knew the house because the school bus he used at the time called there for Richard.

There was corroboration in Lee's recollection of the open kitchen window and the seat of the fire. I also thought the connection between Lee and the deceased also added weight to his admission. We enquired at the local Public Cleansing Department about the presence of paraffin in the grit box but these enquiries were inconclusive. It was known, however, that paraffin was sometimes used to fuel roadside danger lamps.

I was glad that any decision to prefer, or not to prefer, any charge against Lee was a matter for the Director of Public Prosecutions. I knew that any final decision regarding Lee's guilt would be in the hands of a High Court Judge and jury. It mattered not in the final analysis whether I believed Lee or not.

Chapter Twelve

Arthur Bernard Smythe, was 72-years-old and an unmarried ex-merchant seaman. Up until 1972, he owned a small terraced house in the fish dock area of Hull. In that year the house came under a compulsory purchase order from Hull Corporation. Shortly afterwards, he purchased a similar, 'two-up-two-down' house nearby at 33 Glasgow Street. He then lived the life of a recluse and appeared to be in an advanced state of senility, also suffering from gangrene in both legs. He rejected all help offered by the Hull Social Services Department and lived out his days sitting alone in the front room of his house, surrounded by squalor.

Little use was made of any other part of the house. The front room contained an open fireplace, which was rarely, if ever, used. The house was supplied by gas, but the electricity supply was cut off. Smythe used two paraffin heaters for heating and candles for lighting. He had a bed supplied by Social Services Department, but refused to use it and slept in a chair. He was in the habit of collecting his groceries in cardboard boxes and, when empty, stored these in the front room, almost reaching the ceiling.

During the evening of Thursday, 11 October 1973, a police constable was called to the house to attend to Smythe, who was reported to be in a confused state. The constable contacted Smythe's next-door neighbour, Lesley Ann Pooley, who looked after him to some extent. Mrs. Pooley settled Smythe down in a chair in the front room and left him. About an hour later she heard him shouting and returned to find him inside the front room banging on the windows. He broke one of the front windows, leaving a hole covered by a dirty make-shift curtain. Mrs. Pooley left the house, closing, but not locking, the front door.

About 6.45 a.m. the following morning Michael Anthony Greaves was driving to work along Glasgow Street when he saw smoke coming through the roof of Smythe's house. He stopped his car, dashed up to No. 33 and saw the front ground floor room was in flames. He also heard moaning from inside. Mr. Greaves then left for a few moments to telephone the Fire Brigade. Another man came upon the scene, and the two men attempted to get into the house, but they found that fierce heat and choking smoke drove them back. One of the men kicked the front door in, but he could not recall why he found it necessary to kick the door open when, to all intents and purposes, it was unlocked.

The fire call was logged by the Fire Brigade at 6.49 a.m. The firemen found a fierce fire burning in the front ground floor room and attacked the fire with water hoses, very quickly extinguishing the flames. This caused the senior fireman to reach the conclusion that he was not dealing with a deep-seated fire, but, more likely, one caused by an accelerant of some kind, similar to paraffin. He also reported that he found two paraffin heaters in the room, one of which was lying on its back near to the connecting door to the kitchen. Firemen saw that this heater was dismantled and not apparently in current use. Smythe's body was found lying in the room, very badly burned.

Police officers made enquiries into the fire and the Principal (Forensic) Scientific Officer, Kenneth Jones, was called to make an examination. As the fire was confined to the one room, it was apparent that this was the seat of the fire though further, more exact, definition was not possible. There was a coin-operated, two-ring gas cooker in the kitchen but examination of the meter showed that all the gas which had been paid for had been used up. In any case, the fire had been confined to the front room.

The inquest on Arthur Bernard Smythe was held on 21 November 1973 and presided over by the Coroner, Dr. Philip Science. Dr. Percy Mitchell Scott gave the cause of death as asphyxia due to the inhalation of smoke.

In a written report to the Coroner, Mr. Jones stated that the contents of the room had all been affected by fire with charring of the door frames and skirting boards. Part of the lath and plaster ceiling had collapsed onto the floor and much of the very thick plaster had also fallen from the wall. He also noted that there was a smell of paraffin in the room and attributed the smell to a paraffin heater in the room. He could not, however, find any excessive seat of fire damage beside the heater which could be identified as the original seat of fire. Significantly, Mr. Jones also reported that the entire exposed wood surfaces of the room had become charred.

Station Officer Peter Mitchell told the Coroner, 'In my experience I would say that the manner in which the flames were quickly extinguished when the hose was put on them would suggest a rapid fire such as would be caused by ignited paraffin.'

Coroner, 'Is it impossible to say where the fire started?'
'Exactly where it had started, yes, sir.'
'Is it possible to say how the fire may have started?'
'The only thing I can say is, that it was rapidly extinguished, it had not been a deep-seated fire, and I would, however, say that the charring of the woodwork was caused by paraffin, and we did find some evidence of paraffin in there.'
'And how could the paraffin become ignited?'
'I couldn't say, sir.'
'The fire was quickly extinguished, but by the same token it could have been quickly started by the paraffin?'
'I wouldn't like to say, sir.'

The Coroner did not enquire further about the paraffin aspect, nor did anyone else.

The police officer who attended the house earlier that night saw that there was no fire in the hearth and did not see any heater in the room. The officer gave no evidence that Mr. Smythe smoked cigarettes either.

The Coroner concluded by saying that there were two theories as to how the fire started: (1) Mr. Smythe could have gone to bed in his chair leaving either a lighted candle or an unextinguished cigarette, and this could have ignited any of the inflammable material around the house causing the fire. (2) Mr. Smythe may have woken during the night and may have been carrying some naked light or trying to light his paraffin heater or go to the toilet. He was known to be bad on his feet and could have stumbled against any of the rubbish in the room, fallen and set fire to any inflammable material in the room.

With practically no real evidence given as to the actual cause of the fire the Coroner recorded that Arthur Bernard Smythe died from asphyxia due to the inhalation of smoke caused when the living room of his home caught fire. The verdict was misadventure. Coroner Science was left with nothing but conjecture, but surely, a little more probing about the paraffin heater would have been helpful. No one spoke of arson.

Lee was 13 when the Glasgow Street fire occurred. Our enquiries revealed he was then living half a mile away from Glasgow Street, in West Dock Avenue. He claimed that he took paraffin out with him and walked the streets all night. He said he came upon the house, 33 Glasgow Street, early in the morning and described it as a dirty house with some broken windows at the front and an old curtain covering them. He alleged he climbed through the front window and saw an 'old bloke' asleep in a chair. He also spoke of large piles of cardboard boxes in the room. He says he sprinkled paraffin about the room, lit it and left through the front door which Mrs. Pooley had left unlocked. He was asked to point the house out and did so even though many of the houses in the street had by that time been demolished.

The evidence given before the Coroner regarding the presence of an accelerant at the fire now assumed greater significance. Lee maintained he took his own paraffin and could not recall seeing any paraffin heaters. His admission corroborated what was known of the seat of the fire and the wide area of charred wood tended to support his story.

Considering Lee's amazing recollection of Mr. Smythe's house, Prison Doctor Daphne Sasiene's words came flooding back to me: 'We humans all retain a massive store of memory, you know. We all have a much more clear memory of something exciting we have sometime experienced, even though the experience was long ago.' If true, then the fires probably were exciting to Lee. It did not appear, from what I knew of him, that much else had happened in his life to cause any other kind of excitement.

Chapter Thirteen

Humber Buildings, Madeley Street, consists of a series of council-owned two and three-storey blocks of two-bedroomed flats in an area adjacent to the docks in West Hull. No. 50 is situated on the ground floor of one of the blocks.

On Friday, 19 October 1973, the tenant of this flat was a widow, Lillian Brewer, who lived there with her son, David, aged 34 years. He had suffered serious head injuries when he was struck on the head by a crane jib when he was about 18-years-old, and consequently suffered from blackouts and epileptic fits, although he was not known to have had a fit for two or more years. The accident precluded him from gaining regular work and he was registered as unemployed. However, our enquiries revealed that he worked on a casual basis on the night shift at a local fish factory.

Soon after 3 p.m. that day, Mrs. Brewer went out to do some shopping, leaving her son sitting in an armchair in the living room. A fire of coal and logs was burning in the grate. David's mother did not use a fireguard and there were no clothes drying, nor did she have any clothes to dry in front of the fire or anywhere else when she left.

About 4.30 p.m. Herbert Thomas Green, a local coalman, was delivering coal to nearby flats. As he passed the living room window of No. 50, he glimpsed David, who was known to him, knocking on the window. It appeared that Brewer was trying to attract his attention, but Green did not pay much attention to David's actions as he was carrying a bag of coal on his back and he carried on to deliver the coal to a flat across a central paved area between the blocks of flats, presuming that David wanted some coal.

Hilda May Lister lived in a flat immediately opposite the Brewer's, across the paved area and about 100 feet away. Her front door faced the rear of 50, Humber Buildings. Shortly after 4.30 p.m. she heard a loud scream come from the Brewer's flat and ran across the paved area to the flat. She entered by the unlocked door and in the kitchen saw David Brewer in flames from his head to his toes. She soaked several towels in water and pushed him on to the kitchen floor, eventually extinguishing the flames. She also removed David's badly burned trousers, shirt, vest and underpants from his body and, significantly, she left the garments on the kitchen floor. After tending to David, she went into the living room, expecting to see a raging fire, but found that the fire in the grate was low and there was no sign of anything having fallen out. Coalman Mr. Green joined her, saw the state David was in and hurried away to telephone for an ambulance. David Brewer was soon taken by ambulance the short distance to the Hull Royal Infirmary, suffering from extensive burns to his body. He died there eight days later.

By the time the police attended, David had been removed to the Infirmary and was never again sufficiently conscious to relate the circumstances. The police examined the living room and saw there were scorch marks on the arm of the settee, on the carpet and on the linoleum. There was no sign of any other damage. There was no fireguard in the flat but the police saw that ornaments on the mantelpiece were at the back and this gave rise to the conjecture that some article had been hung from the mantelpiece and held in position by the ornaments. No clothing, burnt or otherwise, was found on the living room. The police did, however, recover the burned remains of a vest, shirt, underpants and trousers from the kitchen floor, no doubt believing they were clothes which they guessed had been hanging in front of the fire and not appreciating that they were the clothes Mrs. Lister had removed from David's body.

Dr. Alexander Panton Massie, the Consultant Pathologist, made a post mortem examination and told the Coroner that in his opinion death was due to toxaemia following extensive 2nd and 3rd degree burns. Approximately 50% of the total skin surface was involved.

Hilda May Lister was not called to give evidence but she told the police at the time that, just as David was being taken to the Infirmary, he said something about drying clothes on the fireguard. The police could not find a fireguard and David's mother confirmed there was not a fireguard in the house. The fact that the police noticed there were ornaments at the back of the mantelpiece, which led to the conjecture that clothes had probably been hanging there, was never explored at the Inquest, even though David's mother had earlier denied such a practice.

As Mrs. Lister had stopped the burning by using wet towels, and, presumably, as there was no other burning, no one chose to call the Fire Brigade to give their expert opinion on the cause of the tragedy or considered it worthwhile to ask for the help of a forensic scientist.

No one queried the lack of expert evidence during the Inquest, and the Coroner gave his decision: 'In these circumstances I must record that David Brewer died on 27 October 1973 at the Hull Royal Infirmary and that he died from Toxaemia following extensive 2nd and 3rd degree burns caused while drying his clothes in front of the living room fire. The verdict must be misadventure.'

It was interesting to note that no member of the Brewer family mentioned that David Brewer slept during the day because of his 'unlawful' night-time occupation and, appreciating the family's reluctance to disclose that David was working, the fact that they accepted the Coroner's verdict is not so surprising.

Lee said he sneaked into Brewer's kitchen through the kitchen door, saw the occupier go to the toilet, darted into the living room and sprinkled some paraffin about the floor near where some clothes were drying, lit the paraffin and ran out again. He said he was not far away when he heard the man shouting. He looked back and saw David Brewer on fire running out of the flat. The witness Hilda May Lister's evidence did not mention David running out of the flat at all.

Enquiries into the matter after Lee's first admissions soon revealed that he had not told us everything he knew about David Brewer. Mrs. Lister immediately revealed that Lee had been a friend of her son, Shaun, and that the boys had a common interest in pigeons. Shaun had a pigeon loft at the rear of his home at 25 Humber Buildings, which Lee frequently visited. Mrs. Lister went on to volunteer a good deal of information highly relevant to the fire and Lee. Two days before the fire which killed David, Lee had threatened to wring the necks of Shaun's pigeons. David Brewer, who was present, told Lee he would 'clout him if he tried'. Lee then swore at David Brewer and

Brewer slapped him across the ear. Shaun Lister confirmed this incident. Two weeks later, most of Lister's pigeons were found dead with their necks broken.

Mrs. Lister now claimed that her comment at the time about drying clothes was a guess as she could think of no other cause of the fire. She now recalled that as David Brewer was taken into the ambulance he repeatedly said, 'Who would do this to me?' We asked her why she had not revealed this at the time of the initial police enquiry and she said that she put David's words down to the rambling of a man in dreadful pain.

Despite being given continuing legal advice, Lee was to make a different claim to his involvement in David Brewer's death in the weeks to come. Significantly 50 Humber Buildings suffered no damage, and no person, other than David Brewer, was harmed.

Having examined the initial police enquiry papers relating to the fire at Ros Fenton's home in Troutbeck House, I believed that not enough had been done then to establish its cause. Now, it appeared, in spite of a Coroner's Inquest in David Brewer's case, a similar state of affairs existed here too. In fact my enquiry into David Brewer's death revealed a lamentable standard of professionalism on the part of the police at the time he was killed. How could a man be burned to death in his own home, with nothing but himself and his clothing destroyed, and nothing, absolutely nothing but guesswork as the official answer?

Reading through the Inquest documents, I was not unmindful of the possibility that David's death might have been caused by spontaneous combustion. I knew that, despite the high water content of a human body, experiments have shown that human fat is quite inflammable. The occasional finding of a dead body, ignited by a relatively small source of heat, such as a domestic hearth fire, can become almost completely burned within a short time whilst other things in the house such as furniture are not damaged.

Whether I was prepared to believe Lee's claims or not was of little consequence on this point once I had studied Consultant Pathologist Massie's post-mortem report. David Brewer was not the victim of spontaneous combustion. But it was worth the thought.

Chapter Fourteen

Elizabeth Rokahr was the 82-year-old widow of a chief engineer who had worked on trawlers. She lived at 7 Minnies Terrace, Rosamond Street, a small, two-storey, terraced building in a row of similar houses in a cul-de-sac in the heart of the fish dock area of the City. The ground floor consisted of a front door leading to a hallway, front living room, rear living room and kitchen. There was a toilet in the rear yard. The back door was fitted with a door which led into a narrow passage which in turn led out into Rosamond Street. The yard door was fitted with an old bolt at the top which was ineffective. There were two bedrooms on the first floor.

Mrs Rokahr had very poor eyesight and weak legs. She was forced to use a walking frame in order to move about, but despite her age and infirmities she was apparently mentally alert. She was a regular but not heavy smoker, and, although she lived alone, relatives and friends described her as a competent, careful woman who was well able to care for herself.

According to the papers I found in the Coroner's file, Mrs. Rokahr was often visited by neighbours and relatives. Significantly, I discovered, she was in the habit of leaving her front-door key on a piece of string inside the letter-box. The front door was nearly always locked with the key, and at night was supplemented by an interior bolt. She was also in the habit of leaving the rear door of her home open to allow her cat access. Because of her walking difficulty she slept in the ground-floor rear living room, where she had a bed with its head in an alcove beside the chimney breast and opposite the door. This rear room had an open fire which was used regularly. She had a fireguard and a small clothes line across the mantelpiece. Any drying clothes were always kept to one side of the fire.

Mr. Harry Pratt was a helpful, attentive man who had been Mrs. Rokahr's next-door neighbour for 30 years, and he frequently called to see if she required any help. During the early afternoon on Monday, 23 December 1974, Mr. Pratt made her a cup of tea, did some shopping for her and filled her coal bucket. When he left, Mrs. Rokahr was sitting in a chair, quite alert and fully dressed. The fireguard was in position. He checked the front door and satisfied himself that the front door was locked.

Shortly before 10 p.m. Mr. Pratt smelled smoke. Other neighbours could also smell smoke and realised that it was coming from Mrs. Rokahr's home. Harry Pratt and another neighbour kicked the front door in and ran down the hallway to the connecting door between the hall and the rear living room. This door was closed and, when they opened it, the two men were met by a severe fire and thick choking smoke, giving them no chance of getting into the room. With the help of other neighbours they threw buckets of water into the room but could not control the fire.

An alarm call to the Fire Brigade was logged at 10.09 p.m. that night. On arrival in Minnies Terrace, fire officers wearing breathing apparatus found that the fire was confined to the rear living room and when they got the fire under control they discovered Mrs. Rokahr's very badly burned body lying partially under the bed. They also found that the most severely burned part of the room was at the head of the bed and a pattern was confirmed by the almost total destruction of the old lady's upper half. Officers reached the conclusion, therefore, that the seat of the fire was in the living room, and near the head of the bed. All the furnishings in the room had been destroyed and the fire had burned through the floor and the ceiling. Forensic scientists were not called to the scene, but fire officers concluded that Mrs. Rokahr had either been smoking in bed or that clothes airing over the fireplace had become ignited.

At the Inquest on Elizabeth Rokahr held on 9 January 1975, presided over by Dr. Philip Science, Dr. Scott gave the cause of death as asphyxia due to the inhalation of smoke. Mrs Rokahr's daughter, Annie Elizabeth Wainman, gave evidence about her mother's state of health and, significantly, told the Coroner that, although her mother smoked, she was a careful smoker and always used a fireguard in front of the hearth. Owing to the intensity of the fire, no evidence was available to show if clothes had been airing near the hearth fire; it was also impossible to be sure if Mrs. Rokahr was smoking just before the fire.

The senior fire officer at the scene concluded that there were two possible causes: (1) smoking in bed, or (2) clothes airing over the fireplace becoming ignited from the coal fire.

The Coroner said, 'Thank you, officer. Which theory do you support?'

Fire officer: 'By the seat of the fire, I would go for the smoking in bed, because the seat of the fire was at the head of the bed and it burned through the floor boards.'

The Coroner remarked, 'That is all the evidence we have in this case,' and concluded that Elizabeth Rokahr died from asphyxia due to the inhalation of smoke caused when her living room caught fire. The verdict was misadventure.

At the time it was a fairly common practice to leave front door keys hanging on string which could be reached through the front-door letter-box. Significantly, Lee claimed he knew the key to the front door of Mrs. Rokahr's house was kept on the string and tried to unlock the door by using this key. Somehow, he failed to gain access this way so, he claimed, he went down the passage and into the rear yard, through the insecure door. He found the back door to the house open and crept inside. He saw a figure lying on the bed, but could not say if it was a man or a woman. He sprinkled paraffin on the floor, lit it and left the house the same way as he had entered, claiming he left the scene before the fire gained a hold.

It was not possible for Lee to point out this house because of demolition, but he did point out the area when he referred to this fire. He also accurately recounted the seat of the fire, inasmuch as the floor boards near the bed were burned through. The evidence of the neighbours confirmed a very fierce burning, which is consistent with the use of an accelerant.

I found it interesting that Mrs. Rokahr's cat, which normally had free access by the open rear door, was found dead in the back kitchen. In a slow burning fire, would it not have fled, or did the intruder close the door unintentionally preventing its escape?

When we saw Mrs. Rokahr's daughter she said initially she accepted the findings of the Inquest but afterwards, having thought about it, the findings became more and more difficult to accept. At the time of her mother's death all the family were so distressed that 'they accepted anything'.

We also saw Mrs. Rokahr's son, William, who was employed as a dock porter. No one from the police had been to see him when his mother died. He had seen his mother several hours before the fire in good spirits. He also stated his mother only used the clothes line over the hearth fire to air a towel, which was always put to one side and was quite safe there. Mrs Rokahr's son also told us, although his mother liked a cigarette, she was not a heavy smoker and he had never seen her smoking in bed. She was a very careful woman where fire was concerned, he added.

He was not asked to attend but he accepted the findings of the Inquest merely because he had no alternative. However, forever thinking about the fire, he told us the Coroner's findings became more and more unacceptable. But nothing he could say or do would bring his mother back, so he kept quiet.

Chapter Fifteen

The house, No. 9 Gorthorpe, is situated on Orchard Park Estate in North Hull, the same estate where the Housing Department re-housed Edith Hastie and her remaining family. Many of the houses were occupied by people displaced by the slum clearance programme and the estate is just a few miles from the fish dock area.

No. 9 Gorthorpe is a two-storey building of the terraced type but of the open plan design, and at the end of its row. The ground floor includes a living room, hall, toilet and front door, but these are enclosed and do not form part of the open design, taking up about half of the ground floor area. The other half of the ground floor is open plan and includes the rear door which opens into a dining area, the staircase to upper floors, a cupboard under the staircase and a kitchen. The cupboard under the stairs is of the large walk-in type. The first floor consists of three bedrooms and a bathroom.

In the summer of 1976, the house was occupied by James Vincent Edwards, his wife, Veronica Kathleen Jennifer, and their four children, Jennifer, aged 7 years, David, aged 5 years, James, aged 4 years, and Andrew aged 13 months. Also living at the house then was Mrs. Edwards' grandmother, Mrs. Dorothy Stevenson, who was 77-years-old, and Mrs. Edwards' sister, Carol Boothroyd. Jennifer is a spastic child, unable to speak or walk. James Edwards, Mrs. Stevenson and Carol Boothroyd all carried cigarette lighters. The house was centrally heated by electricity and the gas cooker was fitted with an automatic pilot light.

On the evening of Saturday, 3 June 1976, Mr. Edwards was absent from home playing cricket. About 7 p.m. Mrs. Edwards went out with her sister, Carol, and her son, James, leaving the grandmother, Jennifer, David, and Andrew, still in the house. Despite her age, Mrs. Stevenson was, apparently, lucid and capable of looking after the house and the children. After their mother left the house, the three children were playing in the enclosed living room at the rear of the house, and were supervised by Mrs. Stevenson. Gradually baby Andrew became tired, so his grandmother took him upstairs to bed and put him in his cot in the large rear bedroom. Mrs. Stevenson stayed with him for about ten minutes until he fell asleep. It was later estimated this time was about 8.15 p.m. When she went upstairs with the baby the other two children were still playing in the enclosed living room. Once she saw that baby Andrew was asleep, Mrs. Stevenson came downstairs and saw smoke coming from inside the cupboard underneath the stairs.

The events that followed deeply affected her and she later became resident in a rest home for the mentally ill. Opening the cupboard door under the stairs she found David with his hair on fire. She grabbed the little boy, took him outside and returned for Jennifer, who was still in the living room. The two children were taken into neighbours' houses and the alarm was raised. According to a neighbour, Mrs. Stevenson then stood outside, apparently waiting for the Fire Brigade, when the neighbour asked her if anyone else was in the house. Mrs. Stevenson seemed very vague and no doubt in shock. She did not answer for a minute or so and then said, 'Oh, yes, Good God, the little one is upstairs in bed.' She tried to get back into the house for the baby but the staircase was now a mass of flames. Several neighbours tried to rescue the baby, but failed. One of them claimed that Mrs. Stevenson had mentioned that David had been playing with matches. This assumption, if indeed it was an assumption, was passed on to the police and Fire Brigade officers.

Humberside Fire Brigade found a fierce fire burning on both storeys, and officers with breathing apparatus eventually found Andrew's body in his badly burned cot in the rear bedroom. The seat of the fire was established as the cupboard under the stairs.

Continuing my study of the known facts I could not help but notice that, starting with the fire at Edith Hastie's home, the fire at 9 Gorthorpe was the third fire disaster claimed by Lee where, sadly, a handicapped child resided.

No one called a forensic scientist to the scene even though one constable actually asked his control room for one to attend. Apart from the death of baby Andrew, David suffered an injury, but this was confined to very minor burns to his hair. He was interviewed by the police immediately after the fire in the presence of his great-grandmother. The boy was very badly shocked at the time and appears to have been condemned by the old lady from the outset when she shouted, 'The little bugger has been playing with matches.' In her written statement she said she was unable to understand where David could have got matches from, as she was the only one in the house with matches and 'mine are always in my pocket'. The boy's mother also stated that she did not have any matches in the house.

During further study I noted that Mrs. Stevenson told the police that, when she opened the cupboard door, 'smoke and flames belched out of the cupboard. I pulled David out of the cupboard and took him out of the front door.' But why was David's clothing not burned and why was he not severely burned or choked by the smoke? According to the Inquest file, no one appeared to have asked those questions at the time.

Hearing what Mrs. Stevenson had alleged, the police asked David if he had some matches. 'No,' he answered. 'Tell me what you were doing before the fire?' asked the officer. 'Nanna took my baby upstairs. I was playing hide and seek,' the little boy replied. 'Where were you hiding?' 'Under the stairs.' 'In the cupboard?' asked the officer. 'Yes.' 'How did you see?' 'I saw the fire,' came the reply. 'Where was the fire?' 'In the cupboard.' 'Were you striking matches?' 'Yes.' 'How many did you strike?' 'Two.' 'Can you count?' 'Yes.' 'Count for me,' said the officer. 'One, two,' was the reply. 'Where did you get your matches from?' 'In the cupboard.' 'The cupboard under the stairs?' 'Yes.' 'How many was there?' 'Two.' 'Tell me what happened when you struck the matches?' 'I struck one, then I struck two and the box was burning.' 'What box?' 'A cardboard box.' 'Yes.' 'What was in the box?' 'Papers.' 'Newspapers or comics?' 'Comics.' 'How did they catch fire?' 'With matches.' 'Where did you get the matches from?' 'Out the papers.' 'Were they hidden there?' 'Yes.' 'Did you hide them there?' 'Yes.' 'When did you hide them.' 'This morning.' 'How did you get them?' 'I climbed on the fridge and got them out of the cupboard.' 'What did you do with them then?' 'I put them in papers.' 'The papers in the box under the stairs?' 'Yes.' 'When you struck the matches what happened?' 'Struck one, struck two, then all started burning and it set fire to the comics.' 'Did the full box of matches start burning?'

'Yes.' 'Is that how the comics started burning?' 'Yes.' 'Did you try to put the fire out?' 'Yes.' 'Is that how you burnt your hair?' 'Yes.' 'Did you run out of the cupboard and see your Nanna?' 'Yes.' 'Was it burning hard then?' 'Yes.' The officer obviously asked his questions with the most honourable intentions, and, as might be expected, it was perhaps necessary to ask leading questions of the infant boy. Reading the statement of the interview, however, I was concerned that initially, the question of matches was raised by the officer. The number of matches used was given as two matches in the first instance and then the officer introduced the question, 'Did the full box of matches start burning?' without apparently establishing that a full box, let alone two matches, ever existed. There was no evidence in the file of papers to corroborate that there were matches in a cupboard, near the fridge or anywhere else.

Mr. and Mrs. Edwards, were adamant that Mrs. Edwards' grandmother always kept her matches in the overall pocket she always wore. Mr. Edwards went on to say, 'I can specifically say that my wife and I have only had matches in our house on one occasion in the ten years we have been married. That one occasion was in 1975 when the pilot light on the gas cooker was faulty. I repaired the pilot light myself and threw the matches down the toilet and flushed them away. The reason we never have matches in the house is that we never have cause to use them.'

Great-grandmother Mrs. Stevenson was not called to give evidence at the Inquest on 17 June 1976, but the statement she made shortly after the fire was read out by a police officer. Her statement ended with the words, 'I am still unable to understand where David got matches from, as I am the only one in the house with matches and mine are always in my pocket.' The police officer who interviewed David gave evidence of that interview, but the Coroner did not question the officer.

In his summing up the Coroner remarked: 'It appears that while the great-grandmother was upstairs with Andrew, David, aged 5 years, went into the cupboard under the stairs and started playing with matches he had secreted away. He started a fire in the cupboard, and it was this fire which eventually set fire to the house . . . Under these circumstances, I must record that Andrew Edwards died on 3 June 1976, at 9 Gorthorpe, Hull, from asphyxia due to the inhalation of smoke caused when the house in which he was sleeping caught fire. And the verdict is misadventure.'

The Coroner did not enquire about the availability of matches in the cupboard or anywhere else. No one asked what the circumstances were in the house that morning when David was alleged to have climbed on to the fridge and taken matches from the cupboard. And did the five-year-old boy really take and secrete them away for use later? Here he was quite unfairly damned for causing the fire.

Mr. Edwards told my officers that a few days after the Inquest he and his wife were still mystified as to where David had obtained the matches. Being very uneasy about it, he questioned his son a few days after the fire and David then denied playing with any matches. Both parents have since preferred to let the boy forget about the incident.

Lee, then 15, claimed he sneaked into an end house in Gorthorpe, near to a public house with a white horse sign (The Rampant Horse public house is about 200 yards away from 9 Gorthorpe). He claimed it was still light but getting near to dusk. He could not remember if he entered the house by the front or rear door because, due to the open-plan design, it is difficult to tell one from the other. Neither door was known to be locked. Lee recalled someone moving about upstairs. He sprinkled paraffin under the stairs and set fire to it. He left the house the same way as he had entered and stood a few doors away until the house was well alight. He maintained he saw no one and no one saw him.

No one knows how David Edwards came to be in, or more likely, near the cupboard, but, I reasoned, is it feasible that he was simply attracted to the burning cupboard having been drawn there in the first place by the smoke? No one appears to have explored this possibility at the time. Fire officers later told us that their examination at the time did not reveal the presence of an accelerant in the fire but that one could have been present initially.

I became more and more mindful that in all the cases I had so far studied the people in the houses were incapacitated when the fires started, due to sleep, age or infirmity. I now had four more of Lee's claims to fatal fires to examine. I was also considering asking the most experienced forensic scientist I could find to review all the documents I had, alongside Lee's claims, to see if his claims could be corroborated in a cumulative way.

Meanwhile I found it difficult to accept that in the time baby Andrew was being put to sleep, his home was deliberately set on fire and he was never to be seen alive again. It was also troublesome to believe that five-year-old David had secreted matches earlier in the day, only to set the house on fire with the same fatal result.

Was this another coincidence?

Chapter Sixteen

When Lee was living in 11 Princes Terrace, West Dock Avenue, in the 1970s he naturally spent some of his time with children of his own age. One such family, the Thacker's, lived at No. 9 Princes Terrace. They had a number of sons, including Peter, Robert and Michael Edward whom Lee associated with and they shared a common interest in pigeons.

Gradually, all the houses in Princes Terrace were vacated in readiness for slum clearance and the occupants spread to different parts of Hull. Lee's family moved a short distance away to Irton House flats in 1975, but Lee was still a frequent visitor to West Dock Avenue and so were a number of other youths. In 1976, 22-year-old Peter Thacker was living at 43 West Dock Avenue, situated three houses to the north of the, by now, unoccupied Princes Terrace. Thacker had a pigeon loft in a back yard near Lee's old address in Princes Terrace, which acted like a magnet to children, who brought pigeons and generally frequented the vicinity.

At that time he was living with Karen Lesley Fraser and her two children, Ann Marie, born in 1973, and Kim, born in 1974. There was also a child of the union between Peter and Karen, Katrina, who was just six months old. Peter ceased to co-habit with Karen at the end of 1976 but often visited the house in order to look after his pigeon loft and to see his child, Katrina.

Lee also frequently visited the pigeon loft and on occasions overstayed his welcome. Peter Thacker and Karen stated that Lee often visited the loft uninvited and on at least two occasions actually entered the house uninvited from the yard and through the rear door. Peter Thacker also said that Lee was cheeky to him and Karen and, around Christmas time 1976, Thacker claimed he had cause to strike Lee following an argument.

On Sunday, 2 January 1977, Karen was at home with her three children. Kim was asleep in her cot in the upstairs front bedroom. Katrina was asleep in a carry cot in the ground-floor living room. Karen and Ann Marie were in the room too. Peter Thacker called at the house about 7.10 p.m. and stayed for a few moments before leaving for a friend's house nearby. There was an open fire in the grate quite close to Katrina's carry cot, which was off the floor, on a cot stand in an alcove around the corner, at the side of the fireplace. Karen built up the fire at about 7 p.m., but, after doing so, put ashes from under the grate on top of the coal to keep it safe. There was no fireguard.

About five minutes after Peter Thacker left, Karen and Ann Marie visited the toilet at the rear of the small house. The front door was locked but the rear door was open. Karen remained in the toilet with Ann Marie for about five minutes and when she came out saw smoke coming through the back kitchen from the living room. She appears to have panicked, picked up Ann Marie and run to a neighbour's house, leaving baby Katrina in the living room and Kim still asleep in the cot upstairs. Several neighbours came to her assistance and tried to enter the house, but in the few seconds Karen had taken to go to her neighbour a fierce fire had developed in the living room and there was choking smoke throughout the house. One of the would-be rescuers was Peter Thacker, who showed considerable bravery and determination in his efforts to rescue the two children.

The Fire Brigade found a fierce fire on the ground floor. Officers with breathing apparatus were able to rescue Kim from the upstairs bedroom but were unable initially to enter the living room because of the fire. Kim was treated for smoke inhalation and made a complete recovery. When they brought the fire under control, they found Katrina's badly burned body lying in the remains of the carry cot in the living room alcove. The fire was so intense the room was completely destroyed and the wall plaster had broken off and fallen to the floor. The precise seat of the fire was never defined.

Two possibilities were open to the fire and police officers. Firstly, Karen explained that she had had trouble with a faulty electricity plug, though Yorkshire Electricity Board experts made an examination and found nothing wrong to support an electrical cause. The second and, on the face of it, the most likely cause was the open fire. Significance was properly given to the fact that there was no fire guard there.

Peter Thacker told the Coroner at the Inquest on 2 February 1977 that, when he left the house, the fire was banked up with ashes and there were no flames in the fire. When Karen ran from the house with Ann Marie, she went to her friend, Kathleen Page, who told the Coroner that she ran to Karen's house, saw the smoke, and noticed particularly that there were flames at the back of the couch which faced the fire place with the back away from the direction of any spark from the fireplace. The Coroner did not question this point.

A member of the Fire Brigade told the Coroner, 'In my opinion the probable cause of the fire was a spark or something similar from the unguarded fire in the living room. There is no reason to suspect that the cause could have been from the electricity or gas supplies because the electrical installation was in order and the gas supply to the house had been disconnected.' No evidence was given in respect of anyone smoking in the house and no one thought it necessary to seek expert advice from a member of the Forensic Science Service regarding the origins of the fire.

Coroner, Dr. Science summed up the evidence and gave a verdict of Misadventure.

Neighbours who gathered in the street at the time of the fire saw Lee among the onlookers but had no reason to pay him any particular attention. He claimed the fire as his doing in his third, fourth and fifth voluntary statements. After some deliberation, he recalled that he entered the house by the rear door, 'just as the woman was out'. He sprinkled the paraffin, he says, a fair bit, near the fire in the living room and on a couch and a chair. He dropped a match on it and 'ran out quick' because it immediately flared up. He recalled seeing the carry cot but denied seeing the baby. How was it he went into the house when – by chance – Karen was in the toilet? She had, she claimed, found him in her house uninvited on previous occasions. Lee's recollection of the seat of the fire and the obvious speed and ferocity, I felt, tended to support his claims.

But why didn't anyone consider the possible use of an accelerant in a ferocious and fatal fire which by all account took hold so quickly?

Chapter Seventeen

Wensley Lodge was situated in West Hill, Hessle, and within ear shot of the Humber Bridge. West Hill is a narrow tree-lined and secluded lane in a rather secluded part of Hessle. The Lodge faced south towards the River Humber which was about a quarter of a mile away. The building was formerly two large semi-detached houses of three storeys and a two- storey detached house all of Victorian design. They were converted into one building in the 1950s and became a residential home in 1958. It was owned by the Charterhouse Trust and leased to the County Council.

All the bedrooms were situated on the first and second floors. They were of various sizes and housed between one and four residents. There was a staff duty room on the first floor which contained a call board indicator connected to bell pushes in residents' bedrooms. There were staircases at each end of the main building and two further staircases which led from the dining area to the first-floor bedrooms. The entire building was heated by oil-fired central heating controlled from the boiler room on the ground floor.

The residents at the home were cared for by a Superintendent, his deputy, two assistants and seven care assistants, in addition to domestic staff. A County Council directive ensured that one of the four supervisory officers was resident at the home at all times. The general rule was that the supervisory officer was assisted by two care assistants until 10 p.m. and one care assistant during the night.

During the afternoon of Wednesday, 5 January 1977, the deputy superintendent was accompanied by only one care assistant due to sickness amongst staff. This assistant was working the 2-9 p.m. shift, and the night care assistant was not due on duty until 10.00 p.m. The deputy superintendent was aware that the night duty care assistant normally came on duty at 9.30 p.m. and consequently did not arrange for overtime to be worked for the 30-minute overlap.

During the afternoon of that Wednesday, a plumber, Mr. Steven George Hay, attended at the Lodge after being called to repair a leaking pipe in the ground-floor boiler room. This pipe ran along the northern wall of the building just above the windows in the boiler room. He was obliged to empty the hot water system for the whole building and replace a small section of faulty piping. Whilst removing the faulty pipe and fitting a new piece, Hay had to use a blow torch attached to a propane gas bottle in order to melt solder around the joints. This operation took place about seven inches from the ceiling of the boiler room.

Significantly, the boiler room ceiling was separated from the floor of bedroom 11 above by sheets of asbestos and cement bonded on to sheets of fibre board fixed to the underside of the joists. Hay estimated that he used the torch for about two minutes to dismantle the faulty section and for about one minute 45 seconds to fit the new piece of piping. He finished using the torch by about 2.30 p.m. and then refilled the hot water system, checked the new joint again, drank some tea and left the Lodge about 4 p.m.

The deputy superintendent was relieved at 6 o'clock by the superintendent. This was by prior agreement so that the deputy could attend a social function. From 6 p.m. until 9 p.m. therefore, Wensley Lodge, which that night held 50 male residents of varying degrees of infirmity and senility, was in the charge of only two carers. The sleeping arrangements were such that the least infirm of the residents slept on the top landing, and the remainder on the first and middle landings. Some of the residents began going to bed as early as 5 p.m. and the one care assistant on duty was obliged to physically assist many of the residents to bed. He was engaged with this work until about 8. 30 p.m.

Afterwards, the care assistant made his final check of all the rooms and found that all the men were in bed except four. Of these one was known to be out and three were watching television in the ground-floor sitting room. During his final bedroom check the sole occupant of bedroom 11, Herbert Hunter, was found wandering about in the corridor outside the room, but he was escorted to his room and went to bed. Nothing unusual was noticed, either in bedroom 11 – above the boiler room – or elsewhere. The care assistant reported to the superintendent on the ground floor and went home at 9 p.m. leaving the superintendent in charge.

Just after 9 p.m. the superintendent walked around the whole premises making a routine inspection. He noted that Mr. Hunter was in bed asleep. He had no reason to make a particular inspection of that room and certainly did not sense any undue heat or smoke there. The night care assistant arrived about 9.30 p.m. and the superintendent then retired to his sitting room at the eastern end of the first floor.

The night care assistant, who, it should be noted had no sense of smell, made his way up the stairs to the first floor shortly after he arrived on duty. Upon reaching the first-floor landing he saw smoke and immediately dashed along the corridor to the first-floor duty room, broke the glass on the fire alarm and pressed the button. Nothing happened. He picked up a fire extinguisher and ran down the corridor shouting for the superintendent to telephone the Fire Brigade. As he did so he was frantically opening bedroom doors in a desperate effort to locate the main source of the smoke, eventually arriving at number 11, non-smoker Herbert Hunter's bedroom.

When he opened the door he saw a fire on the bedroom floor near the window. The floor was covered almost entirely with linoleum and there were no power points in the room. The bedroom was full of smoke and he could not see Mr. Hunter. It was not possible to deduce the exact sequence of events immediately afterwards, but apparently the care assistant was joined by the superintendent, the two men roused Mr. Hunter and escorted him from the room. The assistant used a fire extinguisher and almost at the same time there was a surge of heat as, according to the superintendent, flames seemed to leap from one wall to the other. The fire extinguisher, although working efficiently, was quite ineffective against the fire. The superintendent hurriedly took Mr. Hunter from the room as the care assistant continued to use the fire extinguisher against the blaze. He was soon driven back by choking smoke and was unable to see properly as his spectacles became clouded by the heat and smoke. There was no time to check all the rooms to see if there was any sign of fire elsewhere in the Lodge.

There followed a horrifying tale of rescue, attempted rescue, understandable panic and considerable bravery as all the emergency services converged on the Lodge.

It soon became obvious that a major disaster was imminent. Fifty-six firemen and nine officers (including the Chief Fire Officer of the Humberside Fire Brigade) attended from the whole of North Humberside as emergency stand-by firemen moved into Humberside from West Yorkshire. Over 30 ambulances attended the scene and ambulance personnel assisted in rescue and resuscitation of the elderly residents.

The fire spread quickly from the first floor, engulfing the first and second floors of the eastern part of the building. It was totally destroyed and its ruins subsequently demolished. Ten residents were found dead at the scene. Seven of these were relatively unmarked but the other three were very badly burned and subsequent identification was made mainly by medical records. The last body recovered was found under a pile of debris in a first-floor bedroom about 10 a.m. the following morning. An eleventh resident died later in hospital. Thanks to the superintendent of the Lodge and his assistant that night, 74-year-old Herbert Hunter was one of the survivors. A total of 18 residents and six rescuers were treated at Hull Royal Infirmary for shock, slight burns, and other minor injuries.

An investigation into the cause of the fire was carried out by police, fire and forensic experts and 223 statements recorded. It was considered significant that the fire appeared to have started directly above the place where the plumber Steven Hay had been working. The remains of the floor of room 11 were closely examined and experts concluded that a spark from the blow torch had probably found its way through a crack in the ceiling of the boiler room and set fire to a fibre board. The fire had smouldered for over five hours before breaking through the floorboards in room 11 and a flashover occurred when the bedroom door was opened. The fire very quickly raced through service ducts to the second floor and so the fire spread. Neither Mr. Hunter nor any resident who was in possession of his faculties could give any useful information. Actually, Mr. Hunter was one of the few residents who it was thought was sufficiently lucid to commit his story to paper, but, other than saying that he burned the sole of his left foot, he could not give any useful information.

A full Inquest into the deaths of the eleven residents was held before a jury in Hull on 22 February 1977, presided over once more by Dr. Philip Science. Cause of death was given in nine cases as carbon monoxide poisoning; one death as burning, and the final one as hypostatic bronchial pneumonia, aggravated by inhalation of smoke.

Evidence was given to the Inquest on the theory of the plumber's blow torch. This theory, and it was but a theory, was strongly contested by plumber Steven Hay, who was represented by his solicitors, Messrs. Davies, Thornton & Locking, of Hull. Asked by the Coroner if anything had been found wrong with the plumbing, experts agreed that there was nothing wrong with the plumber's work. In fact one expert said, 'I found nothing wrong at all.'

Dr. Science summed up. 'Steven George Hay, a plumber, was called to mend a leak in a pipe in the boiler room of Wensley Lodge, The pipe was located eight inches below the ceiling of the boiler room, and the ceiling of the boiler room consisted of asbestos cemented on to fibre board. Above was the flooring of Room No. 11. Mr. Hay used a blow lamp, and our experts have told us that unfortunately the heat from this blow lamp penetrated a crack or joint in the asbestos and slowly ignited the joists and floor boards of the room above. (N. B. There was no evidence to say which crack or which joint, or whether there was a sufficiently large joint or crack). You have heard that the blow lamp was not faulty in any way, and Mr. Hay completed his job with exemplary efficiency. He was an innocent instigator of the subsequent events. You have heard that both our experts agree that this was the cause of the fire ... As I have already explained before starting these proceedings, you have to ask yourselves, "Was anybody behaving with criminal negligence? That is, was anybody behaving recklessly or dangerously, with wanton abandon, not caring whether there was an accident or not?" I feel sure that you will agree that nobody was behaving in this way, and, if you are so agreed, then I suggest to you that the only verdict possible in this court must be one of Misadventure.' The jury duly returned this verdict: Misadventure. It is apparent that Steven Hay was blamed as the innocent instigator of the fire but no one at the Inquest ever expressed any kind of view on the possibility of arson.

Reading the many statements presented to the jury I believe it fair to say that the verdict of misadventure was a reasonable one. But I wonder if the verdict would have been the same if the Coroner had not made it so obvious what the verdict ought to be. Plumber Steven Hay did not agree then, and never has agreed with it. Being a sensible, keenly observant young man, he saw no cracks in the ceiling or anywhere else near his work. No one was better placed than him in this respect. I found him to be a real 'honest to goodness, salt-of-the-earth character' who knew in his heart that he was not responsible for the deaths of the eleven Wensley Lodge residents. Just think what a difference it would have made to the whole enquiry if a broken window had been found at the time, or someone had been seen inside or perhaps scurrying away from Wensley Lodge about the time of the fire, especially if that someone was seen to be carrying a can of some sort. But then there are thousands of break-ins at premises all over the country, day and night, and only on very rare occasions are intruders actually seen entering or leaving premises. As for cases of arson, I do not recall, in 30 years of criminal investigation experience, ever knowing of an eye witness to an arsonist at work.

So the jury decided, following the Coroner's advice, that the blow torch was the cause. No one at the Inquest appears to have probed the possibility that, if the fire been smouldering for hours on end directly beneath the very old floor boards in Bedroom 11, that there would have been at least some smoke in the room, especially between 9.10 p.m. and 9.15 p.m. when the care superintendent stated he saw that Mr. Hunter was in the room, in bed apparently asleep, only about 15 minutes before the fire was seen blazing in the room. Nevertheless, Steven Hay was publicly blamed for the horrific fire that night. Blamed even though H. M. Coroner said that Steven had 'completed his job with exemplary efficiency'. How could his work be exemplary – serve as an example – and efficient – producing the desired result, if, as the Coroner suggested, he (innocently) caused the fire?

The Inquest was followed by a Committee of Enquiry into the fire, which was formally opened on 5 April 1977, at County Hall, Beverley. They too came down on the side of the experts and once again blamed Steven Hay's plumbing work. With no other evidence before the Committee, what else could they think? Steven Hay has never, ever accepted that the blow torch caused the fire. He claims that he was too far away from the ceiling for the theory to be acceptable. Both he and his solicitor, Mr. John Robinson, have always been strongly of the opinion that there must have been some other cause.

Lee was 16-years-old at the time and was apparently living with his mother and stepfather at Irton House, Hull, which is about three miles away from Wensley Lodge. Wensley Lodge went up in flames three days after the fire at 43 West Dock Avenue, and, significantly, Lee recalled the close proximity of these fires in his admissions.

He said that he took a bicycle from outside a house in Rugby Street during the evening of 5 January 1977. Rugby Street is situated between Irton House and Wensley Lodge. I was particularly interested in the bicycle aspect because I did not think he could ride a bicycle due to his handicap. However, I was soon shown to be wrong when several people who knew him told us they had seen him riding a bicycle 'as well as anyone else in the street'. He told me he had purchased paraffin from a hardware shop and carried it in a metal can. He cycled to Hessle with the can on the bicycle bars with the intention of setting fire to a big house. He claimed he came upon Wensley Lodge, not knowing it was an old people's home. He found it quiet and secluded, laid the bicycle down on grass nearby and walked to the building. Some of the windows were bay windows and some were flat. He kicked in a flat window and waited until he was sure he had not been heard. He climbed in and went up some stairs. He heard old men 'barking', which, he explained, is coughing. He described how he entered a room on the first floor in which he saw a man lying on a bed. He poured a lot of paraffin between the bed and the window and little bits here and there in the room, leaving a gap between the small amount and the large amount. He did this so that when he lit a small amount he would have time to leave the room before the fire trapped him. He claimed he then went downstairs and left by the same window as he came in, sprinkling paraffin about as he did so. He took the metal can away with him and left on the bicycle. He then threw the can into the Humber and cycled back towards home. As he passed Hessle Police Station, about a mile from the Lodge, he saw Police and Fire Brigade vehicles heading towards the fire. He returned the bicycle to the place from which he had taken it and went home.

Although the Wensley Lodge fire received a great deal of publicity, the exact seat of fire could not have been fixed by anyone without first-hand knowledge. The sudden burst of flames encountered by the care assistants is consistent with Lee's description of the method he claims he used to start the blaze. Although the Inquest jury and the Committee of Enquiry accepted the theory of the plumber's torch, they must surely have had some doubts about the length of time the fire is alleged to have been smouldering after the plumber had finished his work. A carer spent some time in room 11 about 8.45 p.m. and another carer visited the room about 9.10 p.m. If one accepts the theory of the plumber's torch, then a fire, which had been smouldering since 2.30 p.m. directly under the old floor boards and which reached such an intensity by 9.30 p.m. that it burned in the manner described, was undetectable either by heat or smoke only 20 minutes earlier. If Lee's claim is correct he entered the building between 9.10 p.m. and 9.30 p.m. whilst the only member of staff on duty was elsewhere in the building. In such a large building it is unlikely that the carer would have heard the window break and is equally unlikely that the three old men watching television would have been prompted into any action, even if they heard it. All the windows in the eastern section of the building, where Lee said he gained entry, were broken in the fire, so any attempt we now made to seek corroboration by this means was impossible. The Committee of Enquiry Report revealed that the contingency plans for a major fire at the Lodge left a great deal to be desired and, whilst this Committee went to great lengths to allay any suspicion that it sat to apportion blame, inevitably some witnesses received adverse publicity. The superintendent, although praised, and rightly so, for his part in the rescue, did not enforce the fire drill plans prior to the fire and there was no doubt in my mind that he saw my re-opening of the case with some trepidation. As part of the case was that an intruder had gained access to the Lodge whilst the superintendent was at his post, his apprehension was not without foundation. In fairness though, how was one man, at night, able to care for every eventuality at the home, let alone give thought to the possibility of an intruder getting in, hell bent on burning the place down?

But, of course, the Inquest jury and a finely educated group of men making up the Committee of Enquiry had decided the plumber was to blame. What a shame for the plumber. However, upon meeting him I found that although he was very annoyed about the Inquest and Committee of Enquiry findings, he bore no guilt and continued to carry on with his plumbing 'with exemplary efficiency'.

I learned from the statements I now had that Room 11 was situated directly above the boiler room. The room was 12' x 14' and there were two single beds, two lockers and two wardrobes in the room. On the floor there were no carpets or matting, only linoleum as the occupants were incontinent. The linoleum was old and well worn. It was frayed and curled up at the edges, and there were numerous gaps in it here and there where it was worn and had been torn by scuffling feet. Around the edges it was possible to see the floorboards. The boiler room ceiling directly below was covered with asbestos cement sheeting, 5 mm thick. The sheets were composed of an inert aggregate consisting of 12% to 15% of clean asbestos fibre, cemented together by an inorganic cement. Behind the asbestos sheeting was a half-inch layer of fibre board which was not apparent in any way from the inside of the boiler room. The asbestos sheeting had also been painted over. According to plumber Hay, he saw no gaps of note in the asbestos sheeting ceiling near to where he carried out his work, or for that matter anywhere else in the ceiling.

There is no doubt, anywhere, that the fire started at the floor above the boiler room ceiling. The night-time carer saw the first flames, 'on the floor near the window' in Room 11 and naturally believed that the floorboards were on fire. The care superintendent confirmed this. The particularly severe fire damage to the floor structure of Room 11 caused part of the floor to collapse into the boiler room below. The floor joists ran in an east-west direction parallel with the outside wall. The joist nearest to the wall was particularly deeply burned and the next two joists had partially burned away. The statements I read also showed that there was similar deep burning within the floor void and the underside of the floorboards.

With no evidence of any kind to point elsewhere it is understandable, due to the way the joists and floor boards had been burned, that the only available explanation for the fire was that there was an accidental ignition of the fibreboard backing of the asbestos cement sheeting through a joint or crack in the ceiling of the boiler room by the torch used by Steven Hay. The Wensley Lodge Inquest did not appear to consider any other possibilities and, of course, the Committee of Enquiry knew of the Coroner's findings before they began their enquiry. Nevertheless, Counsel for Steven Hay did seek to show the Committee that Hay was not 'the innocent instigator' of the fire. Mr. Hay's Counsel urged the Committee to consider other possibilities and the committee quite properly examined the question with considerable care. Although no one put the possibility of arson to them, the Committee, in their wisdom, did in fact consider arson but there was no evidence to support it. The possibility of a cigarette end rolling under the skirting of room 11 was also considered as there was evidence of gaps between the skirting and the floor boards. Whilst this was not impossible, there was nothing to support the theory. The occupant of the room, Mr. Hunter, was a non-smoker and, although the carer who saw Mr. Hunter to bed some time before 9 o'clock was a smoker, he said he was not smoking at the time, and there is nothing to suggest otherwise. One would never know if paraffin had rolled under the skirting board to the joists below. There was no gas in this part of the building and no evidence of mains electric wiring in the vicinity of the seat of the fire. Electricity Board engineers checked the electrical installations, but could find no fault had developed to suggest that the fire was of electrical origin. Accordingly the Committee found the alternatives unacceptable.

Unfortunately, the night care assistant lost his sense of smell during World War 2, so there was no chance of his smelling the paraffin which Lee claimed to have put in Room 11, and it was clearly burning by the time the care superintendent got there. Additionally, as the room was occupied by incontinent men, the smell of urine may well have been greater than the smell of paraffin.

Chapter Eighteen

No. 4 Belgrave Terrace, Rosamond Street, was situated in the fishing district of the City. The terrace was on the west side of the street, almost opposite to Minnies Terrace, where Elizabeth Rokahr died in a fire at her home in December 1974. No. 4 was a two-storey house, occupying the end position of a row of similarly built houses in a small cul-de-sac. It was demolished under a slum clearance programme in the late 1970s.

The ground floor of the house comprised a front door opening into a passageway, which gave access to stairs to the first floor, a large through lounge taking up the majority of the length of the house, and a small kitchen which housed the rear door leading to a yard. The lounge had once been two rooms, the dividing wall having been removed. The ceiling and the walls in the front part of this room were covered with polystyrene tiles, decorated with emulsion paint. Access from the passageway to the lounge was by means of a curtain drawn across a doorway. There was no door fitted to this aperture. Windows were fitted at both ends of the through lounge and the front door was glass panelled. The first floor consisted of three bedrooms, one of which, a small box room at the top of the stairs, was used only for storage. The other two bedrooms faced front and rear respectively. The front bedroom window was of a large sash cord type from which access could be gained to the roof of the front bay window.

The house was purchased in August 1974, by Mrs. Gwendoline Gold, the mother of nine children, only two of whom were resident at 4 Belgrave Terrace, in April 1977, Deborah Pauline, then aged 13 years, who was mentally subnormal and had difficulty walking, and Lana, then aged 9 years.

On Tuesday, 26 April 1977, the Gold family arranged for a friend, Peter Jordan, and his two sons, Graham aged 9 and Mark Andrew aged 7 years, to stay with them that night at 4 Belgrave Terrace, before moving to Chatham, Kent, the following day. The sleeping arrangements were that Mrs. Gold and her husband would use the front bedroom overlooking the terrace, all four children would use the rear bedroom overlooking the yard and Mr. Jordan would sleep on a studio couch in the rear part of the through lounge.

The children went to bed about 10.00 p.m. The Gold's and Peter Jordan had supper in the rear part of the lounge whilst watching television. Mrs. Gold went to bed about 11.00 p.m. leaving Jordan and Gold talking. Gold was sitting on a two-seat settee and Jordan was sitting on a studio couch. About ten minutes later Gold prepared to go to bed. Before doing so he showed Jordan how to switch off the television set, put on an electric fire on the opposite wall to the studio couch, and turned off some electrical pumps to two fish tanks. One of these fish tanks was situated in the front part of the lounge and one on the wall opposite the studio couch, equidistant from the front and rear of the house. Gold turned the pumps off as he thought the noise from the pumps would disturb Jordan's sleep. The switching off of the pumps also had the effect of turning off the fish tank lights. He did not check the security of the house before going to bed, but did say that very little effort was required to effect an entry by anyone wishing to do so.

Both men had been smoking in the rear part of the lounge and used an ash tray on a coffee table. Gold recalled taking his last cigarette upstairs with him and putting it out upstairs. Jordan put out his cigarette in the ash tray, switched off the television and prepared for sleep on the studio couch. He lay on the couch on his side facing the wall. It is worthy of mention here that neither man, nor Mrs. Gold, had been drinking alcohol that evening. Some time after 3.00 a.m. the following morning, Jordan, who was still facing the wall, told of being awakened by what he thought was a bang. 'I laid awake but with my eyes closed, 'he said, 'sort of half asleep wondering if I had imagined it.' He remained on the couch, 'then I heard a noise as though somebody was moving about. It seemed to come from the stairway and I thought perhaps it was Albert or Gwen going out the back way to the toilet.' Jordan was in a state of undress and did not turn over to see who it was as, he claimed, he did not want to embarrass anyone visiting the toilet, which was situated in the rear yard. Some time, perhaps only seconds, later he heard a further more distinct bang and saw a glare on the wall he was still facing. At the same time he felt an intense heat on his back, turned over and saw a wall of flames shooting across the room coming from somewhere between a fish tank and the settee. The flames quickly spread and enveloped an easy chair and caused it to explode in flames.

At this point Jordan jumped up, wrapped himself in a blanket and ran upstairs to warn the rest of the household. He noticed, as he ran through the passageway curtains in the room, that the flames suddenly became brighter. He awakened the rest of the occupants in the bedrooms, wrapped the blanket about his head to protect himself from the heat and dashed back down the stairs. He could not open the front door, either because it was locked or it was sticking, which apparently it was prone to do. In fear for his life he kicked out the glass panel out of the door and fell through the hole. He picked himself up, ran along the street screaming that the house was on fire and ran along to a nearby telephone box to phone the Fire Brigade ,which attended within minutes.

Meantime Albert Gold shouted, 'Get up, kids, there's a fire! Get up! Come on!' They had been sound asleep and Albert had to shake each of them to wake them up. As the four of them awakened they sat up and began choking from the thick black smoke now swirling about the room. He then carefully ushered Mark, Graham, Deborah and Lana out of their bedroom. He was unable to take them down the stairs because the flames were now leaping up the stairway. Intent on protecting them at all costs, he ushered the four of them into the front bedroom towards the window. The heat was now intense and the smoke thick and black, making it impossible for them to see each other. Determined to ensure everyone's escape, Albert and Gwendoline struggled to push open the window and then managed to get Graham and Lana out to the roof of the bay of the lounge. Mrs. Gold dropped her daughter, Lana, and Graham Jordan to the ground below, but then lost sight of Deborah and Mark in the thick smoke and darkness of the bedroom. Meanwhile the draught through the broken glass in the front door downstairs and a then unnoticed broken window and the now open bedroom window, was feeding the fire, which in turn was rapidly engulfing all in its path. Mrs. Gold sensibly remained on the bay window ledge ready to help the two missing children to escape, and kept shouting for Deborah as Albert fought his way back through the dense smoke and heat to look for Deborah and Mark.

It appears that, after being ushered to the window by Albert, brave seven-year-old Mark Andrew Jordan quietly turned away from the window as Mrs. Gold was helping his brother Graham and her daughter Lana off the bay window roof. Known to be a thoughtful little boy and knowing that Deborah had not got out and was not beside him at the window, Mark went back into the smoke to help Deborah to the window. Shortly afterwards, having suffered the heat and smoke belching through the window, Mrs. Gold lost consciousness as she fell to the concrete yard below the bay window roof.

Firemen found Albert Gold semi-conscious, badly burned and crying out in pain lying on the bay window roof. He had endured considerable burning in his effort to save Deborah and Mark but just could not see them. He was very seriously burned from the neck down, and was hospitalised for several months, including a period in the Burns Unit of Pinderfields Hospital, Wakefield. He remained very badly scarred despite numerous skin grafts. Gwendoline Gold remained in hospital for three weeks with head, shoulder, ankle and wrist injuries resulting from her fall from the window. She also suffered from smoke inhalation. Lana Gold was detained for five weeks with burns to her arm and she too received skin grafts. Peter Jordan suffered minor cuts and burns and Graham Jordan suffered from the inhalation of smoke. He also damaged an ankle as he dropped from the window. Firemen wearing breathing apparatus found Mark's body lying on the floor inside the front bedroom just a few feet from the safety of the bay window. They also found Deborah's body lying face down on a bed in the same room. Later the neighbours were all to speak of their rescue attempts and confirm Jordan's testimony of the initial location and intensity of the fire. To prove most important later was Beryl Marion Moore's testimony as, being one of the first to arrive, she noticed that the side-angled window of the bay nearest to the door was broken. In fact the significance of that broken window was not to be appreciated by anyone until two years later when Lee spoke of breaking it. Dr. Philip Science held an inquest into the deaths of Deborah and Mark on 7 July 1977.

Enquiries centred on the through lounge, with particular attention to the central area. Police, firemen and a forensic scientist viewing the scene concluded that the most likely cause appeared to be the careless disregarding of smoking materials igniting the furniture. Jordan very strongly denied this and claimed he went to sleep almost immediately after going to bed. He also reasoned that a cigarette could not possibly cause a fire in the room and burn for four hours or so without his knowing about it.

Witnesses informed the Coroner that the fire had started in the through lounge, involving mainly the upholstery of the easy chair, consisting of polyurethane foam, well-known for its ease of ignition, which had been deeply burnt. The fire had destroyed the settee, and the bottom of the studio couch nearest the passage door had been partly burnt. The remains of a fish tank on a shelf next to the easy chair was apparent. The polystyrene tiles on the ceiling were noted for their ability for very rapid fire spread. The area beneath the fish tanks and beside an electricity plug was quite clean, therefore discounting the possibility of faulty electrics.

The Coroner remarked, 'It would appear that the cause of the fire was a lighted cigarette dropped on the settee.' He went on to say, 'I feel I must publicly praise Mark Andrew Jordan. This brave, kind, and thoughtful little boy turned back into the smoke-filled bedroom to go and assist Deborah, a mentally defective girl. In trying to do so, he lost his own life. I do feel that this gallant action should be posthumously recognised.'

He recorded verdicts of death by misadventure. Albert Gold concluded that the cigarette must have been left by Peter Jordan, and, pre-occupied in hospital suffering from his awful burns, accepted the verdict. Non-smoker Gwendoline Gold was in no position to doubt it.

Peter Jordan, on the other hand, says he knew he had not left a cigarette burning and doubted that Albert Gold had. He put it down to an electrical fault and did not attach any significance to the noises and the feeling of the presence of someone in the room before becoming aware of the fire. He was not happy with the verdict but could not find any answer to challenge it. The Coroner, he felt, did not attach any importance to the bang and the noises: 'I put it down to them thinking it was just the fire starting, but I had it in my mind that it had happened a good few seconds before I saw the glare of the flames. I thought they would think I was imagining things and doubt what I had to say if I mentioned about sensing a presence in the room and blame me all the more.'

The Coroner's verdict distressed Peter Jordan a great deal as it more or less suggested that he had been careless in leaving a cigarette burning when he knew that he hadn't: 'It caused me great distress that my son Mark died in the fire. The only consolation was that the Coroner agreed that he had died a hero trying to save Deborah.'

Lee, now aged 16 was resident at this time at a Local Authority approved house 2, Melwood Grove, Beverley Road, Hull, which is about three miles from Rosamond Street. It was managed by Mrs. Doris Fox, who claimed that her charges had to be in by 11 p.m. but added that no supervision was carried out and they were able to come and go as they pleased.

Lee claimed that he entered the Gold's house during the night by breaking a pane of glass in a window near to a door, removing the glass with his hand and climbing through. He had taken paraffin with him and explained that, when he entered the house, he found a through lounge. He recalled a fish tank in the room and that the ceiling was decorated with polystyrene tiles. He mentioned there was someone asleep downstairs on a couch. He claimed he sprinkled paraffin about the floor and near to the doorway connecting the lounge and the passage, which consisted of a curtain. He lit the paraffin and left the house the same way as he got in.

Once again, without any prompting, and before I had any worthwhile knowledge of the fire, Lee accurately recalled the details. He denied ever being in the house prior to that night and did not know the occupants. He described the general layout of the house, some of the interior decor and the seat of the fire. Beryl Marion Moore confirmed that the angled window near to the door was broken. Some time later I was shown a general photograph of the front of the house taken by the police at the time of the fire. In an endeavour to find corroboration of the broken window the photograph was enlarged, and there, sure enough, I was able to see for myself that the window was broken.

Another female neighbour recalled seeing a youth hanging about the vicinity of Belgrave Terrace during the daytime, about 'the time of the fire'. She described him as young looking with dirty fair hair, of very thin build and small frame with a thin gaunt face. He looked miserable. The description fitted Lee but it was not good enough for definite identification purposes.

How could Lee break the window and climb in with a man sleeping there in the room without disturbing him sufficiently to prompt him to investigate? Jordan greeted Lee's revelation with considerable interest and accepted that it was possible, especially when it was appreciated that there was no other explanation for the broken window.

Chapter Nineteen

In January 1978, Anthony Laurence Dickson, his wife, Christine Viola, and their four young children, Mark Christopher, four-years, Steven Paul, three-years, Michael Ian, 20-months and Bryan, two-months, lived in rather cramped conditions in the terraced house, No. 2 Brentwood Villas, Reynoldson Street, Hull. Reynoldson Street is situated on the west side of Newland Avenue, a major shopping thoroughfare to the north of the City, in the University district. The houses are slightly more modern than those in the fishing quarter of the City, but similar in their very basic design.

Number 2 Brentwood Villas is of two storeys and normal brick construction. It is the second house on the right and, like other houses in the terrace, it is small and was built with a front bay window. The interior of the house is of two-up, two-down design. The ground floor consisted of a front door, painted yellow, opening directly into the living room. A horizontal letter-box was fitted in the centre of the door. There was a connecting door from the living room to the kitchen, from which stairs led to the first floor and a further kitchen door into the rear yard. The first floor consisted of front and rear bedrooms.

On the morning of Friday, 6 January 1978, Christine Dickson woke her husband with a cup of tea about 9.50 a.m. He remained in bed, having taken Valium tablets about 4 a.m. for a nervous disorder. At the time he was off work as a rent collector for Hull City Council as he was feeling unwell. Having given her husband his tea, Mrs. Dickson went back downstairs to attend to her four small children.

About 11.20 a.m. that morning, Christine visited her next-door neighbour and close friend, Mrs. Kathleen Hartley. The two women stood talking in Mrs. Hartley's house for 'just a short time'. Exactly how long Christine Dickson stayed there is of vital importance, but Mrs. Hartley could only use the expression, 'a couple of minutes'. But how often are any friends and neighbours precise in the amount of time they chatter to one another? Nevertheless, however long it was, Christine's four little boys were left alone in the front room of their home and the front door was closed. The boys were confined to this room by reason of the fact that they could not open the connecting door to the kitchen, which was closed to them.

When Christine left her neighbour's house to return to her own home, Mrs. Hartley watched her go towards her front door. Just then Kathleen Hartley heard Christine shout, 'The little beggars have taken my net curtains down. Come and have a look, Kath.' Kathleen Hartley went outside and suddenly heard Christine yell out a frightening scream. At that point she saw that the windows in the Dickson's house were blackened on the inside and there was no sign of the usual net curtains. Christine promptly opened the front door and dashed into the house and out of Kathleen's sight. As she went in, thick black smoke belched out through the doorway. In the midst of it Christine ran out clutching her baby, Bryan, who was covered in black sooty smoke. Without saying a word, Christine hastily put the baby in Kathleen's living room and immediately ran back into her burning home. In an obvious state of terror and probably dumb with fear, her sole concern was getting her three remaining children out to safety. For a moment she frantically shouted for her husband, who was still in bed upstairs, and then ran back into the smoke-filled room.

Just then, and naturally in a state of shock, Kathleen saw, under the rising smoke, what she describes as a 'ring of dancing flames not rising to any great height, about three feet in diameter, similar to what one would get if inflammable fluid was spilt on to the floor and ignited', on the multi-coloured, foam-backed nylon carpet about three or four feet inside the doorway.

Kathleen did not see any of the children there but noticed that the flames were actually burning in the area between the front door and the arm of a settee which stood along the right-hand side wall of the house. A moment later she saw a vast sheet of flame envelope Christine, who gave one final terrified scream before collapsing into the flames. The glass in the bay window shattered, forcing Kathleen back from the door. The whole of the room and door was now a mass of flames.

Kathleen fled into her own house, hurriedly grabbed hold of baby Bryan and, with him tucked under her arm, shepherded her own two infant children out of her house and away from the swirling smoke and flames now threatening her own home. She took her children to the nearby corner shop, and returned to the terrace, still carrying baby Bryan under her arm. She was now joined by neighbour Leonard Milner, who made several brave efforts to gain access to the house by both the front and rear doors, but the now raging fire made access impossible. Despite suffering quite serious burns and with little regard for his own safety, he quickly took two fire extinguishers and a garden hose from his workshop in Reynoldson Street and ran back in a desperate attempt to control the fire. But the blaze was beyond his control. Meantime a neighbour took one look at baby Bryan in Kathleen's arms and said that he looked ill and needed hospital treatment. Another neighbour arrived in his car at the top of the terrace and immediately drove Kathleen and baby Bryan to Kingston General Hospital about a mile away. As they hurried along Kathleen saw that the baby did not appear to be breathing so she opened the car window, gave him the kiss of life and gently slapped his face to bring him around. The little boy began to cough and splutter. The smoke in his tiny body was about to take his life but Kathleen's quick thinking saved him.

Anthony Dickson was not certain whether he woke up naturally or was awakened by his wife's screams. But upon hearing Christine's shouting he realised something was wrong and ran down the stairs to the kitchen. As he did so he noticed some 'wisps of black smoke in the atmosphere'. He opened the kitchen door at the bottom of the stairs into the living room and found the whole of the living room was a blazing inferno. He could see nothing but a mass of flames and smoke. The heat was so intense he was forced back and out into the back yard. Still dressed in pyjamas, he ran round the terrace to the front of the building but could do nothing to save his family.

A neighbour telephoned an alarm call for the Fire Brigade at 11.55 a.m. but unfortunately it was the time of the national firemen's strike so the fire was attended by 'Green Goddesses'. These service personnel were helped at the scene by a number of senior fire brigade officers and by some conscientious firemen who left a picket line in Hull City centre. Fire officers found an extremely intense fire in the living room and the kitchen and were repeatedly driven back by the heat. The whole of the ground floor was now burning, with flames reaching out through the bay window and the front door. The blaze totally consumed most of the furniture, and only the remains of an armchair at the right-hand side of the fire place and a table were recognisable. Even the plaster had been ravaged from the walls. The bodies of Christine and her three sons were eventually found on the living room floor amongst the burnt-out furnishings and plaster from the walls and ceiling. Mother and children were burned beyond recognition. It must be said that, despite the firemen's strike, nothing more could have been done to prevent the deaths. As Christine went in for her children the open door fed the fire with oxygen, which quickly resulted in the massive spread of flames.

The only known factors that were considered at that time are those which I itemise as follows: The fire had started in the front room. The room housed an open grate, and, although no one alive could testify that this held a fire that morning, as there was no other form of heating, it was reasonable to assume that a January morning would merit some form of heating. Fairly conclusive evidence was given concerning the Dickson's use of a well-made fireguard and it was thought that, allowing for the rapidity and intensity of the fire, the grate was unlikely to have been the sole cause. A gas meter was situated in the living room, which had been issuing flames when the fire officers arrived. A gas cooker was installed in the kitchen. A subsequent examination by a gas expert rejected gas as a cause and found that the gas pipe had been ruptured by the fire. Faulty electricity was also ruled out. This simply left the activities of the small children to be investigated.

Christine and Anthony Dickson smoked cigarettes and both used lighters. At the time of the fire Christine was believed to be carrying her lighter, as usual, in her apron pocket. Anthony had his upstairs. He had bought a small can of lighter fuel the day before the fire, but he is convinced that this was put away in the kitchen, out of the children's reach. He and his wife were known to be meticulous about the precautions they took to minimise the chance of the children having access to inflammable materials so it was assumed Christine did not leave matches, a lighted cigarette or a cigarette lighter in the room. Indeed, the day before the fire, she bought a box of matches which she sometimes used to light the gas cooker, and, as if to prove her carefulness, actually left the box full with her friend Kathleen, so that there was no chance of her children getting hold of them. Anthony felt it was unlikely, if not impossible, that, firstly, the children were responsible, and, secondly, that they had access to the lighter fuel. They had clearly not been in the kitchen when Christine was next door. The kitchen door was closed when Anthony got up.

Higher Scientific Officer Malcolm Watson conducted various tests and eventually, with no eye witness to say just how it started, concluded that the probable cause of the fire had been the actions of the children, possibly igniting the lighter fuel. He could only attribute the rapid spread of the fire to the possible involvement of the lighter fuel and the inflammability of the modern furniture in the room. An examination of the fireplace revealed a considerable quantity of coal ash in the open fire grate and the twisted remains of a fireguard. The position of the fireguard suggested that it had been secured around the hearth. Significantly, scientific tests showed that a lighted match dropped on the carpet could not itself ignite the surface. Kathleen Hartley saw the flames coming from 'a ring of flame' on the carpet, just before the whole room went up in flames.

At the Inquest held on 8 February, the Coroner remarked: 'Listening to the evidence it would appear to me that everybody concerned in this tragedy is deserving of praise; from the neighbours, particularly Kathleen Hartley, to the police, the Fire Brigade, and the ambulance men. I would like to mention two people in particular. I cannot speak too highly of Mrs. Christine Dickson. Words are inappropriate. Having rescued her baby she returned to her home and entered this blazing inferno. Her self-sacrifice was that of a mother for her children. There can be no greater love and devotion than this. I must also praise Mr. Leonard Milner for his valiant attempts, at great personal risk, to rescue the occupants of the burning house. His bravery is worthy of the highest commendation . . . The verdict in all four cases must be one of misadventure.'

The Coroner was careful not to actually blame the children for causing the tragedy. There is no doubt he knew that, if he blamed the little boys, his findings rested on non-existent evidence that the children had been playing with lighter fuel which their father, at least, believed was well out of their reach. Like everyone else, Dr. Philip Science could only imagine what had happened and he knew that imagination is never acceptable as evidence.

I now wanted to know more about the front door, particularly the letter-box. I learned that the door opened inwards and to the left. It was old but sound and made of wood, and there was a glass panel in the top half. A curtain was fitted at the top half of the door and hung the length of the glass, with the bottom of the curtain just above the letter-box. The letter-box was fitted in a horizontal position with a loose flap. A postman delivered a sickness benefit cheque through the letter-box and it had dropped on to the living room carpet that morning. Christine took it upstairs to her husband some time before she called upon her friend Kathleen that morning.

Lee was 17-years-old when this fire occurred and was resident at 2, Melwood Grove, about half a mile away. He claimed he frequently walked about the area day-dreaming, and that on 6 January 1978, he was walking about with some paraffin in a plastic washing-up liquid bottle hidden under his coat. He felt the need to cause a fire that day because he had a tingling in his fingers and a 'fire in his head'. He walked under a bridge and turned left into Reynoldson Street past a school and down a terrace on the right.

Lee would not normally be familiar with this area, and Reynoldson Street does not form a through route to anywhere. He claimed he went to the second house on the right, took the plastic bottle from underneath his coat, and squirted it through the letter-box to the right and left and then allowed for a few drips to fall immediately beyond the letter-box. He then lit some paper, pushed it through the letter-box and left quickly. 'You don't hang around after 'cause that's how you get caught,' he remarked.

'Why that particular house?' I asked.

'Don't ask me why I picked on that one 'cause I don't know. See, I remember it was a letter-box job. I put paraffin through letter-box and up it would go.'

'Why in heaven's name didn't someone see Lee in the terrace?' I asked myself. But then, realising that no one saw Kathleen Hartley and Christine when the fire was belching out smoke that morning it was more acceptable that people in the terrace were either away at work, busy with their household chores, or in bed like Christine's husband, Anthony.

Sadly, and if true, Lee appeared to be blessed with incredible luck. I put it to him that, to commit this offence in the middle of the morning, when anyone could have been behind the door, the risk of detection was enormous. He claimed that no one ever took any notice of him, he did not see anyone in the terrace and he was away very quickly, taking his plastic bottle with him. I appreciated, of course, that the daytime burglar in similar surroundings is rarely, if ever, seen by anyone.

Chapter Twenty

I had now completed my study of all the Inquest files relative to Lee's claims. I noted that the quiet, dignified and highly respected Coroner, Dr. Philip Science, had presided over all of them. A few days after completing the study I saw him by chance in Queens Gardens. We spoke about his findings and Lee's claims. 'I, as a coroner, can only proceed on the evidence I am given, and misadventure verdicts were all that was open to me,' he said. 'But don't worry about the findings of the Inquests. Your task is much more important than mine was. I didn't have the benefit of Lee's claims. You do. If Lee is right and he is speaking the truth, then so be it.'

I recall leaving my office late one night not long after. The word 'misadventure' kept coming to mind. Misadventure indeed. I had always looked upon the word as meaning mischance, ill-luck or an unlucky accident. Philip Science had recorded death by misadventure verdicts on no less than 23 poor souls in the Hull area during nine Inquests spanning the best part of the 1970s. Such verdicts are perhaps all too common in Coroners' courts but did these people really die by mischance, ill luck, or in unlucky accidents? Surely not.

Casting my mind back to those inquests I could not help but find the supposed causes of all the fires remarkable. I further considered them in chronological order: (1) The fire at 70 Askew Avenue, was supposedly caused by a possible buildup of gas from a faulty gas pipe. There was no evidence of a faulty pipe and the appliances had only just been examined and found to be in good order. (2) The fire at 33 Glasgow Street, was supposedly caused by a candle or cigarette left burning. There was no evidence that Bernard Smythe was smoking that night. The candles he had been using had burnt down, or indeed out, so his neighbour gave him a torch. (3) David Brewer was seen in the doorway of his home at 50 Humber Buildings, actually in flames from his head to his toes. The supposed cause was clothes drying near to the living room fire. There was no evidence of any clothes drying there. (4) Eighty-two-year-old Elizabeth Rokahr died in the fire at her home at 7 Minnies Terrace. Smoking in bed was given as a possible cause. There was no evidence she was smoking in bed. (5) Little Andrew Edwards lost his life in the fire at his home, 9 Gorthorpe, after he had been put in his cot by his great-grandmother. The cause of the fire was given as children playing with matches. There was no evidence that any matches were available for the children to play with. (6) Six-month-old Katrina Thacker died in her carry cot whilst sleeping in the family living room at 43 West Dock Avenue. The supposed cause was a spark from an unguarded fire. The speed and ferocity of the fire was such that a spark or smouldering ember in the middle of the living room would have been apparent to Katrina's mother long before the fire took hold. (7) The fire at Wensley Lodge killed 11 elderly gentlemen and the plumber working there several hours beforehand was blamed. The Coroner praised the plumber's work and at the same time accepted he was responsible for the fire. Plumber Hay has always known that he was not careless in his work and that there were no sparks from his burner to cause the fire. He will always claim he was not responsible for it. However, with nothing further to consider at the time, the Inquest had no alternative but reach the conclusion it did. But in view of all the circumstances surely the Coroner had a duty to at least invite the jury to consider the possibility of arson? (8) The house, 4 Belgrave Terrace, went up in flames during the early hours of the morning and killed seven-year-old Andrew Jordan and thirteen-year-old Deborah Pauline Gold. The supposed cause was the careless disregarding of smoking materials. There was no evidence to support this conjecture. (9) Christine Viola Dickson and her three sons died in the fire at their home. The supposed cause was that the (dead) children had been playing with cigarette lighter fuel. There was no evidence that they ever had possession of the fuel.

Every one of us on the enquiry found it extraordinary that Lee was claiming the fires as his doing. To put it mildly, his claims required meticulous and careful investigation. Naturally everyone working on the enquiry had every sympathy for the families and friends of the victims, and, whilst we did not wish to bring back the horror of it all to them, it had been necessary for us to question them. Our one aim and consideration was to carefully seek out the veracity of Lee's claims and seek to answer the many questions left high and dry at the Inquests.

A month had gone by without my visiting Lee and I now gathered that several prisoners from Hull had apparently threatened they would 'get Lee and give him a good going over'. I knew that the prison authorities were aware of the threats but nevertheless I believed that an occasional visit from myself would perhaps help to avoid the chance of some harm coming to him. At least now and again I would see for myself that he was not harmed. I told Mr. Pearce of my concern about this almost from the beginning. On Thursday afternoon, 4 September 1980, with Detective Sergeant Martin I saw Lee once more and asked him if he had had any visitors since I last saw him.

'No, but that doctor (Prison Doctor Sasiene) keeps coming to see me and a priest speaks to me when he's got time. A psychiatrist called Dr. Milne from Bradford has been to see me as well.'

As we left him that afternoon I thought about his unhappy life. It appeared no one really concerned themselves with him at any time: brought up in council children's homes, with little schooling, part-time work in a cattle market penning up pigs, scant comfort from his forays into homosexualism and little else. Is this, as he claims, the cause of hellish fire-raising on the people of Hull?

On 25 September 1980, I saw Lee at Leeds prison once more. He said, 'I want to say now, after thinking about all that I've done, that I am truly sorry and want you to take a statement from me saying that.'

I took a statement under caution from him. He said, 'I just want to say now that after looking at the photographs that my solicitor has shown me and reading the dep's, statements or whatever you call them, and now that I've had a lot of time to think about all the people, all the fires, all the families I've split up and all the sorrow and grief I've caused that I am truly sorry.' He continued, 'I want to give the reason that I am pleading guilty is that what I've admitted to you is true and no way do I want to bring relatives into the court to re-live the horror and sorrow of the fires that I've caused. I know the solicitors might want me to plead not guilty, or guilty to manslaughter, but I want to go and plead guilty to arson and murder and that. It's me who is going to do the time. I'm the one who knows, so I'm saying I'm truly sorry and I'm going to do my best to save any relatives more trouble.'

Some time later I asked Dr. Sasiene what she thought about his mental state. 'He certainly knows what he's doing,' she said. 'And he is certainly street-wise. I gather he grew up in Hull in a variety of children's homes from being a year or two old and he's also had periods of fostering. He's told me he's had so many different places to live because, he says, he gets out of hand. He lies within the border-line range of intelligence. He is poorly educated, casual, immature and has an indifferent attitude. He can read and write, although his spelling is poor. Despite his handicaps, he does know right from wrong and is fit to plead whatever he wants to. I shall provide a full report to the court in due course.'

After further enquiries and consultations with members of the Director of Public Prosecution's office, the Director of Public Prosecutions drew up criminal charges and I was asked to prefer these on 15 October 1980, which was the day before Lee was to appear before Hull Magistrates Court for committal proceedings.

So on the morning of that day in company with Detective Constable Paul Bacon I visited Lee in Leeds Prison once again. Upon cautioning him I said, 'Enquiries are now complete regarding the fires and deaths we have spoken about during the past few months. Therefore I am now going to formally charge you, Bruce, with the following offences. Listen to what I say and make any comment you wish:

'That you, on 24 June 1973, in the City of Kingston upon Hull, murdered Richard Anthony Ellerington.'

He nodded but made no reply.

'That you, on 24 June 1973, in the City of Kingston upon Hull, without lawful excuse damaged by fire a dwelling house, 70 Askew Avenue, belonging to Samuel Andrew Ellerington, intending to damage such property or being reckless as to whether such property would be damaged.'

He nodded again.

'That you, on 12 October 1973, in the City of Kingston upon Hull, murdered Arthur Bernard Smythe.'

He nodded again.

'That you, on 12 October 1973, in the City of Kingston upon Hull, without lawful excuse damaged by fire a dwelling house, 33 Glasgow Street belonging to Arthur Bernard Smythe, intending to damage such property or being reckless as to whether such property would be damaged.'

He nodded once more.

'That you, on 27 October 1973, in the City of Kingston upon Hull, murdered David Brewer.'

He nodded again.

'That you, on 23 December 1974, in the City of Kingston upon Hull without lawful authority or excuse damaged by fire a dwelling house, 7 Minnies Terrace, Rosamond Street, belonging to Elizabeth Rokahr, intending to damage such property or being reckless as to whether such property would be damaged.'

He nodded again.

'That you, on 23 December 1974, in the City of Kingston upon Hull, murdered Elizabeth Rokahr.'

He stared me in the face but made no comment.

'That you, on 3 June 1976, in the City of Kingston upon Hull, murdered Andrew Edwards.'

He nodded once again.

'That you, on 3 June 1976, in the City of Kingston upon Hull, without lawful excuse damaged by fire a dwelling house, 9 Gorthorpe, belonging to James Vincent Edwards, intending to damage such property or being reckless as to whether such property would be damaged.'

He smiled and nodded but made no comment.

'That you, on 2 January 1977, in the City of Kingston upon Hull, murdered Katrina Thacker.'

He nodded once more.

'That you, on 2 January 1977, in the City of Kingston upon Hull, without lawful excuse damaged by fire a dwelling house, 43 West Dock Avenue, belonging to Karen Lesley Fraser, intending to damage such property or being reckless as to whether such property would be damaged.'

He smiled but made no reply.

'That you, on 5 January 1977, in the County of Humberside, murdered Harold Akester.'

He made no comment.

'That you, on 5 January 1977, in the County of Humberside, murdered William Beales.'

He made no reply.

'That you, on 5 January 1977, in the County of Humberside, murdered William Carter.'

He made no comment.

'That you, on 5 January 1977, in the County of Humberside, murdered Victor Consett.'

He made no reply.

'That you, on 5 January 1977, in the County of Humberside, murdered Leonard Charles Dennett.'

He made no comment.

'That you, on 5 January 1977, in the County of Humberside, murdered Arthur Ellwood.'

He smiled but made no reply.

'That you, on 5 January 1977, in the County of Humberside, murdered Arthur Hardy.'

He made no comment.

'That you, on 5 January 1977, in the County of Humberside, murdered William Hoult'.

He smiled again but made no comment.

'That you, on 5 January 1977, in the County of Humberside, murdered Benjamin Phillips.'

He made no comment.

'That you, on 5 January 1977, in the County of Humberside, murdered

Percy Sanderson.'

He made no comment.

'That you, on 5 January 1977, in the County of Humberside, murdered John James Riby.'

He smiled again but made no comment.

'That you, on 5 January 1977, at Hessle in North Humberside, without lawful excuse damaged by fire a building known as Wensley Lodge, belonging to the Humberside County Council Social Services Department, intending to do damage to such property or being reckless as to whether such property would be damaged.'

He made no comment.

'That you, on 27 April 1977, in the City of Kingston upon Hull, murdered Mark Andrew Jordan.'

He made no comment.

'That you, on 27 April 1977, in the City of Kingston upon Hull, murdered Deborah Pauline Gold.'

He made no comment.

'That you, on 27 April 1977, in the City of Kingston upon Hull, without lawful excuse damaged by fire a dwelling house, 4 Belgrave Terrace, Rosamond Street, belonging to Albert Gold, intending to damage such property or being reckless as to whether such property would be damaged.'

He made no comment.

'That you, on 6 January 1978, in the City of Kingston upon Hull, murdered Christine Viola Dickson.'

He made no comment.

'That you, on 6 January 1978, in the City of Kingston upon Hull, murdered Mark Christopher Dickson.'

He made no comment.

'That you, on 6 January 1978, in the City of Kingston upon Hull, murdered Steven Paul Dickson'.

He made no comment.

'That you, on 6 January 1978, in the City of Kingston upon Hull, murdered Michael John Dickson'.

He made no comment.

'That you, on 6 January 1978, in the City and County of Kingston upon Hull, without lawful excuse damaged by fire a dwelling house belonging to Anthony Lawrence Dickson, intending to damage such property or being reckless as to whether such property would be damaged.'

He made no comment.

'That you, on 22 June 1979, in the City of Kingston upon Hull, caused grievous bodily harm to Rosabelle Faith Fenton with intent to do her grievous bodily harm.'

He made no comment.

'That you, on 22 June 1979, in the City of Kingston upon Hull, without lawful excuse damaged by fire a dwelling house belonging to Rosabelle Faith Fenton intending to damage such property or being reckless as to whether such property would be damaged.'

He smiled, hesitated for a few moments and then said, 'I'll never set fire

to another dwelling house as long as I live.'
I then gave him copies of all the charges. He thanked me, shook hands and with a smile and a wave he was taken back to his cell. Within a few minutes we were on our way back to Hull.

The following morning, Thursday, 16 October 1980, Lee appeared before Hull Magistrates Court. All the charges were formally read out to him by the Clerk of the Court in the presence of his solicitor, Robert Gunby. Reporting restrictions were not lifted during the 55-minute hearing. Mr. Trevor Pogson prosecuted on behalf of the Director of Public Prosecutions. He tendered exhibits, consisting of photographs of the fire scenes and copies of Lee's voluntary statements, and relevant statements from over 175 witnesses. Copies of all the bundles of statements, exhibits and photographs were also handed to Mr. Gunby and every item of paper in the enquiry was made available for the defence team's examination. Robert Gunby told the court he had no objections or submissions to make except to apply for an extension of legal aid, which was granted by the magistrates.

I watched Lee from my seat in the court as the committal proceedings took place. He was wearing his favourite pink open-necked shirt and his dark grey single-breasted suit. He walked into the court looking a little nervous but quickly looked about him, paying particular attention to the small public gallery, no doubt looking to see if any friend or relative was present. I saw none. I noted that he seemed to take great interest as the various bundles of papers were handed over to his solicitor and he stood up to acknowledge each of the charges as the Clerk of the Court read them out to him. Afterwards he was committed for trial at the Crown Court. No pleas were taken, he was granted further legal aid and again remanded in custody.

That afternoon the *Hull Daily Mail* banner headline was, 'MAN ON MASS MURDER CHARGES'.

A week later on 20 October, whilst in Leeds attending to other matter I called at Leeds Prison where I saw Lee once more. He seemed pleased about the visit and said, 'You know, I'll never do another house fire. Now I can't get my hands on paraffin I'm alright. I was all tense at the committal but you know, now that it's all over what I've been doing, I feel happy. This last weekend has been the happiest I've had for years. It's all out of my mind now. I'm not carrying it with me any more in my head so I feel sort of free of having to be careful what I say and do, not wanting to get caught.'

During the following weeks I had many discussions with my officers, forensic experts, Lee's legal adviser's managing clerk, Dr. Sasiene and others. Meantime the many files of statements were on their way to Mr. Gerald Coles Q.C., selected by the Director of Public Prosecution to lead the prosecution case against Lee.

On Wednesday, 12 November 1980, having heard that Lee was still the subject of possible attack from other prisoners, I went to Leeds Prison to see the prison security officer about his safety and to see for myself that Lee was not harmed. I was assured that he would not be harmed and that he was carefully monitored. I then saw him once more. 'I'll tell you somat, Mr. Sagar. I did do the fire at Hastie's and Wensley Lodge and it's right what I've told you, but, see, they've got me a good barrister and Eric Pearce and Mr. Gunby have been very good to me, done a lot for me they have. So, see, I'm going to plead not guilty 'cause I understand there's a chance if I deny it and act a bit daft I might get into a mental home. That will be better than a stinking prison and anyway I might get away with it all. Mr. Pearce told me there'd be no proof if I hadn't told you, so I'm going to deny it all. Only thing is what frightens me is if I get out and get off with it I'll bloody do it again and kill somebody again.'

Detective Constable Bacon said, 'Even now, knowing what you have done and the grief you have caused, surely you wouldn't light another fire.'

He replied, 'I can't help myself and it wouldn't be my fault if they got me off. It's up to Eric (Pearce) to get me off. You can't blame me for pleading not guilty can you 'cause I'm fed up with this bloody place. There's a good few people going to get me for what I've been doing with fire. Long as you keep coming to see me and they know you are about here I think I'll be alright.'

In view of the fact that I had now been reassured that Lee was separate from and not in any real danger of attack from other prisoners, I did not consider it necessary to spend time visiting him further. Also, in view of the clear indication he had given to me that he was going to plead not guilty to all the charges I believed it wise not to visit him in case those defending him would suggest I had been persuading him to plead guilty. Actually, I was now pleased with his indication to plead not guilty as I wanted to have all the evidence properly tested. There was no better way of doing that than before the Crown Court where a jury could make their own minds up.

Meanwhile my Chief Constable David Hall had been contacted by Yorkshire TV producer Clive Entwhistle who wanted to make a documentary film about Lee. I was not too happy about it, but David Hall asked me to co-operate with the TV crew and provide them with the details they wanted. I reluctantly agreed. I was told to let the producer, Clive Entwhistle, know all there was to know about the case. We had nothing to hide but I was concerned about it as the whole matter was *sub judice*. Unknown to my Chief, I contacted John Walker at the DPP's office and told him about my concern. 'If David Hall wants it to go public and provided the programme does not actually go out before Lee's trial you have nothing to worry about,' was John Walker's advice.

With 'not guilty pleas' on the horizon and with separate trials involving a great many witnesses and legal argument, I knew it would be quite some time, if ever, before the film would go out to the public.

Chapter Twenty One

'Few people will want to believe Lee has admitted what he has, Boss,' remarked Detective Sergeant Mick Trafford. 'Yes, I understand what you mean,' I replied. 'Life would have been so much easier for us if he had only spoken about the Hastie's and Ros Fenton's house fire, but there you are, he didn't.'

'No doubt you are prepared for a good grilling when it all goes for trial,' the sergeant continued. 'I hear he's got Harry Ognall, Q.C., defending him.' Harry Ognall will always be known as a highly competent criminal lawyer and well respected by police officers and criminals alike. Well-known for his tenacity he would never leave a stone unturned. I always relished the thought of his questions. I knew what Sergeant Trafford was thinking and I appreciated that, having been properly advised to plead not guilty, Lee's defence would rely heavily on disproving, in one way or another, that his admissions were untrue. I knew that, to attempt to do this, Harry Ognall would have to cross-examine me at length. Thank God I had no need to worry about the veracity of what I had recorded.

It was now November 1980. Lee had become of considerable interest to prosecution and defence lawyers alike. And, in turn, the lawyers were in consultation with psychiatrists, who were invited to examine Lee in prison. What was this young man's mental state? Concentrating on writing everything verbatim, I don't think I was able to assess it all thoroughly until I was able to sit in my office and study the whole picture. As a teenager, up until the time of his arrest, Lee was living and occasionally working as a normal human being in the Hull community without anyone paying much, if any, attention to him. Mr. Eric Pearce was close to him from shortly after his arrest, and so too, to a lesser degree, was his solicitor, Robert Gunby. They, like myself, obviously did not feel that he was mentally ill. But then, who were we to decide if that was so or not? We were not medically qualified but between us we did have a great knowledge of people, particularly in the criminal fraternity. Apart from his physical disability, he appeared no different from many thousands of other people awaiting trial.

Now, as we were nearing Lee's trial, lawyers and psychiatrists would want to know what was behind all the utterances which I had written in my notebook and written on about seventy A4-size sheets of voluntary statement paper.

On several occasions in the past I had been appointed on behalf of the Home Office and Director of Public Prosecutions to investigate cases of alleged miscarriages of justice in different parts of the country, where men had been charged and convicted of criminal offences following voluntary statements of admission under caution. On more than one occasion I found that the voluntary statements had not been 'voluntary' at all. At their trials, despite protests from the accused, the voluntary element was accepted by judge and jury.

In 1977, I was appointed to investigate allegations of brutality by prison officers upon prisoners after the Hull prison riot. During the course of that enquiry I interviewed all the prisoners who had been in the prison during the riot. They included members of the Birmingham Six and Guildford Four. They were particularly apprehensive about my intentions, but after speaking to other prisoners they agreed to tell me about beatings they had suffered at the hands of some of the Hull prison officers. Paul Hill spent a great many hours giving a long statement to one of my sergeants, Detective Sergeant Geoffrey Chamberlain, and when he was eventually given the seven or eight pages of his statement to read and sign he grabbed it in both hands and immediately tore it to shreds saying, 'That's what I think of bloody police statements. The last time I signed one it was beaten out of me in Birmingham, it was all bloody lies and I got 30 years.' After convincing him that my sole purpose was to seek truth and justice, he calmed down. We carefully sellotaped his statement together and he eventually signed it. He became one of the most articulate witnesses we had in the brutality trial. He and his fellow accused always claimed their confessions about the bombings were false and far from voluntary. I listened to him for many hours and, based on nothing but instinct, I believed him, but no one wanted to hear about it. In fairness to them and to perhaps give them a little hope and encouragement, I actually told Paul Hill (Guildford Four) and John Walker (Birmingham Six) that I believed them. They were in prison for a further 12 years before they were released and cleared of all charges. So much for the criminal justice system. I certainly appreciated the problems and dangers involved in voluntary statements.

    I attended my initial detective training at Scotland Yard in 1962 when I was a detective constable. I was told in that training that a confession was the strongest kind of evidence you could get from anyone. We were all told that any detective who could not get a 'cough' was failing in his job. In fact, I remember that on the training course I was fascinated by the way a 'cough' was banded about as if it had some kind of prize meaning. 'Verballed' was prominent too. I couldn't find it in my Oxford English Dictionary but did find it in a book of criminal slang. 'Verballed' meant the police invented words and then alleged a suspect had uttered them! There is no doubt that for many years the investigative system in respect of uncorroborated voluntary statements, admissions, confessions or 'coughs,' call it what you will, was, to say the least, questionable. In fact, as long ago as 1929, the Royal Commission on Police Powers reported that it had received 'a volume of responsible evidence which it is impossible to ignore suggesting that a number of the voluntary statements now tendered in court are not voluntary in the strict sense of the word'.

    I am the first to admit I am not infallible and, whilst expecting quite an inquisition from Lee's defence team at his trial, I knew that what I had recorded was exactly what was said and written to the best of my ability. But had I really taken all the necessary steps to satisfy myself that he was not mentally ill? Should I have told him, in addition to the formal caution, that it would be best for him to say nothing at all? Would I have been neglecting my duty to the public if I did so? More to the point would I have been failing my responsibility to those people, dead or alive, who were blamed during the Inquests? Should I have refused to write any of Lee's statements down until his solicitors' clerk did attend? What was his IQ? Why didn't I ask the questions and get Sergeant Martin to do the writing? But I was satisfied that Harry Ognall Q.C.'s objective would be to establish the truth, and I was happy with that.

Always being concerned about Lee's claims, his personality and his welfare, I decided, towards the end of November, to see one of Britain's foremost authorities on forensic psychiatry, Dr. Hugo Buist Milne, in Bradford, who had visited Lee in prison and examined him. Dr. Milne told me that he found Lee to be of poor educational attainment but he was alert, always aware of his surroundings and quick to respond to questions. He concluded that he found Lee a most perceptive young man but of limited intelligence. I had not been talking to Hugo Milne for long when he took a telephone call. He turned to me and, looking embarrassed, he said, 'I have just been told by Lee's defence people not to speak to you. I am sorry, but I will probably be called for the defence.' I did not ask how anyone knew I was there or who it was who actually telephoned, or, more importantly, what harm we were doing discussing Lee. I must have been naively ignorant of the defence intentions.

About a week later I saw counsel appointed to prosecute Lee, Mr. Gerald Coles, Q.C. I knew the quietly spoken, well respected barrister quite well. He has a shrewd eye for detail and was the ideal counsel for this case.

I continued to keep in touch with the Coroner He was always very supportive and often told me not to be worried about his Inquest findings. I also contacted Dr. Sasiene, who always reassured me that no harm had befallen Lee.

Early in January 1981, I was informed that Lee was to appear before Leeds Crown Court on Monday, 19 January, for a pre-trial review. This would mean that any administrative matters relating to the trial could be dealt with and a date fixed for a full hearing before a jury.

On the appointed date I attended Leeds Crown Court where I discussed various aspects of the case with counsel. During the day Lee's counsel went to see the Judge, Mr. Justice Tudor Evans, in his chambers because Lee's current instructions caused them anxiety and disquiet. I gathered Lee was now saying that he was pleading guilty. Exactly to what I did not know, but I had not contemplated any guilty pleas at all. However, the reporting psychiatrists for both prosecution and defence agreed that Lee was fit to stand trial, and fit to plead whatever he chose. The case was entered for hearing the following day, January 20 1980, so giving Lee the benefit of further advice from his very experienced counsel.

On the following day, I was approached by Mr. Ognall, who asked if I was prepared to accept charges of manslaughter as an alternative to murder in all the indictments. I said that I was agreeable.

Later that morning Lee stood between two prison officers in the dock as the 26 counts of murder, 26 alternative counts of manslaughter by reason of diminished responsibility, and the 11 counts of arson were read out. To each murder charge, and without any prompting from anyone, Lee answered directly and in a clear positive voice: 'Not guilty'. Similarly, to each alternative charge of manslaughter he also replied directly and in a clear confident voice: 'Guilty'. He also pleaded 'Guilty' with the same air of assurance to each of the 11 cases of arson insofar as he was reckless as to whether life was endangered. A total of 37 charges. All were accepted by the Judge.

During the plea process, and despite his unequivocal pleas of guilty, there was a moment when I felt a great urge to stand up and say out loud, 'Hold on a minute, Judge, don't you think you should hear all the evidence before a jury?' Somehow my self-discipline held out and I kept quiet. No doubt I would have been held in contempt of court had I blurted out my thoughts.

Being engrossed in the activities of the Yorkshire Ripper, few people in Leeds had ever heard of Bruce George Peter Lee and even fewer were aware that he was claiming responsibility for killing 26 people by burning them to death. Almost everyone in England knew about the Ripper's crimes long before he was arrested but no one appeared to know about Lee's achievements before his arrest. Indeed, the people of Hull were not aware of anyone killing by fire, and at random, but just imagine the atmosphere in the City if this had been known during the seven years before his arrest.

The Ripper pleaded not guilty to murder and had been proven responsible for those 13 deaths, exactly half the number Lee admitted. I did so wish the evidence in Lee's case could have been tested. However, after the charges had been read and Lee had pleaded, Mr. Ognall told the court the pleas of not guilty to murder but guilty to manslaughter were tendered on the basis of diminished responsibility.

Prosecuting counsel Gerald Coles said that the Crown took the view that the public interest did not demand a trial and that justice could be done by accepting Lee's pleas. He went on to tell the packed court: 'The mind must have difficulty in encompassing the horror of those fires. When one month short of his 13th birthday in June 1973, Lee had started his first fire, which claimed the life of a six-year-old boy and continued his fire-raising activities until December 1979 when he was 19 years old. Lee was not a happy or well-blessed child and was born with a partially paralysed and deformed right hand and suffered epilepsy. He was not a much loved son and no one ever cared for him. He attended a school for the physically handicapped until he was 16 and spent much of his youth in care. While in care he was introduced for the first time to homosexuality, which led to his downfall. Being low in intelligence, Lee had been unsociable and withdrawn as a youth but had an animal cunning which had enabled him to conduct his fire-raising with some degree of skill and it was a true fact that the fires were his only true achievement in life.'

The prosecution then outlined Lee's statement about buying paraffin and wandering about Hull feeling miserable before launching an arson attack and how he had described his fingers tingling when he knew that meant he wanted to start another fire. He attacked dwelling houses and had almost always used paraffin and his technique had been to make a pool of paraffin and a trickly trail of paraffin back to a small pool which he used as a fuse to set fire to the larger pool to give him time to get away. Mr. Coles told the court that Lee had chosen houses at random without knowing who was inside. On only four occasions could there be said to have been a motive, but the grudges he held against those victims could only be described as trivial.

Interestingly, the prosecution said all Lee's victims had been incapacitated either by old age, extreme youth or disability. The fires had been either lit knowing that people were in the houses or were lit in rooms where people actually were. On one particularly gruesome occasion Lee had poured paraffin on the body of a sleeping man. Over the years Lee had, according to Mr. Coles, developed an expertise such as to mystify police and fire officers as to the nature of the fires. Time and again, Inquests had returned verdicts of misadventure in the deaths.

Mr. Harry Ognall said, 'No words represent this crippled and solitary young man. He was a pathetic nobody who had achieved notoriety through his deeds. For the most of the material time he was in the care of the Humberside County Council. We have had, with their courtesy, the advantage of examining all relevant records, and fairness demands that I say these records disclose that throughout the whole of that period they treated him and reared him with fairness, compassion and concern.' Then he added, 'Would that his parents had done the same.'

Significantly, Mr. Ognall, like ourselves, was unable to produce any evidence from the Humberside County Council records to show exactly where Lee should have been at the time of the fires.

Mr. Justice Tudor Evans said he was satisfied that Lee was suffering from a psychopathic disorder to such a degree that it warranted detention in hospital. He then ordered Lee to be detained without limit of time at Park Lane Hospital, near Liverpool, under section 60 and section 65 of the Mental Health Act 1959 for the protection of the public, considering the risk of further offences.

So Bruce George Peter Lee was told his fate and escorted from the dock by no fewer than five prison officers. Glancing at him for the first time during the hearing, I saw that he appeared relaxed and I could only guess that he was satisfied with being taken to Park Lane Special Hospital, near Liverpool, instead of 'a stinking prison'. Lee's performance in the dock, the way he appeared so alert, the way he spoke confidently and the way he pleaded so clearly and consistently left me in a state of considerable anxiety. Despite his pleadings of guilt, was he really guilty of all the charges? I believe that, had he pleaded not guilty to one or two of the charges, Mr. Justice Tudor Evans could well have decided to take not guilty pleas for all of them due to the complexity of the evidence. Although I believed that had Lee been found guilty of the Hastie case and that of Ros Fenton, the remainder would quite properly have been 'left on file'.

Oddly enough, I could not help noticing that a newspaper reporter kept looking towards me and across to Lee standing in the dock as the indictments were read out and his pleas taken. I did not look at Lee, even for a second, during the 20 minutes or more it took the Clerk of the Court to read out and take the pleadings.

Having said goodbye to prosecuting counsel and the Director of Public Prosecutions I drove back to Hull. Taking my time for a change, driving along the M62, and into Hull, I simultaneously thought of the fire victims and of those previously blamed, particularly plumber Steven Hay. I thought about the Inquests. I also thought about Lee. Poor little devil, I thought, he's never had a chance. His 20 years on this earth had not done him any favours but his passion for fire had. Obviously the concern, fairness and compassion of the good people within Humberside County Council Social Services was not enough.

Upon my arrival at Hull Central Police Station in Queens Gardens, I found that news of Lee's guilty pleas were banner headlines in the *Hull Daily Mail*, 'HULL MAN ADMITS 26 FIRE KILLINGS'. A large picture of Lee, which must have been taken a month or so before his arrest, made him look quite hard and ruthless. There was also a small photograph taken when he was nine-years-old, not long before he claimed that he set about his deadly fire campaign. I do not know where the newspaper obtained their photographs but at least they revealed that someone, at some time, was interested in him.

That night Yorkshire Television broadcast the 40-minute programme in which the Chief Constable of Humberside had authorised police material, in effect, to be put in the public domain. The programme was prepared in advance, ready for transmission as soon as Lee's trial was over. Producer Clive Entwhistle had done a good job without being unkind to anyone. In front of the camera Lee's mother said for all to hear that she had been 'on the game' when Lee was a child. Several local people, in their interviews before the cameras, said they knew Lee was a fire-raiser but didn't tell anyone! 'You just can't go accusing, can you?' said one woman. 'You can't tell a policeman that a lad has started a fire.' In front of the TV camera in 1981, she said she had had her suspicions since 1973, immediately after she saw David Brewer burned to death. Why she chose not to inform the police is beyond me.

The next day the *Hull Daily Mail* reported that two Hull M.P.s, Mr. James Johnson, West Hull, and Mr. Kevin McNamara, Central Hull, were calling on the Government to set up top-level inquiries into the 11 arson attacks. They were concerned that Lee was able to carry out several of his attacks while still in local authority care. I shared their concern but it was my duty to discuss my views with the Director of Public Prosecutions and prosecuting counsel, not Members of Parliament.

Mr. Johnson, according to the press, was planning an all-party deputation including Mr. McNamara and Patrick Wall, M.P. for Haltemprice, to see Mr. William Whitelaw. 'The constituencies of the three M.P.s have all suffered in one way and another from these serious arson attacks,' said Mr. Johnson. 'I feel that a public enquiry into these tragic events should be held in order to allay widespread public disquiet.' The newspaper also reported that Mr. Edward Park, Humberside's fire chief at the time of the attacks, said he would like to see fire investigation procedures made even more thorough in the future. These were eventually made more thorough but there was to be no public enquiry of the kind suggested by the Members of Parliament.

A week after Lee's Crown Court appearance I received a letter from Eric Pearce: 'The enquiry and presentation required extra care and thought by all concerned and the final result was in the best interests of Bruce Lee. I enjoyed the challenge and also the working relationship throughout the enquiry between ourselves (the defence) and all the officers engaged with you in the various spheres of the long enquiry. I wish you well for the future and hope that any of our future ventures will be conducted with the same good sense, honesty and a bit of humour to flavour the mixture.'

Bless you, Eric. When you put pen to paper you had no idea how important your kind words were going to be in the Royal Courts of Justice in London six years later. Although I could not have imagined it then, material was already being gathered in a determined effort to destroy me.

Chapter Twenty Two

On Monday morning, 26 January 1981, immediately after I arrived at my office and less than a week after Lee's Crown Court appearance, a colleague showed me an article published the previous day in the *Sunday Times*. It was headed: 'CALLS GROW FOR PROBE OVER THE "SIMPLETON" WHO FOOLED EXPERTS'.

When I read it I particularly noted the question: 'What convinced police that Lee – with mental and physical disabilities – was able to be agile enough to force windows and break in to start some fires, and to commit arson without arousing suspicion?'

What 'convinced police'? I was certainly not convinced about everything regarding Lee's activities. That should have been a matter for a judge and jury.

The article continued: 'Unease over the case is summed up by Edward Park, chief fire officer for Humberside at the time of several of the fires and now retired. He says, "Because this lad confessed to starting fires, all the details of what he did were not subjected to the thorough public airing that accompanies a not guilty plea. The police obviously accepted that he was telling the truth but there was no opportunity for anyone else to see precisely how he got away with it for so long."'

How does anyone get away with any crime? The answer is simple: well over 70% of criminals get away with it because the whole of the investigative system is not effective enough. If it were, we would be living in something of a police state, and I would not want to be part of it.

The *Sunday Times* report went on: 'Hull child psychiatrist Dr. Peter Benyon was reported as saying, "I am not suggesting it happened in this case but it's by no means unusual for someone who has a low level of self-esteem and feels himself to be a nonentity to seize on some activity, be it criminal or otherwise, and pretend that it was their doing to give themselves importance and inflate themselves".'

The article claimed that Lee was interviewed after 'being found loitering at public lavatories'. Lee was not arrested loitering at public lavatories, but in Hull City centre, where he was found playing a gaming machine in the Collier Street Crystal Rooms.

Ironically, on Friday, 23 January 1981, two days before the *Sunday Times* publication, the Director of Public Prosecutions, Sir Thomas Hetherington, wrote to the Chief Constable of Humberside commending everyone on the Lee investigation for the 'meticulous, careful and efficient way in which the evidence for the prosecution was marshalled'. The Chief Constable added his congratulations to Sir Thomas's remarks and my team was commended.

Accounts in many newspapers of the way criminal investigations are conducted usually show little knowledge of what really happens and they give little inkling of the methodical system, patience, thoroughness and accuracy that are crucial to solving most crime, let alone murder. In my view the *Sunday Times* article not only showed a lack of that understanding but also implied that the whole of the enquiry, and my handling of it, was suspect. I did not know it then, but the newspaper was about to mount a campaign to clear Lee and do its damnedest to condemn me.

The day after I read the article I was appointed to investigate several allegations of corruption in the South Yorkshire Police at Sheffield. I was told that my Chief Constable had seen the newspaper, but no one of senior rank mentioned it to me and I decided to keep my own counsel. I was naturally concerned about the newspaper story and began to look back over the whole of the enquiry to the night Edith Hastie found her home ablaze. In fact, I began to question my every move and it became something of a preoccupation when I travelled to and from Sheffield on my new assignment. I thought about the morning the Hastie fire investigation got under way, and the sad days that followed as the three boys died. Several well-meaning Hull citizens suggested to me then that I must be under a lot of pressure to solve the matter. They apparently did not have a clear understanding of the job I was doing or the type of nature I have. I was not under pressure either from within myself or from anyone else. As it happens, I know of no murder enquiry where any senior investigator has 'been under pressure' to produce a result, a situation which owes more to journalese than to reality.

From day one I gave a great deal of thought to the type of person who would set a house on fire with human beings inside. My officers and I had collected, evaluated and recorded every scrap of information we had and we had pondered over minute clues and weighed up chance remarks.

I knew from experience that many fire-raisers had mental problems. Experience also told me that in most cases arson is committed by young men aged between 16 and 25; the frequency curve decreases during adult years, but, I had learned, surprisingly increases again towards old age. Culprits are usually to be found at the bottom of the social ladder living in very poor home circumstances. I also knew that there seemed to be several motives for an arsonist's action. Some set fires for pleasure; others had a desire to do something spectacular, or to destroy traces of another crime, or to claim insurance money, and some set fires simply to kill. But often an arsonist would not fall into any particular group.

The *Sunday Times* article also took my thoughts back to the times when Lee told us what he wanted to say. I recalled the way he sometimes stared at me with intolerable directness. I thought about his regular, vapid smile, his sharp watchful look at my writing and the times I had seen him in his cell in Hull Central Police Station, sitting there completely relaxed reading the Bible. I believe he got a great deal of solace from his readings and I was fascinated by his ability to recall some of the passages he read.

After completing all his many statements, I studied his admissions many times. I was satisfied with his claim about Edith Hastie's house in Selby Street. We had found ample corroboration for that, but the remainder presented a much more difficult problem. In an endeavour to assess the truth of his statements and to seek corroboration of all his words in the remainder of the fires, I decided that one sure way of knowing something concrete about his claims was to allow forensic scientists to study them in detail. I wanted to see if the scientists – who could carry out any experiment they wished – would consider it at all possible that the way he claimed to have started any of the fires was, in fact, possible from the scientific point of view. Therefore I arranged for all Lee's voluntary statements and all the evidence of his interviews to be passed to two Home Office scientists for their opinion. I also told Lee's 'on hand' legal representative, Mr. Eric Pearce, what I had done. He agreed, saying, with a wry smile, that with luck the scientists could well decide that the whole set of statements was pure fantasy!

I knew that it would be difficult to conduct an experiment recreating the exact circumstances of Wensley Lodge, as the scientists did not have the same room properties or furnishings. The objective was to see whether paraffin could cause underfloor burning like that at Wensley Lodge, and whether it was possible to maintain burning on top and underneath a floor. I knew, of course, that in conducting any experiment, account would be taken of the fact that the floor would not have the original floorboards, lino and joists of the ill-fated Room 11.

In due course I was told that the Wensley Lodge experiment was complete and the conclusion drawn from this particular experiment was that one could have underfloor burning (of the kind found in the floor at Room 11) from a liquid accelerant (paraffin) poured from above. So there was a certain amount of corroboration, albeit small, to support Lee's claim. Curiously, from the scientific point of view, what Lee claimed he did, was not, therefore, ruled impossible.

Two months before Lee appeared before Leeds Crown Court, I received statements from Mr. Roy Cooke, and Mr. Graham Devonport, the two scientists who studied all Lee's claims and who were responsible for the experiments relative to them. Both scientists concluded that consideration of all their findings led them both to believe that they cumulatively corroborated Lee's admissions. They also mentioned that in all Lee's fire claims, the people harmed were incapacitated when the fire started because of age, sleep or infirmity.

My one-time distrust, which lay mainly in the inherent improbability that some of the fires Lee talked about ever happened, began to fade as factual evidence was uncovered. The scientists' corroboration had been helpful in this respect, but they did not, and could not, rule out entirely the possibility that the Wensley Lodge fire could not have been started by the accidental action of plumber Steven Hay.

Two questions were uppermost in my mind from the time I learned the full facts about the Wensley Lodge fire, and will remain without sound answers for ever, no matter how often they are pondered over. Why did Lee make his rather detailed claim to the fire? What would the result have been at the Inquest and Committee of Enquiry if the plumbing work had not been carried out?

Chapter Twenty Three

Within two weeks of Lee's Crown Court appearance it was reported that Home Secretary William Whitelaw had agreed to see a joint deputation of North Humberside M.P.s about Lee's case. 'We have a great many points to put to Mr. Whitelaw,' they were reported to have said. Mr. James Johnson, M.P. for West Hull, said that he was not bringing into question the activities of the police or local authority.

About that time I received an anonymous telephone call from a man who was obviously a member of the criminal fraternity. I recall his words: 'One of them newspaper chaps is looking for material to ruin you, Mr. Sagar. This chap from one of the London papers is looking to find anybody you might have planted evidence on, or anything corrupt you have done.' He appeared to be about to ring off as he added, 'You done me a favour and saved me going down the road a few years back, so let's just say I'm returning you one now.' There were no proverbial skeletons in my cupboard, and, unless someone manufactured some kind of 'evidence' against me, I thought that any such journalist would be wasting his time.

A day or so later I saw a cutting from the *Hull Daily Mail* headed, 'FORGIVE LEE, PLEADS VICAR'.

In it the Rev. Allan Bagshaw, vicar of St. Matthew's Church on Anlaby Road, near to Selby Street, described the three young Hastie brothers, Charlie, Peter and Paul's deaths as heinous crimes and a tragedy. But he added, 'Please remember Lee in your prayers'. Thank God for Allan Bagshaw, I thought.

In between my Sheffield corruption enquiry I was now invited to join a working party for a series of joint discussions to be held between Humberside Police, the Humberside Fire Brigade and the Forensic Science Service. The purpose was to examine the difficulties in recognising arson and where responsibilities lay in this area. Indeed, it was thanks to Lee's claims that the combined agencies formed the working party and now recognised that something they should always have known – there was no clearly defined investigation responsibility in many fires.

Many practical difficulties were examined by the working party and everyone agreed that the investigation of fires is complex and multi-disciplinary with a need for an awareness of the technology of fire scene searching and damage interpretation skills. The evidence is frequently imprecise, and suspecting that arson exists from physical remains at the scene is often only a matter of conjecture, and insufficient evidence may be adduced to prove arson.

The working party reported its findings, which were passed on to the Home Office and eventually taken up nationwide as the problems now appreciated in Hull were relevant in many other parts of the country. Lee would be proud to know that some good was produced from his admitted wrongdoing.

On 11 February 1981, the large black and bold banner headline splashed across the front page of the *Hull Daily Mail* read: 'LEE: QUESTIONS NEED ANSWERS.' The article read: 'Home Secretary, Mr. William Whitelaw, was asked today to re-open a public examination of the Wensley Lodge fire which killed 11 men. The call comes from Central Hull M.P. Mr. Kevin McNamara as a result of the admission by Bruce Lee at Leeds Crown Court last month that he was responsible for the fatal, 1977, Hessle old people's home fire.'

Mr. McNamara was also reported as saying that, because of the failure to detect arson in any of the Lee fires between 1973 and 1979, he was urging Mr. Whitelaw to ensure that the full details of the confessions were made available to the Forensic Department and the fire services so they could analyse the efficiency of their investigations. Mr. McNamara was rightly concerned, but he did not appear to realise that I had asked the forensic science people to examine the admissions before Lee's case was dealt with. I and my officers had also discussed a great many aspects of Lee's claims with fire brigade officers.

The same day as the *Hull Daily Mail* article, the *Guardian* reported that Mr. Edward Park, the former Chief Officer of the Humberside Fire Brigade, did not believe Lee's story about Wensley Lodge. Two days later the *Hull Daily Mail* reported that Hull M.P.s 'had left Home Secretary William Whitelaw to ponder over nagging doubts raised by the Bruce Lee fire attacks'. And so various newspaper reports continued with a variety of journalists from the national newspapers asking me for comment. I thought that all that could be properly said was said at the Leeds Crown Court and I said so. None of the people quoted in the newspapers ever contacted me.

Six months after Lee's Crown Court appearance, the *Hull Daily Mail* of 26 June 1981, reported under a headline, 'BRUCE LEE: STILL DOUBT': 'An extensive inquiry by Home Secretary William Whitelaw into the case of Bruce Lee still left questions about forensic science unanswered,' a Hull M.P. has claimed. Central Hull M.P. Mr. Kevin McNamara said he welcomed improvements in procedure between the police, fire and forensic services outlined by Mr. Whitelaw in a reply to a group of M.P.s who raised questions about the Lee investigation and court hearing. But Mr. McNamara was quoted as saying, "Mr. Whitelaw's inquiry still leaves a number of matters of a forensic nature unanswered and the methods about how these conclusions were arrived at have still to be examined."'

The report also stated that the Home Secretary invited the M.P.s to see him again if they felt they needed to raise any further points. Mr. James Johnson, M.P. said he was hoping to contact his parliamentary colleagues to take up Mr. Whitelaw's offer and described the Home Secretary's statement as something of an 'apologia'. But he too welcomed the tightening of links between the police, fire and forensic science services. Our working party's conclusions had obviously been well received in Whitehall.

I was engaged on the Sheffield investigation for the remainder of 1981, but I was frequently receiving messages from ordinary members of the Hull public, members of the legal profession, one or two journalists, and several members of the criminal fraternity claiming that a *Sunday Times* journalist was doing 'all sorts' to blacken my name and prove Bruce Lee innocent. One Hull villain, who would often be happy to shop one of his own kind, telephoned me early one morning before I left home. He said he had heard that 'a London journalist was looking for any criminal Sagar could have fitted up'. My caller was laughing when he told me and he added, 'It's a funny old world, ain't it, Boss, we all know you are doing your bit to nick crooked cops in Sheffield, and back here in Hull a newspaper man is out to nick you. What have you done to upset him? Maybe if you gave him one of them exclusives newspapers is always looking for he'd leave you alone.' I agreed with him but 'funny old world' was an understatement. A few weeks later I heard that 'some people' were seeking out the possibility that perhaps I had had an affair with a prostitute. They – whoever they were – had no chance of discovering anything of that sort either. But such talk was worrying.

Something of a breakthrough was presented to the *Sunday Times* journalist about a year later. Five members of the Humberside Drug Squad were committed for trial at York Crown Court, charged with drug conspiracy charges. The charges arose from the words of a one-time drug dealer and informer but his evidence was rejected by the jury and the officers were acquitted on 5 March 1982.

During the drug squad officers' case it was alleged that Bruce Lee had been paid £300 to damage the house of a neighbour of the Hastie's, as part of a dispute over drugs, and that Lee had set fire to the wrong house.

The *Yorkshire Post*, in a leading article on Saturday, 6 March 1982, asked 'WAS THERE A LINK WITH FIRE DEATHS?' and went on to cover Bruce Lee's fire claims and the Hull M.P.s' concerns. The *Yorkshire Post* also appeared to take great pride in the fact that they had tracked the informer down to the island of Corsica where he had gone into hiding in a futile attempt to avoid giving his ill-founded evidence against the drug squad officers. I knew the informer and was not surprised to hear that the twelve York jurors rejected his evidence out of hand.

Two days after his evidence was thrown out the *Sunday Times* printed a story headlined, 'DRUG VENDETTA LINKS CONTRACT TO KILL WITH ARSON DEATHS'. It claimed that it could now reveal 'disturbing evidence' that the motives for one of Lee's fires might have resulted from a vendetta in the Hull drugs world and that Lee himself claimed he was paid to carry out the revenge attack. The newspaper also alleged that 'by the end of March 1980 the pressures on Sagar to solve the Hastie killings were intense. He still had more than twenty men on the investigation and the police bill for police overtime alone approached £100, 000. Yet the investigation was getting nowhere, until it suddenly changed tack. We have been able to establish that the police had considerable evidence that others were involved. This was immediately forgotten when Lee confessed, claiming sole responsibility. But the evidence still is that Lee was not alone.'

Anyone who took the time to read the story, and, if they gave it any credence at all, would naturally be concerned about what they read. Any intelligent reader would also see that there were many inferences there too. Several people told me it was obvious 'the *Sunday Times* was out to destroy (my) reputation'.

I read the story and treated it with the contempt I believe it deserved. But I also wanted to denounce the report and tell everyone that it was inaccurate and distorted. Common-sense, however, told me not to play into the newspaper's hands. I knew I was never under intense pressure from anyone, and the amount of the police bill for overtime did not worry me. As a detective superintendent I never received overtime payments and, in my view, considering the long hours, unpleasant working conditions, and some of the unsavoury people they were dealing with, my officers deserved whatever payment was due to them.

Chapter Twenty Four

On 14 March 1982, the *Sunday Times* devoted two pages and thousands of words, with drawings and a picture of Lee, to their allegations about Lee and my handling of his case. This time the heading was 'BRUCE LEE. THE CASE FOR THE DEFENCE? A year-long Insight (*Sunday Times*) investigation reveals that the confession that sent him to a mental hospital for life was deeply flawed. If the prosecution case had been tested in court, Lee could not possibly have been convicted,' the sub-heading claimed.

The story continued, 'Lee was frequently alone with Sagar and his colleague Detective Sergeant John Martin. Other police officers on the investigation were not allowed to talk to Lee and forensic experts re-examining the fires were not allowed access to Lee.' Complete and utter rubbish, I thought. I found the many allegations now being published were downright lies. I well appreciated what my anonymous caller was meaning when he told me a year earlier that there was a move afoot to ruin me.

The day after the two-page *Sunday Times* story, the *Hull Daily Mail* naturally took the same story on board but without the same vindictiveness. The *Mail* banner headline read: 'LEE: CALL FOR FULL ENQUIRY. M.P.s AND COUNCIL PRESS WHITELAW'. It told its readers: 'Mounting pressure for a comprehensive and independent enquiry into the conviction of mass fire killer Bruce Lee was being levelled at Home Secretary Mr. William Whitelaw today as a new controversy raged over a Humberside Police investigation into the case.

'A year-long investigation by the *Sunday Times* alleges there is now "reasonable doubt" Lee was not responsible for all the arson attacks of which he was convicted at Leeds Crown Court in January 1981. The dossier, prepared by *Sunday Times* reporters is to be handed to the Home Office. The dossier alleges there were flaws in evidence which ended Lee's fire raising attacks and that at least two other people were involved.'

As well as Humberside M.P.s McNamara, Johnson and Sir Patrick Wall, Humberside County Council leader Councillor Michael Wheaton also entered the controversy. He was quoted in the *Hull Daily Mail* as saying, 'Public disquiet will certainly be aroused by the *Sunday Times* article. Our concern is largely for the investigative and judicial systems which played so large a part in this case; but also in the interest of everyone – not least those of the police – that an immediate investigation be mounted into the precise details of the investigation, arrest and subsequent conviction.'

A week later, on Sunday, 21 March 1981, the *Sunday Times* published another Insight article headlined: 'I DEMAND A RETRIAL SAYS MASS KILLER'. It announced that it had sent its 12,000-word dossier, which highlighted 'worrying defects' in the police investigation, to 'Whitelaw'. It was claimed that the dossier showed that my officers did not re-interview vital witnesses and that their evidence was ignored. The most wicked claim I read in the story was that Lee was suggestible. This implied that I had deviously suggested crimes to him in such a way that he admitted being responsible for them and, therefore, my evidence was false. Anyone with even the slightest knowledge of criminal law procedure would know such behaviour was downright criminal. It would necessitate a whole system of lies in the evidence and an outrageous ability to deceive the whole of the criminal investigation process and the courts. I am not in that league.

I could not help but notice about that time that, whenever I returned to Hull Police Headquarters from the Sheffield enquiry, most senior police officers in Hull did their best to avoid any mention of the Bruce Lee publicity and my concern about it. There was always a kind of stifled apprehension in the air whenever I saw any one of them. An atmosphere of 'You are in trouble but don't involve me' existed. Yet, officers who had been engaged on the enquiry often spoke about it. One said, 'If you were a member of the Police Federation (which consists of all ranks up to and including Chief Inspector) you could sue that damned newspaper. You know, if we were to tell lies we'd get done for perjury; if a newspaperman tells lies he makes money.' I was not telling lies and I was not thinking of instituting legal proceedings against the newspaper. I was too busy trying to solve other people's problems, particularly in Sheffield.

The national press now picked up the *Sunday Times* story, but they were clearly not in the business of attacking me. In fact, the *Guardian* reporter, Malcolm Pithers, claimed in his article on 29 March 1982 that Home Secretary William Whitelaw had not yet studied the *Sunday Times* dossier. Furthermore, Pithers stated that the dossier had not revealed any new and substantive evidence.

A few days later I was busy in South Africa, with my colleague Detective Sergeant Kevin Sutton. We were seeking evidence from potential witnesses out there to help prove or disprove serious allegations of police corruption in Sheffield. I had time on the long-haul flights to reflect on what I had read in the *Sunday Times* of their 'investigation'. I also thought back, yet again, to the evening early in December 1979 when I volunteered to take over Bob Dixon's on-call duty, that quiet Monday night when neither of us expected other than a peaceful night. The newspaper did not know that it was by sheer chance I was called to investigate the Hastie fire, but that was irrelevant now. It was obvious that the *Sunday Times* was out to engineer my downfall whether I deserved it or not.

My thoughts were compounded by the fact that the reporter had not asked to see me, at least to point out what his 'new' evidence was. And I knew from my experience in other major enquiries that, where journalists' intentions were honourable in that kind of enquiry, they at least queried their information with the senior investigating officer.

At that time it was normal practice for flights on the Heathrow to Johannesburg route to make refuelling stops in Nairobi. Just a few minutes after taking off from Nairobi on our way back to London one night in April 1981, the 747 jet developed serious engine trouble. The Captain told everyone on board about the problem and explained that in the interests of safety, the fuel he had just taken on board would have to be jettisoned. That would take about 28 minutes and the fuel would be jettisoned high over the wilds of Kenya and would cause no problems for the wildlife 20,000 feet below. When the operation was complete, all being well, we would be returning to Nairobi. Practically everyone on board knew that having to jettison practically all the fuel meant there was a possibility of a crash landing and that the fuel was being dumped to lessen the fire risk. Looking around, I saw many passengers gripping their seat arm rests. No one spoke and there was a fair amount of tension in the cabin. My sergeant, Kevin Sutton, was oblivious to it all as he slept off the effects of the generous supply of whisky which a delightful stewardess chose to ply him with during the four-hour flight up from Johannesburg earlier in the night. It may sound foolish now, but, as the fuel was being jettisoned during those rather long 28 minutes, I wondered what the *Sunday Times* journalists would have made of my demise had the plane crashed and killed us.

I gave Sergeant Sutton a shove, woke him up and told him that there was just a possibility that we were about to find ourselves in a crash landing. We needed to weigh up those passengers around us who looked best able to help should the worst happen. But we landed safely amid an amazing amount of excited hand-clapping from our 400 fellow passengers. Funnily enough, on the flight out to Johannesburg I read the book written by Earl Moorhouse entitled, *Wake Up – It's A Crash*. It's the story of the first 747 jumbo jet disaster, which happened at Nairobi Airport.

We had only been back in Hull a few days when I heard more about the *Sunday Times* endeavour. Detective Constable Mick Sothcott told me that a reporter had approached him outside his home and asked him to 'spill the beans' on the Lee enquiry. Mick told him that 'the beans' had already been spilt in the Crown Court!

Mick, bless him, died from cancer in 1995. He was one of the best ferreting kind of detectives I knew and he was one of the officers I kept on the Lee enquiry throughout. He also told me that he had heard that, apart from everything else, the newspaper was going to attempt to prove that I could not have written the number of words which I had, in fact, written in the time I had done so. I had not thought about it before but I knew, for example, I had written Lee's voluntary statements contemporaneously and in a manner I have previously described, at the rate of a page of about 100 words every ten minutes or so.

As I write this I recall that, whilst it was always my practice to write voluntary statements under caution and interview notes contemporaneously, it was not until 1984 that it became compulsory for all police officers in England and Wales to make all their interview notes contemporaneously. I, and many of my colleagues, could never have been satisfied with the reliability of such notes in any other way. But then in those days we did not have the benefit of tape recorders, video's and all the other safeguards for both officer and suspect which the Police and Criminal Evidence Act of 1984 introduced.

On 23 May 1982, the *Sunday Times* published another story about Lee. This time it was headed: '"MASS KILLER" LEE LODGES APPEAL AFTER INSIGHT PROBE'.

It stated that Lee's chances of an appeal hearing were thought to be good because the *Sunday Times* dossier revealed major flaws in my investigation. Was the newspaper man trying to be a better lawyer than Lee's defence counsel, Mr. Harry Ognall, I wondered. Flaws indeed! My sanity, my job, and my good name were on the line because of those ill-founded 'major flaws'.

But quietly I was happy that an appeal appeared to be on the way.

About this time I heard that, apparently at the journalist's instigation, Lee had now changed the solicitor who acted for him from the time of his arrest to conviction. I did, however, gather that Mr. Harry Ognall was still acting for him. His continued presence was pleasing for he knew all there was to know about the case.

On Tuesday afternoon, 29 June 1982, I returned to Hull from Sheffield and, at his request, I saw Chief Constable David Hall in his office. He told me that Mr. Vivien Brook, an assistant Chief Constable from South Wales, had been asked to enquire into the *Sunday Times* dossier on behalf of the Court of Appeal. The Home Secretary had passed the papers to the Court of Appeal in view of an application from Lee's new solicitor for leave to appeal. Many questions posed in the dossier were apparently ambiguous and had not been made clear. David Hall told me that no one had made an official complaint against me or my handling of Lee's case and in any event it was policy that official complaints against the police were never taken purely from newspaper reports alone. Mr. Hall then announced that Vivien Brook had arrived at Hull Police Headquarters that day and was about to start his work. I was glad it had not been left to the media to inform me. I was asked to assist Mr. Brook in whatever way I could. I had not met him before but I knew his reputation as demanding, unforgiving and of the highest integrity. With a fair amount of trepidation in my heart, I met him a few minutes later.

Did Mr. Brook believe what he had read in the dossier, I wondered. No, I reasoned. Knowing a little about him, I knew that he would believe nothing without corroboration. He weighed me up as I introduced myself to him. He looked stern and tough and I thought, 'Well, after so much journalistic rambling it now appears that this is the start of a thorough review of my investigation.' The final result would be a full and proper legal inquisition in the Court of Appeal before three distinguished High Court judges. I thought I could now see the glimmer of a light at the end of it all.

I spent several days being questioned about every aspect of the enquiry. Everything, from the moment I volunteered for the on-call duty the night Edith Hastie lost her three boys to the last time I saw Lee, was covered. In due course my note books were examined word for word. Numerous statements and enquiry forms were subjected to electrostatic document-analysis testing. This could help to prove the authenticity of everything from confessions to written telephone messages by suggesting the police records had, or had not, been made contemporaneously.

A day or so after Mr. Brook's arrival, I found that I was getting more messages from the Hull underworld, national newspapermen, and even some members of the legal profession, telling me that the *Sunday Times* reporter was leaving no stone unturned in his attempt to prove Lee innocent. On one occasion a national newspaper journalist telephoned to tell me that the man was preparing 'a two-page spread' about Lee and that the article would allege I had altered some of the evidence in the case. The article would be published next Sunday, 4 July 1982.

I took this opportunity to ask my journalist friend how it was that his daily newspaper and the other nationals had not taken the Lee story up in the same way as the *Sunday Times*. He answered promptly: 'We are all satisfied there is nothing for us to find, so we are leaving the *Sunday Times* crowd to stew in their own juice.' That, at least, pleased me, but I knew that I was still being subjected to a witch hunt of the kind I could not muster in any legally based criminal enquiry. I am not in any way a privileged human being. I was not the perfect detective, either; I don't know anyone who is, but I was the *Sunday Times'* target with the newspaper's journalists behaving like hungry dogs savagely biting at a bone with imaginary meat on it.

I was naturally apprehensive when I awoke on Sunday, 4 July. By now I was expecting several telephone calls from well-meaning colleagues and friends, about newspaper delivery time, should there be any notable item printed which affected any enquiry I was involved in. It was a quiet day and there was no sign of the expected report.

The following Friday, 9 July, I spoke to prosecuting counsel in the Lee case, Mr. Gerald Coles, and discussed the ever-increasing likelihood of our attending the Appeal Court. I was now treating the information that the newspaper was going to accuse me of altering evidence as nothing but gossip. There was nothing on Sunday, 11 July, but the following Sunday morning, 18 July 1982, I was dismayed when I received my first telephone call of the day. My well-meaning caller told me that the *Sunday Times* had published a long and detailed story about Lee. Soon afterwards one of my officers called at my home and showed me the *Sunday Times* report. The headline read: 'Bruce Lee: HOW VITAL EVIDENCE WAS ALTERED'. Apart from describing, in considerable detail, the first few months of the enquiry in Selby Street, and questioning my every move at the time, the article showed a sketch of Selby Street with a Rover car and two men running from Edith Hastie's house. There was also a photograph of the man who claimed to have seen the Rover, a photograph of Bruce Lee, and an old press photograph of myself. It went on to support its headline by alleging that 'police persuaded the so-called Rover car witness, a key witness, to sign a false statement after Lee had confessed'.

Everyone on the enquiry knew we had never been satisfied that the Rover story was true and we had discontinued it some time before Lee was arrested. The false statement allegation was a lie and, by inference, it accused me of serious wrongdoing. This latest article made me angry – and that normally takes a lot of doing. The re-hashed Rover story naturally brought back the whole of the savagery of the fire at Edith Hastie's home and would obviously bring awfully sad memories back to her, so my heartache and anger was nothing compared with her feelings. How I wished Lee had pleaded not guilty so that all the masses of evidence could have been published.

The 'evidence altered' story also reported Vivien Brook's presence in Hull and stated that he was enquiring into the case. The following day several national newspapers reported that Mr. Brook's enquiry was underway. Kevin McNamara was reported as saying he welcomed the police enquiry. 'Public confidence in the police can only be restored by such an investigation,' he said. He added that he hoped Lee's lawyers would be successful in their attempts to win a fresh trial.

More newspaper articles appeared throughout the summer of 1982. I was still fully engaged investigating a number of serious allegations from members of the criminal fraternity against South Yorkshire police officers. Several detectives were suspended there, and I found that, although my work in Sheffield demanded every moment of my time and consideration, as time went on so the Sunday newspaper reports were niggling away at me and, when I was travelling, they were becoming something of a preoccupation. One day a man who read the *Sunday Times* articles wrote to my Chief Constable saying it was 'essential' that I be dismissed. I wondered if he had ever sat on a jury and found someone guilty when there was no evidence, or someone not guilty when there was. I was not dismissed.

Rumour, speculation and gossip were plentiful. Had I been suspended? Was I suspended? When was I going to be suspended? Members of the criminal fraternity, where I had many informers, were often commenting on my situation and several were offering their street-wise advice should matters get much worse. I considered taking legal action against the newspaper but delayed making a decision as I believed that the Court of Appeal would eventually resolve the matter. Most of my senior officer colleagues remained deadly silent on the subject, not wanting to be contaminated by an officer under suspicion.

In October 1982, I learned that an Appeal Court judge was to consider an application from Lee's new solicitor and counsel for legal aid to prepare for a full appeal against all his fire convictions. I so very much hoped they would be successful with the application. There was now only one way I could see to clear the air once and for all and that was a hearing in the Court of Appeal.

On Sunday, 20 March 1983, another sickening piece of unfounded reporting appeared when the *Sunday Times* published yet another report. It was headed: 'THE CASE FOR RETRYING BRUCE LEE'. The story simply repeated much of what had already been written but this time it was penned with even more of a sinister motive in mind. Lee falsely confessed, it read. Confessions were heard by detectives only. The story went on to say that the Wensley Lodge fire could only have been started by plumber Steven Hay.

The weekend of 20 March was a rest period for twelve Sheffield jurors who had already spent a week in Sheffield Crown Court, listening to a drug conspiracy charge I had brought against a Sheffield detective sergeant. They listened to the evidence I gave about the sergeant and about my interview with him, and they listened as I told them how the sergeant made a voluntary statement under caution confessing to his illegal dealings with a heroin dealer. There was no doubt that some of the jurors, and even the trial judge and lawyers there, read the *Sunday Times* that weekend, and now, the following day, I was standing before them in the witness box being questioned about my interview with one of their detective sergeants. If a newspaper, and the *Sunday Times* at that, doubted my integrity, would twelve good people from South Yorkshire believe me now in this important trial? I had no idea. No one talked about the Lee case in the Crown Court but outside in the corridor one Sheffield police officer did have the audacity to mutter something about the *Sunday Times* making sure that I found myself accused in court before long.

A week later the detective sergeant was found guilty and sentenced to three years imprisonment. I am not a gambler, but the chances were that the latest *Sunday Times* lies were timed to cause me the utmost embarrassment at a most delicate time in the case against the detective sergeant.

During an enquiry into another quite separate criminal allegation against the South Yorkshire Police, a local solicitor, representing a man making the allegation, approached me one afternoon. He said, 'I have read about you in a Sunday newspaper regarding this man Lee and your enquiries about him. It makes me wonder if you are a fit and proper person to be carrying out the enquiries for my client.'

I asked the obvious question. 'Are you referring to the *Sunday Times*?'

'Of course I am,' he replied.

'I am surprised that someone from the legal profession is so taken in by an uncorroborated item in a newspaper. The truth is said to make the devil blush you know and I put you in that category.'

He made no further comment about the Lee saga.

About ten days later the Deputy Chief Constable of Humberside told me that the Chairman of the Humberside Police Committee had spoken to him about the *Sunday Times* reports, and, in view of the allegations, suggested that I should be suspended from duty. I was not suspended then, or at any other time.

A few days afterwards, although I knew unofficially, the *Hull Daily Mail* announced that Mr. Vivien Brook's enquiry was now complete. 'A spokesman for the Director of Public Prosecutions confirmed today (24 March 1983) that the report has been with them for two to three weeks and is now being considered,' the *Mail* said.

Several of the more humorous junior officers I know read the *Hull Daily Mail* and asked me what charges were going to be preferred against me when the DPP had considered the findings of the Brook enquiry. 'If a newspaper as influential as the *Sunday Times* says you are crooked then it must be so, and we have got you all wrong,' said one with a laugh. Quoting Mark Twain, he added, 'Are they going to hang you anyhow – and try you afterwards?'

'It seems they have already done it,' added Detective Constable Mick Sothcott.

Time rolled on. The Humberside Police Authority eventually called a special meeting to discuss facts connected with the Lee case and Police Committee Chairman Charles Brady was reported to have told the media, 'There is too much speculation going on. It is time to clear the air. We are not going to discuss the Bruce Lee case because that is *sub judice*. It is a very sensitive situation where someone has made an appeal against a sentence. He pleaded guilty and has been put away because of that. The Chief Constable is going to give the Committee facts to clarify the position and end speculation.'

Charles Brady had not apparently got his facts absolutely correct insofar as the appeal was concerned, as the proposed appeal was against conviction and sentence, even though Lee had pleaded guilty. His legal advisers were also seeking to call fresh evidence, and to seek ultimately a retrial. I just hoped they would be successful, at the very least with a Court of Appeal hearing. I did not know it at that time, but Charles Brady was to save my neck several years later.

I was still considering legal action against the *Sunday Times*, but, in view of the pending Court of Appeal hearing, it was inappropriate, in my view, to take any civil action before then. Nevertheless I forwarded a file of the most relevant statements to my Superintendents Association in London with a view to seeking advice on my proposed civil action. In due course I was advised that the meanings in the articles were highly defamatory of myself and that they were largely allegations of fact to which justification would be the only defence. I was advised that it was essential that the criticism made by the *Sunday Times* be closely examined before proceedings were threatened or commenced. Clearly, I needed to wait to clear my name.

Finally, as summer turned to autumn I received official word that Lee's long-awaited appeal hearing was to take place before three Appeal Court judges (Lord Justice Ackner, Mr. Justice Glidwell and Mr. Justice Leggatt), commencing on 14 November 1983. I was well pleased. I could hardly wait, as I would now have an opportunity to answer any question, from the *Sunday Times*-generated nonsense to the cumulative brain power and experience put to me by the three highly distinguished judges.

And, importantly, Bruce Lee would now be able to receive the justice he was entitled to, despite his guilty pleadings at Leeds Crown Court.

Chapter Twenty Five

The Appeal Court hearing was delayed by a week but finally began on 22 November 1983. It was now nearly three years after Lee's appearance before the Crown Court and three and a half years since he was arrested. His lawyers had quite properly drawn up Lee's Grounds of Appeal, notwithstanding the expiration of the normal time limit, for leave to appeal against his convictions. In the premises, Lee's Grounds of Appeal were threefold:

1) That his pleas of guilty were ill considered and were significantly out of accord with the evidence.
2) In the circumstances, in the absence of the alleged confession, there was no evidence in respect of any count on any indictment upon which a jury could safely convict, and in the context of the case and the state of mind of Lee and the evidence which he would seek to adduce the validity of the confessions was called into question.
3) The learned Trial Judge erred in accepting Lee's pleas of guilty and failed to put the Crown to strict proof.

The Court of Appeal was told that Lee's convictions related to 11 fires and the deaths of 26 people, including the 11 men at Wensley Lodge.

Mr. Gerald Coles, Q.C., for the Crown, said Lee's application should not proceed and that, if the evidence had been defective, or if Lee had been overborne by the police, then an adjournment could have been requested. But there were no such applications before the Crown Court. The case had proceeded in the normal way and Lee went to hospital. He accepted the situation, buckled down to his incarceration and had, albeit erratically, continued to admit he was an arsonist. It was not until March 1982, said Mr. Coles, that the article in the *Sunday Times* 'started a hare' and led him to believe that there was a chance of regaining his freedom.

Lord Justice Ackner said that the Court was empowered to hear fresh evidence – despite the unequivocal pleas of guilty – if it was expedient and necessary to do so. He added that the Court did not want Lee's case in this respect to be regarded as setting a general precedent but the Court regarded the case as 'wholly exceptional, if not unique'.

'We have read the account in the *Sunday Times* and can well appreciate the public concern that the articles must have occasioned,' Lord Justice Ackner said.

Mr. Gerald Coles told the three judges that the police had uncovered other evidence to connect Lee with other fires but he stressed that the Crown was not trying to add to Lee's list of convictions (I had good evidence to connect him with other fires, but none of those fires caused harm to anyone and I did not consider it worthwhile pursuing enquiries further.) It was not part of the Crown's intentions to put or keep this young man's name in the Guinness Book of Records, continued Mr. Coles, but it was very much part of the Crown's concern to ensure that a dangerous arsonist was kept in the right place. The fires, he said, had all the hallmarks of arson. Some of the victims were people against whom Lee had a grudge. It would have been wicked and monstrous for the police to have put all the facts relating to the fires into Lee's mind.

Mr. Harry Ognall told the judges that the case, if not unique, was highly unusual and should cause the court 'profound anxiety'. Lee, though he had made a total of 12 written confessions and pleaded guilty, was now seeking late permission to appeal against his convictions, to call fresh evidence and to seek, ultimately, a retrial. He would also seek leave to give evidence himself so that he could explain his confessions. Furthermore, he added, it was the unanimous opinion of doctors that Lee had a severely disordered and psychopathic personality.

'Lee had achieved a harmonious relationship with a very senior policeman, Detective Superintendent Sagar, between June and August, 1980 – a kind of relationship he had never enjoyed before. Whether he had been prompted to confess and become the homicide record holder one would never know,' Mr. Ognall commented. 'But even before the trial those representing him were gravely troubled as to whether his motives stemmed from an acknowledgement of genuine guilt for these appalling crimes or not. We think it is essential to call Lee to explain why he pleaded guilty. He will also give his version of his many interviews with the police. He is a greatly changed young man. He has, in fact, mentally improved and he is physically almost unrecognisable from the pathetic creature with whom I had so many encounters,' said Mr. Ognall.

He told the judges that the circumstances of the case betrayed very curious features and there must, at the very least, be substantial doubt as to his responsibility for these crimes – if they are crimes at all'. Mr. Ognall went on to say that it would be part of Lee's case that police had suggested parts of his confessions to him, in fact, he said, 'It will be our contention that he had words put into his mouth.'

When I heard this I was annoyed but not really surprised, for the newspaper campaign was always aiming to hit me right between the eyes with this kind of allegation. But was I really hearing those words? I was actually being accused of manufacturing a series of interviews; of making up confessions; of conspiring to pervert the course of justice; of committing perjury. Indeed, it would have been wicked and monstrous for the police to do such a thing.

Acting on instructions Mr. Ognall said it was all too clear that for 'police' one should read Detective Superintendent Sagar. For the life of me I could not see what motive I could have had to do such a thing. Mr. Ognall urged the three judges to order a retrial for Lee rather than determine the appeal themselves. There was in his opinion a legitimate public interest in the case which demanded that the verdicts should be in the hands of a jury and not in the hands of three judges.

I was not concerned whether the case went before a jury or the three judges as long as the matter was properly resolved and my name was cleared. It was now abundantly clear that Lee's admissions would be open to a very strong challenge from Mr. Ognall and I knew that, whoever listened to the challenge, could do nothing but accept the truth.

On Tuesday, 22 November 1983, the second day of the hearing, the Appeal Court refused Lee leave to appeal against his convictions for arson and manslaughter relating to the fire at Edith Hastie's home in December 1979. The decision followed a ruling that Lee's counsel could not call evidence relating to his confessions to starting other fires, in an attempt to show that his confession to the Selby Street fire was unreliable. Mr. Ognall then abandoned the Selby Street appeal and told the Court that he would not be calling any new evidence in respect of Selby Street. So the arson and three manslaughter convictions in respect of Selby Street stood firm. It was, in other words, accepted, at least by the court, that I had not 'put words into Lee's mouth' in relation to Selby Street.

Lord Justice Ackner ruled that the hearing before him and his two fellow judges should resemble as closely as possible the trial which would have taken place at Leeds had Lee pleaded not guilty. In my discussions with Crown Counsel in late 1980, it was agreed that the Crown case at Leeds would start with the Hastie arson and manslaughter charges, and details about the other fires would not be mentioned until the Hastie case was over, as such evidence was inadmissible and, of course, unfair to Lee. The Appeal Court now ruled that the same would apply in the appeal hearing. Mr. Ognall told the judges that justice demanded that the court examine all the fires, and, added, 'It would be utterly wrong that this man should languish in a special hospital with one more homicide than is justified, to his name. I could not agree more. The court then decided to deal with the fire at the home of Ros Fenton at Troutbeck House, near to where Lee was then living. Bruce George Peter Lee was then called to give evidence. He was flanked by two uniformed prison officers as he stood and affirmed that he would tell the truth. I was surprised that he did not swear on the Bible but, of course, affirming serves the same purpose.

'I want to ask you straight away about Ros Fenton's flat at Troutbeck House,' he continued.

'Did you set fire to that flat?'

'No.'

'It is said against you that, on the night of 22 June 1979, you set fire to that flat by dropping a lighted paper inside the doorway of Ros Fenton's flat. Is there any truth in that allegation?'

'No.'

'Did you know where Mrs. Fenton's flat was?'

'Yes.'

'At 407 Troutbeck House?'

'Yes.'

'Is it correct, as the judges have been told, that you lived quite nearby?'

'Yes, I lived in the next block.'

'Thank you. We know that Mrs. Fenton had a next-door neighbour, Mrs. King. Did you know that lady?'

'Yes.'

'How well did you know that lady?'

'Fairly well. I knew her two children as well.'

'Did you know in June of 1979 that Mrs. King had fallen out with, or had a quarrel with, Mrs. Fenton?'

'No.'

'How well did you get on with Mrs. Fenton, if and when you saw her?'

'Well, I only saw her to say hello and that.'

'Did you ever have any quarrel with Mrs. Fenton?'
'No. I had no cause to.'
'On the night of 22 June 1979, on the evening of that day, were you at any stage anywhere near 407 or 409 Troutbeck House?'
'No.'
'Not at all?'
'No. I was in my house.'
'I do not know, Mr. Lee, but there may be evidence that at some stage of that evening you were on the balcony outside 407 Troutbeck House in Mrs. King's company. Do you understand?'
'Yes.'
'If that evidence were to be given to this court, what do you say about it? Were you ever on the balcony that evening?'
'Well, I can't remember, but as far as I know I was in the house.'
'When did you become aware, if you did, that there had been a fire in Mrs. Fenton's flat?'
'The next day.'
'Would you please tell the court how you got on with Mr. Sagar during those interviews?'
'Fairly well.'
'What was his attitude towards you?'
'Regarding?'
'Regarding you as a person. How did he treat you?'
'He treated me all right.'
'Did you like or dislike him, or did you have no feelings about him at all?'
'Well, I didn't dislike him.'
'Can you remember how many times you were questioned by that officer and his colleagues?'
'No.'
'Was it a lot?'
'Too many.'
'Why do you say too many?'
'Well, I was going from Leeds prison and also coming from Hull down to Leeds as well.'
'To see you?'
'Yes.'
'So, sometimes you would be taken from the prison at Leeds and other times they would visit you at the prison?'
'Yes.'
'What I wanted to know, if you can assist us, is why you said, "too many times"?'
'Because it was. It was more than once or twice a week – if you understand.'
'How did you feel about these large number of meetings you had with the police?'
'Well, afterwards it just got me down and that is the main reason really.'
'You say that is the main reason, because it got you down. What is it the main reason for? What you are telling us.'
Lee then said, 'I am not trying to say nowt against the police, but there

was times when he would just come up and put things—you know, he would ask his questions, but rather than asking he would be putting things into my head, sort of like: "Would it be possible that you did this sort of thing this way?" and just for argument's sake and because of the lengthy time I did admit it, you see, because it was a long time. I just said, "Yeah."'

'When he put things to you and you just said "Yeah", as you told us, were you telling the truth or not?'

'No.'

'Then why did you say yes when he put these various things to you, if by saying yes you were not telling the truth. What is your explanation for that?'

'Well, I was fed up with him asking me all the different questions at the time really.'

'Mr. Lee did you realise in saying yes, as you have told us, in making these admissions, how serious you were making your position, or not?'

'No.'

'It is now nearly three and a half years since you were arrested, Mr. Lee. You remember that. Is your memory of the events between yourself and the police still clear, or has it faded?'

'It has faded in some parts. There is parts where if I had been able to – if I had been able to remember those parts I would have been able to tell you – you know things.'

'Do you mean that you have forgotten some things.'

'Yes.'

'So you cannot tell us about them now. Is that what you are saying?'

'Some things I will be able to tell you. If not, I will just say I can't answer.'

'Very well. I am going to ask you about Troutbeck House and your conversations with the police about Troutbeck House . . . First of all, was it you who first mentioned Troutbeck House to the police, or was it the police who first mentioned it to you?'

'The police.'

'Do you remember, and I am not asking you for the exact words, but the sort of thing they were saying to you about Troutbeck House?'

'No.'

'You do not? Were they suggesting you were responsible or not?'

'I don't know. You see, there was one time, I can't remember which fire it was at, but there was one time. They asked if I done a fire and I said, "No." This was the Saturday I think. I went out on to the courtyard for a walk and this policeman was walking around and he is going: "Come on, admit to this fire. One more."'

'Which policeman was this?'

'I can't remember which policeman, I'm sorry.'

'I would like you to think about Troutbeck House in particular and your conversations with the police. You say you do not remember what allegation the police put to you, but I want to remind you, Mr. Lee, of what the police say you said about it. Will you listen to me carefully. The police say that you said this to them, "Look, I did do that one, but it wasn't through the letterbox." Now did you say that, or words like that to the police?'

Lee shook his head.

Mr. Ognall said, 'You shake your head. Please answer.'
'No.'
'Before I go into further detail, did you, by your own mouth, admit the fire to Troutbeck House to the police, or not?'
'No.'
Mr. Ognall, addressing the judges, said, 'My Lords, I am not, in the light of that answer, going to go *seriatim* through the whole of the conversation unless you believe that I would be acting improperly.'
Speaking to Lee, he continued,' I want to remind you of one or two passages about Troutbeck House which the police say you said. They say that you said this: "I just opened the door, see. It wasn't shut properly and I just got some paper, set it alight with my matches and then threw it well inside the door. It went up in no time." Did you say those words, or anything like those words, Mr. Lee.'
'I can't remember.'
'You cannot remember.'
'Under pressure I might have done. I don't know.'
'You were asked this by Mr. Sagar: "Why fire Ros Fenton's house?", and you replied, according to Mr. Sagar, "I like fires. I do. I like fires." Do you remember whether or not you said those words?'
'No.'
'You do not remember. Very well. Do you think you might have said those words, or words like them, or can you not say?'
'I can't say, sorry.'
'Do you like fires?'
'No.'
'Or watching fires?'
'No.'
'The police say that, in a later interview, Mr. Lee, this is what you said about Troutbeck: "Thank God someone saw the flames at Troutbeck or there'd be more killed and that. All them flats so close together." You heard those words. I have just read them out. Did you say those words to the police?'
'I don't know.'
'I want to ask you one or two general questions first, Mr. Lee.'
Mr. Ognall then went on to question Lee about the voluntary statements he made and whether he read them before signing them. He continued: 'Did you know that what you were being asked to sign were admissions that you set fire to those places. Did you know that?'
'Not at the time, no.'
'What did you think you were being asked to sign then?'
'I didn't know. I mean as I said, all he did was turn round and say: "Sign this."'
'Had there been a lot of writing down on paper before you were asked to sign it?'
'Yes.'
'Who by?'
'Mr. Sagar.'
'What did you think he was writing down, Mr. Lee, on these occasions?'

'I don't know. I didn't ask him. I mean, I didn't know what he was writing down.'
'And you never asked what you were being asked to sign?'
Lee did not reply.
'It appears that you accept that you did sign these statements although you did not know what they were?'
'Yes.'
'I am going to read out to you what appears in one of these written statements you signed. Will you listen to me carefully please: "I like fires and you will think I am a fucking fire bug."'
'Did you say anything like that to the police officers?'
'I don't know,' replied Lee, who then sighed loudly.
Mr. Ognall continued his examination of Lee and the voluntary statements. Lee denied uttering the words contained in them. Mr. Ognall then moved to Lee's appearance before Leeds Crown Court. Addressing Lee once more, he asked, 'This court knows, Mr. Lee, that in January 1981, you remember, you came to court in Leeds?'
'Yes.'
'And you there pleaded guilty to causing a large number of deaths by setting fire to a large number of premises?'
'Yes.'
'First of all you pleaded guilty?'
'Yes.'
'Did you understand clearly what you were pleading guilty to: that is killing these people by setting fire to the places where they were?'
Lee shook his head but made no reply.
'You shake your head. What is your answer?'
'No.'
Lord Justice Ackner asked, 'Is his answer: 'I did not understand what I was pleading to?'
Mr. Ognall, 'My Lord, I will deal with it again because it may be of importance.'
Addressing Lee, he said, 'Did you understand the charges that you were pleading to?'
'No.'
'Why not?'
'Because of my state of mind at the time. I wasn't myself and after all the police and things people were saying: "Do this. Do that." You yourself (Mr. Ognall) you did try and persuade me to plead not guilty which I was going to do anyway. But I have changed my mind so many times.'
'Stop please. Did your Lordships get that?'
Lord Justice Ackner: 'No, I did not. I got the phrase: 'To plead not guilty which I was going to do anyway.'
Mr. Ognall: 'That is right. It was referring to me, my Lords. Then he said: "But, I have changed my mind so many times anyway." I am sorry to have to put it in this personal sense, my Lords, but I can see no way out of it.'
Turning to Lee, Mr. Ognall continued, 'Why, if I had done my best to persuade you to plead not guilty, Mr. Lee, did you on the morning of that day

in fact plead guilty?'

'Because I didn't want a lengthy trial. I couldn't have stood a lengthy trial.'

'Had you any idea, on that day, where you were likely to be going when the proceedings on that day were finished, in other words, whether you were going to prison or a hospital?'

'I knew, yes.'

'Where did you believe you would be going to?'

'Park Lane.'

'The hospital in Liverpool?'

'Yes.'

'How did you feel about that, as opposed to remaining in the prison in Leeds?'

'I would have preferred prison if that's what you mean.'

'That is exactly what I wanted to know. Why then, if you preferred to stay in prison and you knew that you would be going to a hospital after you had pleaded guilty, did you plead guilty?'

'Because I told you, because of the state of mind I was in . . .'

'Were you relying, Mr. Lee, on anybody's advice, other than your barrister's advice when you pleaded guilty.'

'No.'

Cross-examined by Mr. Coles, Lee was asked, 'You knew you were not guilty when you were being interviewed by Mr. Sagar?'

'What do you mean?'

'You knew you were not guilty when you were being interviewed by Mr. Sagar?'

'Yes.'

'Did you at any time try to persuade him that you were not guilty?'

'Yes.'

'You did. Did you at any time tell him that you were not guilty?'

'I cannot remember.'

'You cannot remember. Mr. Sagar, you say, you still do not dislike? Is that right?'

'Yes.'

'In fact, you got on really rather well with him, did you not?'

'That's what I said before, yes.'

'Were you surprised how kind they were?'

'Yes.'

'You were. Did you tell them that?'

'I can't remember if I did or not.'

'Might you have done so?'

'I might have.'

'Did you at one stage ask Mr. Sagar if he would provide you with a Bible?'

'Yes.'

'What did you want to do with that?'

'Read it.'

'Your reading was up to that, was it?'

'I could understand it and if I didn't I'd ask.'

'And Mr. Sagar was kind enough to provide you with one?'
'Yes.'
'Did you, at the time you were talking, about that, ever say: "Look, Mr. Sagar, I didn't do Troutbeck House?"'
'I don't know if I did or not.'
'You said to my Lords a short time ago that it was afterwards that it got you down. It was not anything that happened in any particular interview that upset you, but just the great number of interviews, one after the other?'
'That's it.'
'Did you ever say to Mr. Sagar, or any one of the other police officers: "I'm fed up with this. You are always coming and asking me questions. Stop it!"?'
'I don't know if I did or not. I might have done, I might not.'
Mr. Coles went on to ask, 'Is it right to say, Mr. Lee, that the more you agreed with the police officers the more questions they asked?'
'Yes.'
'Then if it was pressure of the interviews that was getting you down, why did you go on saying yes?'
'So they could finish and I could get back to my cell.'
'But you are not foolish and you have just agreed with me, the more you said yes, the more questions they asked?'
'Yes.'
Mr. Coles then questioned Lee about his affidavit, prepared by his legal advisers, for the purposes of the appeal: 'You say (in the affidavit) that shortly before your Crown Court appearance Dr. Sasiene told me that there would be a place specially waiting for me at a special hospital in Liverpool if I pleaded guilty to manslaughter on the basis of diminished responsibility. At the time this prospect seemed more attractive . . . Is that right?'
'Yes.'
'I have two questions about that. Why is it that you told their Lordships this morning that it was the prospect of going to prison that was more attractive?'
'I thought you meant now. I'm sorry. I didn't understand what you were asking.'
'I see. You mean now that you have been to a special hospital you think you would rather be in prison?'
'Yes.'
'Did you understand what was written down here (in the affidavit) about pleading guilty to manslaughter on the basis of diminished responsibility?'
'No.'
'You understood, did you not, that if you pleaded guilty to murder you would go to prison?'
'I understood that.'
'And you understood that if you pleaded guilty – let's leave it at this – to something else, you would go to hospital?'
'Yes.'
'You knew you had a choice, did you not?
'Yes.'
'Your lawyers were trying to persuade you to plead not guilty?'

'That's right.'
'And you went against that advice?'
'That's right.'
Mr. Coles, continuing to ask Lee about his appeal affidavit, said, 'You say that you accept that on many occasions Detective Superintendent Sagar appeared to be taking notes . . . Is that right?'
Lee nodded.
'You nod, Mr. Lee. Is that true of the interview about Troutbeck House. He was always making notes, was he not?'
'Yes.'
'You used to make jokes about it, did you not?'
'Now and again.'
'Do you remember going out in motor cars and you used to make jokes then about him forever writing in his notebook?'
'Yes.'
'When you were interviewed, it is said by Mr. Sagar that you said, "I like fires. I do. I like fires." Might you have said them?'
'I don't know and if I did I don't know why I did for the simple reason that I don't like them anyway.'
'Did you say to Mr. Sagar: ". . . you will think I am a fucking fire bug"?'
'I've just answered your question. I said I don't know.'
'Throughout all this Mr. Sagar was very quiet in the way he spoke, was he not?'
'Yes.'
'He speaks quite slowly and gently?'
'Yes, but one or two places he tried to ask me two questions – difficult questions at the same time, and you cannot answer it with one answer.'
'He always let you explain everything, did he not?'
'Not all the time, no.'
'He spent very long hours with you, did he not?'
'Yeah.'
In answer to further questioning by Mr. Coles, Lee denied confessing to the fire at Troutbeck House, or having any interest in it. Mr. Coles ended his cross-examination by asking Lee, 'Was it sheer coincidence that the fire was so near to your home and you did not even have an interest in it?'
'It had nowt to do with me, did it?'
Lee was then re-examined by his Counsel, Mr. Ognall. 'You have been asked a number of questions about how Mr. Sagar treated you? You have heard those questions?'
'Yes.'
'I want to remind you of one conversation which, it is said, you had with Mr. Sagar and see what you tell us about it. Did you appreciate Mr. Sagar's interest in you?'
'Most probably.'
'Had many people in your life shown interest in you, Mr. Lee, before then or not?'
'Not many. There is a few, or there was a few.'
'Mr. Sagar said you said this and tell me if you remember saying it, please.

You said to him: "Do you know somat, you are the only bloke I know who shows any interest in me." Do you remember saying words like that to him?'
'I might have done.'
Lord Justice Ackner then referred to Lee's voluntary statement regarding Troutbeck House: 'At the bottom it is said that it is your handwriting?'
'Yes.'
'There is this: "i Bruce George Peter Lee—with the spelling, apparently, as you have put it — "i have read the above statement and i have been told that i can correct alter or add anything i wish this statement is true i have made it—"and then the word "on" is crossed out and initialled by you— "of my own free will". It is signed: B. Lee. Do you see that?'
'Yes.'
'Do you remember writing the bottom of the statement in your own handwriting, the phrase that you read it, that you had had an opportunity to correct or alter anything and that it was true?'
'Yes.'
'Well, why did you write that out in your own handwriting?'
'I don't know.'
So Lee's evidence was concluded.
The following day I was examined by Mr. Coles. I had not been in court to hear Lee give his evidence and, consequently, I did not know what he had said. As I walked into the court room I saw him for the first time for many months. He seemed quite calm and observant and faintly smiled as he watched me take the oath.
Mr. Coles asked if the fire at Troutbeck House had been dealt with by the police initially, and had I visited Ros Fenton before interviewing Lee.
I told the court that the police had dealt with the fire initially and I had in fact seen Mrs. Fenton and had read the statements my officers had taken. I then gave the evidence of my interview with Lee. Asked if I took a contemporaneous note of the interview I told the judges that I had taken a contemporaneous note, but the pace of the interview was very much slower than that which I was now giving the evidence.
Asked what I knew about how the fire started I answered: 'I do not think I knew anything for sure. I had read the statements. I felt concerned about the lack of (investigative) activity by the police at the time of the fire and I think I was more inquisitive about Lee than what I might have read.'
I gave the whole of the evidence relating to my interview with Lee about the fire at Troutbeck House.
Asked about Lee reading his voluntary statement and then adding the last paragraph in his own handwriting, I said, 'I had a card and I read it to him. I told him what was required and he then copied the card. Of course he read the statement beforehand.'
Mr. Justice Leggatt asked, 'Did he sign the statement anywhere?'
'Yes at the bottom of each page, my Lord.'
'Did Lee appear articulate, Mr. Sagar, or did he appear confused?' asked Mr. Coles.
'He certainly did not appear confused.'
'Did he appear nervous?'

'Most certainly not. Frankly, he appeared relieved.'

Mr. Ognall began his cross-examination of my evidence.

'No doubt, as the officer in charge, you had cause to make a number of inquiries about him before this series of interviews started on the 26th?'

'Of sorts, yes.'

'Well, you would want to know, I suggest, as much as you could properly find out about him, to know the sort of young man you were or might be dealing with.'

'Yes.'

'Did you know before 26 June that he was described by some people as "Daft Peter"?'

'It may well be that I did, but, in fairness, I cannot swear to it.'

'Did you know before 26 June that he was a young man with a history of mental subnormality?'

'No.'

'It was perfectly obvious that he was, to a degree, physically crippled was it not?'

'He has a badly spastic right arm, I believe'

'A spastic right arm, yes.'

'Did you have any information of any kind before 26 June as to his mental state, or the reputation he enjoyed as to his mental state?'

'I had heard something of his reputation, but I had not seen anything in the way of any medical reports.'

'Did you know that by repute he was thought by lay folk to be a bit deranged or disordered in his mind?'

'No.'

'Did you know that for virtually all of his life until he reached 18, that is to say, from three until eighteen, he had been in legal care and under the physical control of the local authorities in various foster homes or institutions?'

'No, but I knew that he had not had a normal upbringing and I knew something of his mother. I knew he had had quite a rough life.'

'But in particular, I am asking specifically: Did you know he had spent it in the care of the local authority? You must have known surely?'

'Well, he was in the care of the local authority. He was in and out of local authority homes. He was not exactly in their care all the time.'

'All I am asking about this for is this reason. You knew, I suggest, before 26 June, that you wanted a reasonably accurate account or assessment of Bruce Lee and you knew where to go and get it?'

'If I had wanted it, yes.'

'Bearing in mind that he was to be interrogated, it seems, with regard to murder and arson, did you not think it appropriate to make all proper enquiries about his mentality before you started to interview him?'

Turning to their Lordships, I answered, 'I do not want to play with words, my Lords, but he was not interrogated as such, he was spoken to.'

Mr. Ognall then said, 'I am very sorry. There was no pejorative implication behind my question, but would you apply your mind to the spirit of the question rather than to the letter of it. Did you think it right to make enquiries of the local authority to see if they could throw light on this young man who, you may have known as "Daft Peter" and whom you knew had been in care of the local authority for something like 15 years?'

'Not in any detail before the end of June.'

'So you did not make those enquiries until after those interviews, which included his alleged admissions to the fire at Troutbeck House?'

'No. I spoke to his solicitors about my concern for him, that is all.'

'Why was that? Why was it that you deferred doing that until after those interviews?'

'I did not defer doing it until after the interviews; it just did not happen. My concern became so very much greater after those interviews.'

'Do you maintain, Mr. Sagar, that during those three weeks before you first visited him at Her Majesty's Prison at Leeds, you did not countenance that you might be dealing with a mentally disordered person.'

'That is what I am saying, yes. I might add that I have interviewed many people who I would describe as being in mentality and appearance very much like Bruce George Peter Lee.'

'Yes. I mean not to be offensive to him or to anybody gratuitously, I hope, but this court is seeing him three and a half years after you interviewed him. He looked an odd young man at the time, did he not? Do you know what I mean by that?'

'Yes, but I am sorry, I do not really agree with you. He did not look an "odd young man"; he looked as if he had had something of a rough upbringing. He even looked undernourished. But he certainly understood all that was going on about him. I have never had any doubts on that score.'

'Did it ever occur to you that, in terms of his temperament or mentality, he might be an attention seeker?'

'Certainly, later, but I cannot say exactly when. A matter of days afterwards, when I took him out into Hull, I began to wonder whether he was not just saying things to draw attention to himself.'

'Thank you, you are an officer of considerable experience. Does not the fact that he is disposed to do that, in your judgement, suggest that something is rather odd mentally about him?'

'No. I spoke to his legal representatives and, in fact, some days later, I took him out to the scene of a fire, which I had asked my staff to find, that he had not mentioned to me. This was in view of the fact that I wondered whether he was not just saying things for the sake of it. On approaching a particular address in Anlaby, on the outskirts of Hull, he denied it and simply did not want to know anything about the fire which I understood had occurred at that address.'

Mr. Ognall continued, 'When, if at all, did you discover his IQ as being assessed somewhere between 75 and 78?'

'A long time after interviewing him.'

'Did you not think it part of your duties in this, I would suggest, most peculiar case, Mr. Sagar, to make those sort of enquiries at the earliest possible stage?'

'I discussed Lee with his legal representatives and, on several occasions when I visited Leeds Prison, I spoke to the Prison Doctor (Dr. Sasiene) about him.'

'Without, I hope, improperly bending the rules, were you, in making these enquiries, seeking to satisfy yourself that he was mentally competent enough to cope with your questions, or what?'

'No. I did not need to do anything like that in relation to my questions. My questions were put and Lee simply answered them.'

'I appreciate that, but that was not the thrust of my question. Did you not think it right, in the light of what little you may have known of him before 26 June, to make further enquiries as to his mentality and his intelligence quotient, or his assessment educationally?'

'I took it that he was no different from the vast majority of people one deals with in respect of the intelligence level.'

'You appreciate, of course, Mr. Sagar, that there are administrative directions, or direction, touching on the questioning of mentally subnormal persons, do you not?'

'Yes.'

'And it did not occur to you when, as you have told the court . . . albeit that I accept this was at a later stage . . . you considered the possibility that he might be an attention seeker? It did not even cross your mind then to see that he was protected by the presence of some other independent person during your interviews with him?'

I answered, 'Quite clearly, my Lords, he understood the questions that were being put to him. It did not occur to me, and I do not accept that it was necessary, to have some friend, welfare officer or someone of that kind present. Within hours of Lee's arrest, literally hours of his arrest, I obtained legal advice for him. If I thought for one moment that it would be necessary to have someone present, it would have been such an easy matter for me to do so. His solicitors, at no time, suggested or hinted in any way at all that someone of that kind should be present and, on talking to the Prison Medical Officer, and the Probation Officer at the prison, such a suggestion was never made by them either.'

'Did you notify his solicitors of each occasion that you were intending to take a statement from him thereafter?'

'Yes. There was constant communication with the solicitor and/or solicitor's clerk.'

'Did you notify his legal representatives of each occasion when you intended to take a statement from him?'

'I said there was a constant communication with the representative. Whenever I was going to Leeds Prison, I notified his solicitors. On the occasion Lee was remanded to the police from Leeds Prison, the solicitor was present in the Magistrates Court. He was told that the prosecution would ask for a remand to the police station for further interviews, and he agreed and accepted that.'

'That is to say, the solicitor accepted it?'

'Yes. Well, he stood in court and had no objections.'

'There were, I think, —and you will correct me if I am wrong—something in the order of 28 interviews in all, between yourself and Lee and between 26 June and some time in September . . . Is it probably true to say, Mr. Sagar, that you did your very best to build up a relationship of confidence between yourself and Lee?

'I do not know about "build up confidence". I feel that the relationship was probably no different to talking to any other accused person, apart from the fact that I felt some degree of pity for Lee due to his upbringing.'

'And you made plain to him verbally your compassion for him and your concern did you not?'

'Yes. I certainly mentioned his upbringing.'

'Am I right in thinking, Mr. Sagar, that with the exception of the person who may have attended with you in order to, if you like, corroborate your account for obvious reasons, you and you alone conducted all the interviews with Lee?'

'Yes.'

'There was never a single occasion when any other officer, of whatever seniority or rank, was to interview him about any question of fires or deaths. That is right; is it not?'

'Yes. It certainly happened that way.'

'With respect, Mr. Sagar, I suggest it did not just happen. I suggest that it was a deliberate policy decision on your part to ensure that only you, together with your note takers or observers, interviewed Lee and nobody else. That is right; is it not?'

'Yes. I might add that there is nothing unusual in that.'

'You took the view that the matter (Troutbeck House fire) was woefully inadequately investigated by the police at the time. Is that right?'

'Yes.'

'And so you were going to renew the enquiry. Is that right?'

'Certainly look at it.'

'The reason that I ask you these questions as to how much you knew is this. The applicant himself has given evidence to this court and he says of this interview – indeed of such interviews about Troutbeck House as you had – that all the facts which appear in your records of the interviews came initially from your mouth; that you were putting propositions to him and inviting him to assent or dissent. Do you understand?'

'I understand what you are saying only too well.'

'And, although the record, as you have given it in evidence here, suggests that they were words that spontaneously came from his mouth, I put it to you that in fact the details came initially from you and he merely assented to them as you put them to him. What is your answer to that?'

'No. Most certainly not. If that was the case, I would record the interview in that manner, but it did not happen that way.'

'How satisfied were you of his capacity to read his voluntary statement.'

'I was satisfied that he knew what I was writing and I was satisfied that he understood what was happening. It did not become a situation where one was for forever asking oneself: "Can he understand, or can he not understand?"'

Lord Justice Ackner said, 'Mr. Ognall, can you help me on this? Is it suggested to this officer that Lee had not the capacity to read?'

Mr. Ognall replied, 'All I can rely on is the applicant's evidence about this matter. I am not in a position, as I am sure your Lordships know, to put that. All I am seeking to do, I hope properly, is to test this officer's state of mind and his attitude towards Lee at the time of these interviews. It would be quite wrong of me to say one way or the other.'

Lord Justice Ackner, 'Thank you.'

Mr. Ognall continued, 'Mr. Sagar, Lee has said that, although you were writing things down, he has told my Lords that he did not read his statement over himself. He was merely asked to sign it. What do you say to those allegations?'

'I find the allegation quite frightening. Such a situation did not occur and I would be totally irresponsible if I asked him to sign what might as well have been just a blank piece of paper.'

'Did it occur to you, as a senior policeman, that if the contents of his first statement were true, or might be true, there was something mentally abnormal with the young man you were going to further interview?'

'By the mere fact that someone, anyone, could be causing the fire at the Hastie household, obviously, in my humble opinion, had something wrong. But in respect to him being a person who did not, or could not, understand what he was doing, so far as the Judges' Rules are concerned, no, he clearly understood what he was doing. He clearly understood what was happening, and clearly, in my view, he read the statement.'

'Mr. Sagar, did you take the view that if you, so to speak, broke the bond of your personal relationship with Lee by allowing other officers on the scene, this young man might not talk to you any more and, let us say, not confess to any further fires?'

'Let us make no mistake about this, sir. Other officers did see Lee. They did not interview him about other matters. He would be exercised in the police station. What I sense as perhaps a sinister view is just not so at all. It was perhaps, in my mind, a matter of efficiency, let alone anything else, that one or two officers be involved in this matter as opposed to a dozen officers waiting to give a little bit of evidence here and a little bit of evidence there.'

Mr. Ognall, 'Well, Mr. Sagar. . . .'

'Might I continue, sir? In relation to this most unfortunate man, Bruce Lee, what is being said is in fact that I was extremely irresponsible and unkind to Bruce Lee in allowing him to sign statements that he did not understand or had not read. That is just not so at all. I have always felt—perhaps wrongly— a great deal of pity for the man and the way he has been brought up. To do something of the sort that you are now alleging, with all due respect, is so very, very far from the truth.'

'I take it that that is your complete answer, officer. May I say something now?'

'Yes, thank you.'

'What I was putting to you was merely that you took no steps to satisfy yourself that he had read and understood those statements. That is the nature of my suggestion, Mr. Sagar. What steps did you take to satisfy yourself that he had read and understood the statements?'

'Initially by the question and answer situation and, as the statements were being taken, by the obvious fact that he was dictating those statements word for word. He could see how the handwriting was progressing across the lines of the statement paper.'

'When you interviewed him on these large number of occasions that I have put to you, I think it is right to say that, on more than one occasion, you yourself were concerned, so you say in your witness statements, that he should not make admissions to things he had not done. Is that right?'
'Yes.'
'That happened, I think, on more than one occasion, did it not, that you said that? Am I right about that?'
'Yes. I, as a mere human being, could not help but be concerned about what he was saying.'
'The reality, I suggest, is that you put that proposition to him because you entertained then, as you entertain now, serious doubts as to whether credence could be attached to at least some of his confessions. That is why you kept putting the proposition to him, I suggest. Is that unfair?'
'No, it's not unfair. I would go along with that.'
Mr. Ognall finished his cross-examination.

Earlier Mrs. Ros Fenton told the Appeal Court that she saw Lee outside her home shortly before the blaze started. She said she saw him through the glass panel of her front door. She had been on her way upstairs when she heard her letter-box rattle. She looked through the glass panel and saw Lee standing near to the door, she said. 'I shouted at him to go away,' she said. She went to bed, but a few moments later she heard what she thought was rain, then she heard someone shout, 'Fire!' She went on to the landing and saw a 'big orange ball of fire, like an explosion rolling up the stairs'. She told the judges that she suffered 'massive burns' and lost the baby she was expecting.

Cross-examined by Mr. Harry Ognall, she denied that she was a heavy smoker. Under further questioning from Mr. Ognall, Ros agreed that she had not mentioned seeing Lee when she made her original statement in hospital where she was recovering from her burns.

Ros Fenton's friend, Mrs. Gail Lenny, also told the judges that she had seen Lee outside Mrs. Fenton's house. Gail had visited her friend, Ros, that evening and actually left shortly before the fire. Cross-examined by Mr. Ognall, Mrs. Lenny denied she left the house with a lighted cigarette in her hand. 'I was not smoking,' she said. But she said that word had been put about the Cavill Place area of West Hull that she was responsible for the fire at her friend's house. She said that she was so concerned about the rumour that she went to see someone who she knew had seen her leave Ros Fenton's house that night. Ironically, she said that someone was Bruce Lee. 'When I saw him he agreed with me that I was not smoking,' she commented.

Mr. Thomas Ellis, a former Hull Fire Brigade divisional commander, told the judges that he investigated Ros Fenton's house blaze. He had felt unhappy about it at the time and he said there was a possibility that the fire had been started by an 'induced agent'.

Called by the Crown, Forensic Scientist Roy Cooke, told the judges that Lee's confession was remarkably similar to his analysis of how the fire started. He rejected Mr. Ognall's suggestion that the fire could have started by a cigarette being dropped on to the nylon carpet. He also rejected the suggestion that a cigarette, dropped into a cardboard box in the hallway, could have started the blaze in the time between Mrs. Lenny leaving and the fire being discovered. The Court knew that no forensic scientist was called to the scene at the time of the fire, and therefore Mr. Cooke's analysis was a valuable piece of evidence from the corroborative point of view.

During the afternoon of 25 November 1983, five days into the appeal hearing, and after much legal argument and discussion, the Court of Appeal rejected Lee's application for leave to appeal against his conviction for the arson at Ros Fenton's home at Troutbeck House.

The three Court of Appeal judges also refused leave to appeal against the convictions in respect of arson and manslaughter at: 2 Brentwood Villas, Reynoldson Street, 4 Belgrave Terrace, Rosamond Street, 33 Glasgow Street, 50 Humber Buildings, 9 Gorthorpe, Orchard Park, and 7 Minnies Terrace, Rosamond Street.

Three cases now remained, namely: Wensley Lodge; 43 West Dock Avenue; 70 Askew Avenue.

Having rejected the indictments that afternoon and the indictment regarding the Hastie fire earlier, Lord Justice Ackner told Mr. Ognall that he had the right to elect which of the three remaining cases he wished to proceed with first, adding, 'and we will no doubt assume, without any surprise, that you would like to go ahead with Wensley Lodge'.

Mr. Ognall then spoke about the Wensley Lodge case and, due to the complexity of the evidence, requested more time to prepare his presentation.

At last, thanks to Lee's appeal, the slow process of the law was making its way to a thorough examination of all the evidence now available in respect of Wensley Lodge. It was now almost six years after the fire.

Chapter Twenty Six

On Tuesday, 29 November 1983, the three Appeal Court judges continued the hearing.

I felt a sense of relief that we were now at the beginning of the end of the Wensley Lodge affair. I believed that Mr. Harry Ognall would make his main thrust at the scientific evidence as that was the main weakness in the Crown's case. However, we considered it important to call Miss Helen O'Shea, a housemother at St. Vincent's Children's Home in Hull. Miss O'Shea told the court that she knew Lee, because he was at one time friendly with a teenager at the home. She also said that after the fire Lee told her that the fire at Wensley Lodge was 'no accident and that the police had got it wrong'. She did not quiz him but felt at the time that he was saying what he did to gain attention.

Lee again repeated his allegation that the voluntary statements I took from him were obtained under police pressure. He denied causing the Wensley Lodge fire, saying, 'I did not burn the Hessle home.' He denied that he ever talked to Miss O'Shea about the Wensley Lodge fire and he certainly had not said that the fire was not due to an accident.

Crown Counsel Mr. Coles said, 'You pleaded guilty, Bruce Lee, because you were, weren't you?'

Raising his voice he denied that he was guilty.

Called by the Crown, plumber, Steven Hay, told the hearing that he had been working with a blow lamp in the Wensley Lodge boiler room. He strongly denied that he could have inadvertently set material smouldering which spread and engulfed the building hours later.

Mr. George Pearson, the care assistant at the Home on the night in question, told the three judges about his experiences during the night of the fire and spoke of fighting the blaze until he was driven back by the intense heat.

Mr. Ognall called expert evidence from Mr. Henry Bland, a former Home Office forensic and chartered chemist, who now specialised in a private capacity, in fire investigation. Mr. Bland did not attend the fire at the time but said that he was originally asked to investigate the Wensley Lodge fire by the *Sunday Times*. He stated that it was significant that the first signs of a fire were seen in Room 11 at Wensley Lodge, the room directly above the boiler room, and concluded the fire was started by the plumber's blow torch.

The Crown also called Former Hull Deputy Fire Prevention Officer, Mr. Geoffrey Hirst, a man with 30 years' fire-fighting experience. He had investigated the Wensley Lodge fire wreckage and explained that in his view there was clear confirmation of his theory that the blaze was not a case of arson. He relied upon the pattern of burning; to him it was obvious that the fire had begun below the floor of Bedroom 11 and had occurred in the void of the ceiling of the boiler room. The slow burning fire would have become a free-burning, unconfined fire involving the whole room due to oxygen entering the room when the door of the room was opened. It was not possible to know with certainty, if, or how often, the door of the room was open during the six hours from plumber Steven Hay carrying out his work to the time the fire was discovered.

Mr. Hirst told said that Mr. Hunter, the occupant of Room 11, was extremely lucky not to have died of smoke inhalation. He had no detailed knowledge of the air ducts in the building, but considered that some smoke might have gone up them. The fire spread east-west and he thought the fumes would have gone up the duct in the north-west corner of bedroom 11. From what he saw, and all the reports he had read, the fire bypassed the second floor and went into the roof. He assumed that the fire had spread through a duct or ducts, straight up into the roof void, and this seemed to confirm the existence of a flue or chimney which went from the first floor into the roof void.

Mr. Graham Devonport, a forensic scientist with well over 20 years experience investigating fires, said that he had also examined the wreckage of Wensley Lodge. His view, previously given to the Coroner and Committee of Enquiry, was that the fire had been caused by the plumber's blow torch. He now told the Appeal Judges that, having heard the alternative suggestion, in 1980, of the ignition of paraffin poured on the surface of the floor of Room 11, he no longer held the opinion which he had previously expressed. He had re-appraised the evidence, in particular the nature of the burning of the ceiling below Room 11, and, in addition, carried out important experimental work. He now assessed the pattern of burning beneath the floor as that of a free-burning fire with a restricted ventilation, and he now considered that the nature of the char showed that the fire had been burning downwards. The other reason for altering his view was the result of tests that he had carried out in order to see whether paraffin ignited on a wooden floor could cause a fire in a roof void below. To this end, he made up a double-sided floor section, 7' x 5'4", using tongued and grooved deal boards fixed to either side of 4" x 2" joists, sealing one end up against a brick wall and fastening the other end with a piece of boarding. This model was not intended to simulate the floor of Room 11 at Wensley Lodge. Fifty per cent of the area was covered with cardboard to sustain the flame to ignite the paraffin. Of course, cardboard soaked with paraffin is more inflammable than linoleum. In the model, cracks (a quarter of an inch maximum width) were induced between the floorboards at unspecified intervals over the floor area. In the first test, when only 1½ pints of paraffin were poured on the upper surface, no fire in the joist space was observed, although parts of the lower board were wet with paraffin. In the second test, to simulate the presence of debris, a small quantity a cardboard was placed in the space between the joists and about 2½ pints of paraffin were poured on the unaffected reverse floor. After 3½ minutes, some burning on the underside of the boards was observed; some 2½ minutes later, the wood below the floor was burning vigorously on the upper and lower faces of the joist space. Five minutes later, flames were penetrating from the lower surface to the upper floor surface. Nineteen minutes after the test began, the lower face of the joist space was burning very well, and, one minute later, when the test terminated, carbonization was almost complete on some of the top floorboards. The final appearance of the floor surface was that of intense charring of the boards with the joists showing considerable variation in their surface burning.

Mr. Devonport said the result was a surprising one. Prior to the experiment he thought that, if paraffin had been poured on a floor and set alight, it would have been consumed on the floor and would not ignite what was below the floor, as indeed had been demonstrated in the first experiment. The second experiment had demonstrated that, if a floor has cracks in it, the pouring of sufficient paraffin on to it, which is then ignited, can create inter-floor burning. This burning will cause premature collapse due to the enhanced exposure to the flame of the floorboards. The quantity of paraffin necessary to achieve this appears to be in pints rather than cupfuls.

The pattern of the char in the model was, in Mr. Devonport's view, similar to the pattern seen in the joists below Room 11 in Wensley Lodge. He visualised a quantity of paraffin being poured onto that floor, with edges of the holes in the linoleum acting as wicks when the paraffin was set alight, with burning drops of paraffin falling into the void and igniting debris accumulated over the years. In answer to Mr. Coles, Mr. Devonport conceded that he had to assume that there were gaps in the floor boards of Room 11. However, he had not noticed gaps when he examined the wreckage after the fire. He concluded that what he saw at Wensley Lodge fitted 'quite conceivably' into a paraffin fire commenced as Lee had described.

Mr. Devonport told the Court that, even before he carried out the tests, he had appreciated the difficulty in accepting the slow-burning fire theory, namely that the occupant of Room 11 had survived despite the smoke and poisonous fumes which the fire created. Previously he had in mind the dissipation of those fumes through the ducts and the squared-off alcoves. The alternative explanation of the fire caused by the use of paraffin did not involve that difficulty. Whilst he was satisfied that the duct in the north-west alcove led nowhere, that is, that it ended at the ceiling of Room 11 and could not therefore have provided a flue or a chimney, he had not examined the other possible outlets for the fumes and, in particular, he could not help about the flue from the boiler.

In a well-sustained cross-examination Mr. Ognall established that Mr. Devonport did not draw either to the Coroner's attention or to that of the Committee of Enquiry the two difficulties which confronted the slow burning theory, namely that, although slow smouldering fires produce a substantial amount of carbon monoxide and smoke, the occupant of Room 11 emerged unharmed by the fire, and that there was an absence of smoke in Room 11 whilst the fire was developing. In his opinion, arson by use of paraffin was no more than a possibility. He could not, however, exclude the possibility of a slow burning fire. In fact he considered that both explanations were indeed possibilities.

The Crown called no further expert evidence.

Called to give further evidence I described to the judges my police car journey with other officers when Lee directed us to West Hill and Wensley Lodge. I told how he claimed to have gained access to the building by breaking a window and how he claimed to have spilled paraffin about. I asked him why he had chosen Wensley Lodge.

He replied, 'I just picked on that house because it was nice and quiet. I didn't mean to kill 11 people, it just happened like that.'

Mr. Coles asked, 'What was his demeanour at this time?'
I replied, 'I tended to think he was boasting.'

Addressing the three judges, Mr. Coles submitted that, on the totality of the evidence, any doubt as to the guilt of Lee would be unreasonable. He contended that, if the judges were satisfied that Lee had lied to the court about the way he had come to make his admissions, both oral and in writing, lied about directing the police to Wensley Lodge, lied to his conversations long before the police came on the scene with Miss O'Shea, the housemother of St. Vincent's Children's Home, and lied as to how he had come to plead guilty to the crime, that should conclude the matter. Mr. Coles also stated that the Court of Appeal should not consider the findings of the Committee of Enquiry as absolute since they did not have the benefit of Lee's confession. He added that the scientific evidence now given, bearing in mind also the evidence of Steven Hay, was inconclusive. The fire could have been caused either by a blow torch or by Lee using paraffin in the manner he described. In that situation, it was Lee's admissions, given that these were voluntarily made and properly obtained, and Lee's plea of guilty in disregard of the 'very firm and detailed advice' given to him by Mr. Ognall, which should be decisive.

Mr. Ognall submitted that if, on the totality of the evidence the judges had a 'lurking doubt', then the convictions on the Wensley Lodge indictment would be unsafe.

I listened to Mr. Ognall with more than my usual interest in counsel's speeches. As always, in my opinion, Harry Ognall chose his words with great care and legal simplicity. 'Lurking doubt,' he said. In all the circumstances now before the hearing the phrase was perfect. I am sure everyone who listened to the Wensley Lodge evidence during those days in the Royal Courts of Justice would agree that indeed there was a 'lurking doubt'. Mr. Ognall continued, saying that a lurking doubt could be less than a reasonable doubt, since it could be a doubt which was based, not on reason, but on a feeling of unease, a gut reaction, he unpoetically called it. He submitted that, however adverse a view the judges might form of Lee's explanation for his many and various admissions, the state of the forensic evidence in the Wensley Lodge case gave rise to an inevitable sense of unease.

Lord Justice Ackner agreed with Mr. Ognall when he announced: 'We think that the convictions on Indictment 810048 (Wensley Lodge) are not safe. They will accordingly be quashed.'

He continued: 'We desire, however, to make the following matters clear at this stage: (1) That we have no doubt that Lee made the statements, both oral and in writing, attributed to him; that these were voluntarily made; that they were properly obtained by Detective Superintendent Sagar and that he recorded Lee's own words in the way he said he did. (2) That Lee's statements and in particular much of the circumstantial material which they contained as was accurate, together with his repeated statements in 1978, which was long before his admissions to Detective Superintendent Sagar, made to Miss O'Shea that he knew the Wensley Lodge fire was not an accidental fire, coupled with his pleas of guilty, persisted in contrary to the advice of his counsel, provide very powerful support for the validity of his convictions. (3) That the doubts which we entertain arise essentially from the unsatisfactory state of the scientific evidence given both to this court and in 1977 to the Committee of Enquiry set up by the Humberside County Council. The Committee of Enquiry should have been informed that the theory that the plumber's blow torch had caused a slow burning fire to develop under the floor of Room 11 which had remained undetected for some six and a half hours suffered from the following potential weak points:

Although slow smouldering fires produce a substantial amount of carbon monoxide and smoke (a) the occupants of Rooms 11 and 20, immediately above Room 11, emerged unharmed by the fire (b) there was an absence of smoke in Room 11 whilst the fire was developing. Had these important points been disclosed, the structure of Room 11 and those in the immediate vicinity would have been carefully investigated to ascertain whether a flue or vent existed which would have carried any of the poisonous fumes and smoke into the roof or out into the air, by-passing Rooms 11 and 20.'

Lord Justice Ackner continued, 'At this point in time no certainty can be achieved as to the position. On the basis of plans drawn to our attention by the Crown all that can now be said is that there may have been an escape route for these flames and smoke. As to the experiments carried out following the confessions made by Lee, these were based on assumptions that may or may not have been justified. The quite inadequate consideration which was given to the possibility of the fire being a paraffin arson resulted in an inadequate consideration being made of the floorboards in Room 11, or the adjoining rooms, with the result that there was no evidence of the extent of the gaps, if any, between the floorboards or the precise nature or condition of the linoleum on that floor. In all these circumstances, none of us think that it would be safe to allow the (Wensley Lodge) convictions to stand.'

There was then a short adjournment while Mr. Ognall conferred with Lee in the cells.

Upon his return to the Court Mr. Ognall told Lord Justice Ackner, Mr. Justice Glidwell and Mr. Justice Leggatt that Lee now withdrew the final two applications for leave to appeal. These related to the fires and deaths of six-year-old Richard Anthony Ellerington at 70 Askew Avenue, Hull, and six-month-old Katrina Thacker, at 43 West Dock Avenue, Hull.

Lord Justice Ackner, who presided throughout the hearing, said, 'We think that is a very sensible course to adopt. We will give our judgement in full, we hope, some time next week.'

Naturally I was pleased to hear the judges' comments on my evidence. However, listening to the great many words of wisdom spoken throughout the hearing, I could not help but smile to myself about the 'Simpleton' label attached to Lee by the *Sunday Times*. I watched Lee closely in the grandeur of the Royal Courts of Justice, where for the most part he listened intently, as he was discussed at length by a grand array of legal minds and brain power. Yet, despite their endeavour, Bruce Lee, despite his low IQ, was the only person there who knew the real answer to his self-confessed guilt! I also noted that at no time during the hearing did Mr. Ognall rely upon the allegations in the *Sunday Times* relative to the Selby Street fire, that I, or any of my officers, persuaded a key witness to alter crucial evidence; that we had convincing evidence until literally minutes before Lee claimed responsibility, that it had been started by several people who drove away in a Rover car; or that the fire might have resulted from a vendetta on the Hull drug world.

As I travelled back to Hull by train that afternoon I reflected on the whole of the enquiry which led me to Bruce George Peter Lee, alias Peter Dinsdale. Volunteering to be on call that Monday night had gradually become a nightmare with dreadful unfounded allegations of malpractice being publicised everywhere. Never before, as a senior detective, had I had cause to seriously dispute national newspaper stories in respect of any major investigation I conducted. I also thought about the victims of the fires and particularly the inadequacy of the investigation of the death of David Brewer in Humber Buildings in 1973. If only more questions had been asked then, perhaps Edith Hastie would not have lost her sons, and I would not have felt the need to ask for her husband Tommy's release from prison. And the likeable rogue would not have died on that motorcycle.

As I walked from the train at Paragon Station that day, I recalled that in the past I had often seen the Hastie boys larking about in the Paragon Station concourse, but their fun and mischief were no more.

Chapter Twenty Seven

On Friday, 9 December 1983, Lord Justice Sir Desmond Ackner, Mr. Justice Glidwell and Mr. Justice Leggatt, returned to the Court of Appeal to give their judgement. I looked forward to it and was ready to hang on to every word.

Lord Justice Ackner described the events surrounding the fire and deaths of the Hastie brothers, Charles, aged 15 years, Paul aged 12 years and Peter aged 10 years. 'It has never been open to doubt that this was a case of arson,' he said. 'The fire had been deliberately started, using paraffin as an accelerant. That paraffin had been poured through the letter-box and then ignited. Accordingly a murder enquiry began.' The Judge went on to speak about the lines of enquiry relative to the Rover car and the suggestion that the wrong house was fired in revenge for a double-cross in a drugs deal, which proved fruitless. He continued, 'Detective Superintendent Sagar then considered whether the motive for the arson attack might have some homosexual connection. Lee and other homosexuals were interviewed, but only Lee admitted homosexuality with Charles Hastie. On 18 May 1980, a statement was taken from Lee and, although much else in these (appeal) applications had been the subject matter of challenge, no suggestion has ever been made that this statement was other than a voluntary statement properly obtained and contained the truth. In that statement Lee explained how he came to meet Hastie. He gave details of their homosexual practices and how Hastie would, from time to time, ask for money following their sexual activities.

'On 6 June 1980, Lee was arrested. Later that evening he was interviewed by Detective Superintendent Sagar, who made a contemporaneous note of his questions and Lee's answers. During that interview Lee admitted that Charles Hastie had been demanding money from him for taking part in their homosexual activities, that this made him angry and that he therefore set fire to the house. He gave a detailed account of how he poured paraffin through the letter-box and caused the fire. At the conclusion of this lengthy interview he agreed to provide a statement in writing. This he dictated to Detective Superintendent Sagar, signing the caption at the commencement of the statement that he wanted someone to write down what he said, confirming that he had been duly cautioned, signing each page of that lengthy statement, and not only signing the statement at its conclusion, but in his own writing confirming that he had read the statement, that he had been told that he could correct, alter or add anything and that the statement was true and made of his own free will.'

Continuing the judgement, Lord Justice Ackner said, 'On the next day, 7 June, Detective Superintendent Sagar told Lee that he believed he should have legal advice. Lee eventually selected a solicitor and, it being weekend, the solicitor's clerk was contacted. Lee then arranged to show, and showed, the police where he had burned the plastic container which had contained paraffin and also where he had stood under the flyover that night. Later, on 7 June, he saw a representative of the firm of solicitors who were to act for him both up to his trial and for some little time thereafter. In the presence of the solicitor's representative Lee identified the nature of the two-litre soft drink plastic container which he had used to pour paraffin through the letter-box of 12 Selby Street. Two days later, on 9 June, there was a further interview at the conclusion of which he agreed to make a further statement regarding the purchase of the paraffin which he had used. A statement was duly taken down in writing and signed and he confirmed this in a like manner to his first statement.

'A little over two weeks later, on 22 June 1980, after Detective Superintendent Sagar had made enquiries into another fire, namely at 407 Troutbeck House, which occurred on 22 June 1979, there was a further interview with Lee. Lee, in the course of that interview, admitted that he had set light to those premises and, at the conclusion of that interview, agreed to make a written statement. In the course of that statement he admitted guilt for other fires and further admissions were made and written statements obtained in subsequent interviews. In due course 11 indictments were served on Lee, all of which, except the fire relating to Troutbeck House, contained not only counts of arson, but counts of murder.'

Lord Justice Ackner then went on to detail the various charges contained in the indictments to which Lee pleaded guilty before Mr. Justice Tudor Evans, on 20 January 1981.

'Lee's pleas were accepted and Lee was ordered to be detained without limit of time at Park Lane Hospital, under section 60 and section 65 of the Mental Health Act 1959. Despite the extensive confessions made by Lee it was not anticipated that he would plead guilty. Indeed, in the papers sent to us by the Director of Public Prosecutions and, of course, provided to Lee's legal advisors, is an account by Detective Superintendent Sagar of a conversation between him and Lee when Lee said in terms, on 12 November 1980, in Leeds ". . . I'm going to plead not guilty, see, 'cause I understand there's a chance if I deny it and act a bit daft I might get into a mental home, that'll be better than a stinking prison, and anyway I might get away with it all. Mr. Pearce told me there'd be no proof if I hadn't fucking told you so. I'm going to deny it all . . . Anyway, I'm not going to go into the fucking witness box so it's up to Eric Pearce to get me off with the barristers."'

The Judge continued, 'The case was therefore listed for a hearing of a pre-trial review on 19 January 1981. However, Lee instructed his counsel, Mr. Harry Ognall Q.C., that he wished to plead guilty. At the request of Mr. Ognall the judge saw counsel in his chambers and we have, at the instance of Lee's advisers, been provided with the benefit of a transcript of what took place. Mr. Ognall informed the judge that his then instructions caused him anxiety and disquiet. He said it was difficult to get instructions from Lee, who had shifted his ground as to his guilt, the present change being about the fourth change of his instructions. Mr. Ognall pointed out that one of the factors causing anxiety was the conclusion of a public enquiry of the cause of one fire, the Wensley Lodge fire in 1977, when 11 elderly men met their deaths, as accidental. The following exchange took place: Mr. Justice Tudor Evans, "I suppose if I were of the view that on some counts the pleas are not very clearly answered I ought to say a plea of not guilty is to be entered."

Mr. Ognall, "That would be our submission."

Mr. Justice Tudor Evans, "The difficulty will arise if, for example, he pleads guilty to (a), (b) and (c), and not guilty to (d), (e), (f), etc. as to whether I should say there is a plea of not guilty to them all."

Mr. Ognall did not suggest that course, but remarked, "I am not being difficult when I say I do not think I can assist further. I did feel it was my duty to my client and to you, as well as to ourselves, to draw these matters to your attention."

'However,' Lord Justice Ackner continued, 'the reporting psychiatrists on both sides all agreed that Lee was fit to plead and, accordingly, the case was called on the following day, January 20, thus giving Lee the benefit of further advice from the very experienced counsel appearing for him. On the following day, when the case was called, the pleas were made consistently and were quite properly accepted by the learned Judge.'

The Judge then went on to relate to the reasons given by Lee for his late leave to appeal, particularly by reason of enquiries made by the *Sunday Times*, where, it was said, there were now grounds for believing 'in respect of most if not all of the deaths the subject of several indictments, the Applicant had untainted alibis'. An example was given in relation to the fire at 50 Humber Buildings, Madeley Street, Hull, in October 1973'.

Continuing the Judgement his Lordship detailed a statutory declaration made by Lee on 29 October 1982, which I noted, was during the time when the *Sunday Times* was in full flight with its own particular style of investigative journalism. I listened intently to the words accredited to Bruce Lee, in his statutory declaration, the words in fact of the young man described as a 'Simpleton' by the newspaper. The Judge read the declaration out as follows:

'It had been my intention to plead not guilty to all charges on all indictments and to the best of my knowledge and belief preparations were being made for my defence at trial. The indictments against me were due to be listed for pre-trial review before the Honourable Mr. Justice Tudor Evans on 19 January 1981 at Leeds. By the 19th January, some seven months had elapsed since my arrest. I had been interviewed at great length on many occasions by the police and had been examined and interviewed on more occasions than I can remember by medical men and by representatives from my instructing solicitors. It was, and still is, my case that I had been badgered into admitting the offences and each of them by a prolonged and remorseless interrogation by Detective Superintendent Sagar. Throughout the various interviews he kept suggesting to me ways in which I could have started the various fires. I was extremely drunk when arrested and during the course of my first interview (in respect of the Hastie fire) I was feeling unwell. I admitted that offence in order to obtain respite from the pressure of the interrogation, and having made one admission I thought there was little point in failing to admit anything else that was put to me. It seemed to me that the police would not accept any denials and it was easier for me simply to accede to their suggestions rather than to refute them.'

It had been said that I knew Lee better than anyone. I do not know if that is right or not, but I do know that in all the thousands of words Lee uttered to me, he did not use words of the kind written in the statutory declaration. Furthermore he was not 'badgered' or subjected to 'prolonged and remorseless interrogation'. I found it extremely difficult to accept that he used the words 'respite', 'accede' and 'refute', but more were to follow.

The Judge continued to read more from Lee's statutory declaration: 'When my case was due for pre-trial review I felt depressed at the enormity of my situation and I was feeling the strain of the previous seven months and had lost the will to fight. I felt that I could not face a trial, or series of trials, and was very much influenced by the fact that shortly before my first Crown Court appearance Dr. Sasiene told me that there would be a place specially waiting for me at a special hospital in Liverpool if I pleaded guilty to manslaughter on the basis of diminished responsibility. At this time the prospect seemed more attractive that further periods on remand facing murder charges. I, therefore, on 19 January 1981, decided to plead guilty and on this day informed my legal advisers of my intention. I must emphasise that up until this day my legal advisers had no reason to believe other than that I intended to plead not guilty to all charges. I acknowledge that I was prevailed upon by both my counsel and my solicitor to reconsider this decision but my mind was made up and therefore the case was heard as a plea of guilty the following day.'

Lee's declaration went on to mention that he could not give any details of alibis save that of 12 Selby Street, maintaining that he was at home during the night of the fire. In conclusion, in his declaration, it was stated that he 'could only respectfully repeat and emphasise that his pleas of guilty were tendered, not because they represented the truth, but because he felt so overborne by the pressure of events generally that he felt that he could not take any more'. Obviously my evidence relative to the course of my interviews with Lee told quite a different story.

Lord Justice Ackner referred to Lee's provisional grounds for appeal, submitted some time before the final statutory declaration, noting that, 'unlike the provisional grounds for appeal, the declaration makes a serious attack upon the police. That, unlike the provisional grounds for appeal, the motive for pleas of guilty was not expressed to be a desire for notoriety and publicity. The pleas were said to have been made because Lee felt depressed, had lost the will to fight and preferred to go to a special hospital in Liverpool than face a trial with remands in prison.'

In continuance of the Judgement, Lord Justice Ackner said, 'It is necessary in the interests of justice that we should allow – in a case where no evidence at all was called before a jury – evidence which would, or could, have been called if the applicant had, by pleading not guilty, caused the trial to take place. Super-added to the application to call that evidence are, of course, applications to call evidence which has, since the convictions, become available. Obviously the answer to this question depended upon the particular circumstances of the case. The decision which we made was not intended to provide any general precedent. Indeed, it is our view that the occasions on which this court will allow evidence to be called, after there has been an unequivocal plea of guilty, will be very rare. However, this case is, as was accepted on both sides, wholly exceptional if not unique.

'We have read the *Sunday Times* articles, they being part of the voluminous material put before us. We can well appreciate the public concern that these articles asserting Lee's innocence must have occasioned, not only on the ground that in respect of some of the arsons it was alleged that they could not have been committed by him, but much more because of the serious and sinister allegations as to how his confessions had been obtained and how it had been sought to corroborate his account.'

The Judge went on to speak at length about the admissibility of the evidence in respect of one fire being relevant to the others. He stated that by hearing all the evidence on all the indictments at once was a course which could not have been adopted if Lee had accepted advice and entered pleas of not guilty. Referring to several stated cases, the Judge ruled that on the trial of the counts in the Selby Street indictment, Lee's confessions relative to the other ten fires, the primary facts concerning those fires and the expert evidence based on those primary facts as to the cause of those fires, were all inadmissible evidence.

'In short,' he said, 'despite our having granted Mr. Ognall leave to call all relevant and admissible evidence, he declined the invitation. Since we were thus provided with no material to support the contention that the convictions on this indictment were either unsafe or unsatisfactory, we dismissed the applications.'

'However, before proceeding to deal with the next stage in this most unusual of cases, we should put on record the following matters: (1). That Lee's case in relation to Selby Street, as is apparent from the grounds of appeal and his declaration, was that he made none of the admissions, either oral or in writing, as recorded against him. All the detail had come from Detective Superintendent Sagar. Lee had merely answered in the affirmative to every question asked because he did not feel well enough to say no. (2). That he also claimed that he had an alibi in respect of that occasion. (3). That in the written submissions provided to Lee's advisers and to the court by the Director of Public Prosecutions, supported by voluminous documents, it was stated that the following features of Lee's admission make it appear true: (a) his motives stem from the fact that every time he was involved in sexual activity with Charles Hastie, Hastie demanded money; (b) the letter-box at 12 Selby Street was, as described by Lee, located in a wide piece of wood between two pieces of glass at the side of the door; (c) there was, as described by Lee, a net curtain draped on the inside of the door of the house; (d) he described dropping two burning matches and there were two on the ground; (e) paper was, as described by Lee, used to ignite the paraffin; (f) it was, as described by Lee, breezy and drizzling on the night in question; (g) a police car did drive in the area, as described by Lee, just before the fire; (h) a young couple did, as described by Lee, walk down Selby Street, about that time; (i) there was, as described by Lee, a man walking there with his dog shortly before the fire; and (j) he described hearing fire engines very soon after the fire began and they were on the scene very quickly. 'Thus, even if evidence had been called about the Selby Street fire, it is apparent that the prosecution had a strong case supporting Lee's confessions.

'We should also record that at no time did Mr. Ognall seek to rely upon the following allegations made in the *Sunday Times* article relative to Selby Street: (1). That the fire might have resulted from a vendetta in the Hull drug world. (2). That the Hull police persuaded a key witness to alter crucial evidence that they had initially accepted as the best line of enquiry. (3). That until literally minutes before Lee claimed that he and he alone had started the fire, the police had convincing evidence that it had been started by several people who drove away in a Rover car.

'From the material provided both to this court and to Lee's advisers by the Director of Public Prosecutions, these serious allegations were without any valid foundation and should never have been made. The drugs motive theory had been eliminated by January 1980. The man who made the Rover car allegation was not one of those witnesses whom the applicant even contemplated calling. The police had, by May 1980, after exhaustive enquiries, abandoned the Rover car enquiry after being satisfied of the unreliability of the witness who initially gave the information involving the Rover car anonymously.

'Having dismissed the applications in respect of the Selby Street indictment, we enquired of the prosecution as to the course which they would have adopted on the assumption that, following a trial on the Selby Street indictment, that had achieved the same verdict of a jury as the pleas which were offered and accepted. As we anticipated, Mr. Coles informed us that they would have next proceeded with the fire at Troutbeck House on 22 June 1979. This fire was the next in point of time before Selby Street. Detective Superintendent Sagar raised with Lee his involvement in this fire some two weeks after his confession to the Selby Street fire. This fire was the only one of the 11 fires which had not resulted in a fatality. It had, accordingly, not been the subject matter of an inquest and Detective Superintendent Sagar, who first applied his mind to that fire after Lee's confession to the Selby Street fire, concluded that it had been inadequately investigated by the police.'

Lord Justice Ackner then proceeded to detail the case of the fire at Ros Fenton's home at Troutbeck House. In respect of the evidence of my interview with Lee he said, 'Quite apart from the inherent improbability of this evidence being accurate, we heard Detective Superintendent Sagar give his evidence at length, and being subjected to a very competent and searching cross-examination. We are quite satisfied that Lee made his statements in the interviews as described by Detective Superintendent Sagar, who made contemporaneous notes of each interview at the time, and that Lee provided the information in his statements. In short, the statements were voluntarily made and properly obtained. The suggestion that Lee suffered from a mental handicap such as required his being interviewed only in the presence of someone other than the police officer, e.g. a social worker, is not even supported by his then solicitors. They came on the scene within hours of Lee's arrest, knew when the police interviews were due to take place, were even present at some and were provided with copies of statements made by Lee. At no stage did they make the suggestion, nor was it made by the prison medical officer or the probation officer at the prison, nor has there been any application at this lengthy hearing to support it by medical evidence.

'The genesis of this criticism of the police appears to be the article in the *Sunday Times* of 14 March 1982. It was an irresponsible allegation.

'Lee stated in his evidence (before the Court of Appeal) that he did not understand what he was pleading to, he was not himself when he made the plea, he was mixed up and did not know what he was doing. We totally reject this. He had the advantage of very clear and efficient advice. We note in particular that when he gave evidence to us, the suggestion that he pleaded guilty in order to obtain notoriety was never mentioned.

'Returning to Lee's grounds of appeal: (1) We reject his alibi. (2) We reject his allegations as to how his confessions came to be made. (3) There is considerable evidence to support the view that the fire was started in the way he confessed.

'We do not think that the conviction was either unsafe or unsatisfactory. We had no doubts, lurking or otherwise, that Lee was guilty of the arson at 407 Troutbeck House to which he pleaded guilty.'

Continuing the Judgement, Lord Justice Ackner then referred to items of correspondence between Lee, Hull solicitor Robert Gunby and the Registrar of the Court of Appeal in March 1981. The most material paragraph was contained in a letter from Robert Gunby: 'We have now received a letter from Lee in which he requests our assistance, mentions Members of Parliament who are trying to sort out whether or not he did the fires and he then goes on to say that he had done some of the fires but not all of them, and indicates three cases of arson including the Wensley Lodge fire which took the lives of 11 males, which he did not commit. It was no real surprise to instructing solicitors that a letter couched in these terms was written by Lee, or on his behalf, because ourselves and counsel have expressed grave concern as to whether the pleas which Lee insisted on tendering to all the indictments were in every case the proper pleas. This concern was particularly strong in respect of the Wensley Lodge fire.

'We accordingly dismissed the applications in respect of the indictments concerning 33 Glasgow Street; 50 Humber Buildings; 7 Minnies Terrace, Rosamond Street; 9 Gorthorpe; 4 Belgrave Terrace, Rosamond Street; and 2 Belgrave Terrace, Reynoldson Street. Thus, at the conclusion of the first week of the hearing of these applications, Lee's applications to appeal against eight of the eleven arson convictions to which he pleaded guilty, and the manslaughter of 13 people, apart from the near death of a mother and her daughter and the death of an unborn child (Ros Fenton), had been dismissed. Although it could make no conceivable difference to the sentence, Mr. Ognall desired to continue, certainly with his application in relation to Wensley Lodge.

'We asked ourselves whether it was necessary or expedient in the interests of justice, in the light of the dismissal of the applications previously referred to, for evidence to be allowed to be called as to this fire. In view, however, of the public interest which had been generated, albeit by articles in the press which included a number of unfounded and serious allegations concerning the other fires, we thought it desirable to give Mr. Ognall an opportunity to call his evidence. The prosecution having achieved the verdicts which they thought appropriate on the Selby Street and Troutbeck House fires would have asked for the other indictments to lie on the file, not to be proceeded with without the leave of the Crown Court or the Court of Appeal, and this would no doubt have been assented to by the defence.

'It is however, very easy for misunderstandings to arise and we considered that the better course was to allow the remaining three applications to be ventilated if that was the course desired.'

Lord Justice Ackner then described at length the circumstances of the fire at Wensley Lodge. He also referred to the evidence given at both the Inquest and Committee of Enquiry.

'The Committee referred to measurements which were taken under their supervision with a gas cylinder standing on the actual chair used by Mr. Hay. With the hose stretched taut, the nozzle of the blow-torch was seven inches from the ceiling. They concluded, therefore, that it was just possible that there was direct contact between the flame and the ceiling which could have ignited the fibre board. From this we infer that they were satisfied that the length of the flame could have been as long as seven inches.'

The Judge then referred to the occasion when Lee claimed responsibility for causing the fire, using an accelerant: 'I did that old blokes' home at Hessle. I don't think anybody will believe I did, but I did.'

Detailing Lee's claims in respect of Wensley Lodge, Lord Justice Ackner continued, 'On 29 July 1980, in the presence of his solicitor, Mr. Gunby, and his clerk, Mr. Pearce, Detective Superintendent Sagar said, "On 5 January 1977, three days after the West Dock Avenue fire, a fire occurred at Wensley Lodge, West Hill, where 11 elderly gentlemen died as a result of the fire. You have admitted responsibility for that?"'

Lee replied, "Yes."'

The Judge then detailed Lee's evidence which he gave before the Court of Appeal, and the evidence I gave in respect of my interviews with him. The Judge also referred to Lee's comments to Miss Helen O'Shea and her query to him with his reply, 'Because I know.'

The Judgement continued,' We must now return to the scientific evidence, because the contention put forward on behalf of Lee is that the scientific evidence is strongly against the use of paraffin as an accelerant, and strongly in favour of the conclusion reached by the Committee of Enquiry as to the cause of the fire.'

Lord Justice Ackner went on to detail fully the scientific evidence given before the Court of Appeal and continued, that in a well sustained cross-examination, Mr. Ognall established that neither the Coroner's attention or that of the Committee of Enquiry was drawn to two difficulties which confronted the slow burning theory, namely that, although slow burning fires produce a substantial amount of carbon monoxide and smoke, the occupants of Room 11 and 20 immediately above, emerged unharmed by the fire and there was an absence of smoke in Room 11 whilst the fire was developing.

'It was conceded,' said the Judgement, that 'the whole picture had not been put before the Coroner and the Committee of Enquiry. The possibility of the smoke and poisonous fumes exhausting themselves through the ducting was in his (the scientist's) mind, but he carried no detailed investigation of the available ducting in relation to Room 11 or Room 20 above. The question of deliberate ignition was in his mind, including the use of paraffin, it being a common accelerant.

'There is a glaring deficiency in the Crown's expert evidence given both to this court and to the Committee of Enquiry in 1977.'

He continued by saying that, if the scientist had given proper consideration to arson by the ignition of paraffin poured on the floor of Room 11, then he, or others, could, no doubt would, have carefully examined the state of that floor. 'We would then have known the extent of the gaps – if any – between the floorboards, and the nature and condition of the linoleum on that floor. It could well be that either the absence of gaps and/or the state of the linoleum would not have permitted any, or any sufficient, paraffin to drip into the void between the floor and the boiler room ceiling, so as to permit a fire to take place under the floor.

'While we have to bear in mind that it would be remarkable that Lee should have made so many and such detailed admissions, despite the incredulity expressed from time to time by Detective Superintendent Sagar, unless he was the instigator of the fire, we have also to bear in mind that the coincidence of Mr. Hay working below with a blow lamp so close to where the seat of the fire was subsequently found, is also surprising . . .

'We wish to make it clear that we are far from satisfied that he did not set Wensley Lodge on fire. However, accepting as he does and did, responsibility for the majority of the fires, he might have fantasised his part in this fire in order to revel in the publicity which this would, and did, give him. We cannot, therefore, reject the possibility that this fire could have been the result of an accident. Not withstanding his unequivocal pleas of guilty, we are thus left with doubts, the benefit of which must be given to Lee.'

At the conclusion of the Judgement, Lord Justice Ackner said, 'We have made it clear, not only in the course of this judgement, but in the announcement of our decisions as the hearing of these applications continued, that the very serious attacks made on Detective Superintendent Sagar were wholly unwarranted. Being without foundation, this could already have been acknowledged in the Sunday newspaper which led the attack and mounted the campaign. Now that we have drawn attention to the matter in our judgement, we are confident that the criticism of the officer will be immediately retracted. Common fairness requires no less.'

So ended the two-and- a-half-hour Judgement.

I did not expect the Judgement to consider, let alone mention, the newspaper retraction. But I appreciated Lord Justice Sir Desmond Ackner's comments greatly. Fundamentally I am an optimist, and, appreciating that there is a certain amount of common fairness in all men, I thought there would be something of an apology hidden away in the many pages of the *Sunday Times* on 11 December 1983; that being the case, I would not go on with my thoughts of civil action for libel. I was wrong. I had not bargained for the unyielding, unapologetic attitude of the *Sunday Times*.

Chief Constable David Hall telephoned me at the Court of Appeal offices after the judgement and offered his congratulations on the Judge's comments. Word had quickly got back to Hull.

Chapter Twenty Eight

The following Sunday, 11 December 1983, the *Sunday Times* boasted on its front page, '150,000 new readers rise to the quality of the *Sunday Times*'. The front page carried a story under the heading, 'Hitler Hoax – the full story', about the Hitler diaries hoax which continued on page 2. There it was written that on 24 April 1983, the *Sunday Times* announced the discovery of Hitler's 'secret testimony'. 'Two weeks later, the diaries were revealed to be certain forgeries'.

Ironically, appreciating my belief in the falsity of the allegations the newspaper had published about the Bruce Lee case, immediately beneath the Hitler forged diaries story was a two-column item with the underlined heading: 'Bruce Lee' 'On Friday, Lord Justice Ackner called on the *Sunday Times* to apologise to Detective Superintendent Ronald Sagar for "very serious attacks" this newspaper is alleged to have made in respect of his investigation of Bruce Lee who was convicted of 26 manslaughters and arsons entirely on his own pleas of guilt. The judge referred to "sinister" allegations in the *Sunday Times* as to how Lee's confessions had been obtained and how corroboration of his account had been sought. It was an "irresponsible" accusation that Lee had been improperly interviewed by Sagar because Lee suffered from a "mental handicap" which required him to be interviewed only in the presence of someone other than a police officer. The editor of the *Sunday Times* made the following statement yesterday: "Our investigation into the Bruce Lee case revealed major flaws in his confessions. After hearing Lee's appeal against conviction for one particular fire, Wensley Lodge old people's home, the Court of Appeal up held the *Sunday Times* view and quashed the conviction. The court was faced with overwhelming evidence, much of it gathered by the *Sunday Times*, that Lee's confession was untrue. In our original article of March 14 1982, we said that important leads were neglected in pursuit of evidence that could corroborate Lee's confessions. We stated that vital witnesses were not re-interviewed and gave, as an example, Geoffrey Hirst, the fire officer responsible for the original investigation of the Wensley Lodge blaze. Hirst's evidence was entirely at odds with Lee's confession but, at the time of the police investigation, he was not afforded the chance of making his comments known. He was a witness at Lee's successful appeal against conviction for the Wensley Lodge fire. We also took the view that, because of his low intelligence, Lee should have been interviewed in the presence of a third party, such as a relative or a social worker. But only detectives were present during Lee's confessions. Yet his last recorded IQ at the time of his arrest was 68, putting him within the educationally-subnormal range. Unfortunately the judges have turned down applications for leave to appeal against conviction for starting several fatal fires on which Lee's lawyers have independent forensic reports doubting his involvement. But the *Sunday Times* sees no reason to apologise to anyone.'

My optimism quickly evaporated.

So editor Andrew Neil rejected Lord Justice Sir Desmond Ackner's call. In Andrew Neil's opinion the unwarranted, unfounded and serious attacks were justified. I was not surprised at his attitude, but, glancing through the rest of his newspaper, I saw an article under the heading, 'A Plot To Destroy Us,' by George Jerrom, national officer of the National Graphical Association. The article began: 'Your four page Focus of last week deserves to be challenged, but more particularly, what needs answering are the gross inaccuracies in your editorial that went with it. . . .'

I read Neil's Bruce Lee article for a second time and carefully considered what I should do. With a touch of cynicism in my mind I decided, there and then, that the *Sunday Times* deserved to be challenged for the stance now being adopted in relation to their inaccuracies and quite unfounded reports about my handling of the Hastie arson deaths and Bruce Lee. I took it for granted that to simply write to Andrew Neil would be a waste of time. But how could I possibly challenge the big and mighty Rupert Murdoch's *Sunday Times* and win? I would still need to think about it, but, after all, my integrity was at stake. In addition, I owed it to many people to show that, beyond all doubt, my intentions in respect of Bruce Lee, as with everyone else I dealt with, were entirely honourable.

My son was working hard at Leeds Medical School during the whole of the time of the *Sunday Times* attacks. My daughter was studying at Cambridge University and then articled to become a lawyer. Many of their peers were in what the *Sunday Times* described as the ABC 1 social classes and no doubt some, at least, smirked at the stories they read, thinking that Sagar senior was allegedly crooked. My wife, Phyllis, knew well that my intentions were always honest and, to be fair, she had put up with the long and uncertain hours of her senior detective husband often enough without having to put up with the sinister stories circulating in the *Sunday Times*.

However, from the professional aspect, I was very concerned about the men and women under my command for if, as the *Sunday Times* alleged, evidence had been altered or concocted in any way, then there was a possibility that their careers could be polluted by even the mildest cloud of suspicion hanging over their integrity. Equally I owed it to all the many people involved, in one way and another, with the fires: the dead; the survivors; those who had been suspected of playing with matches; those suspected of smoking in bed; and those who, for one reason or another, blamed themselves for not taking enough care or whatever. I also owed it to the police service, the legal profession and to the sad figure of Bruce Lee himself. I had to do something about it.

My resolve was strengthened by the knowledge that every member of the enquiry team during those final weeks of the enquiry when Lee came into the picture offered their unstinting support for they, above everyone else, knew the truth and honesty of purpose we always enjoyed in respect of all our endeavour. Sadly the same could not be said for many senior officers. 'Don't pollute me with anything to do with the Lee business, it might affect my future,' was their continuing if unspoken message. In fact, anyone who thinks that police join forces to protect each other when bad publicity strikes does not appreciate the reality of such problems. In fact, whilst occasionally attempting to seek out the views of my seniors as to the best way forward at this time I recall how more than one of my seniors would tip-toe towards the exits and on through the tulips outside Police HQ in Hull's Queens Gardens.

During 1982, when the *Sunday Times* published their allegations, I knew that word had spread among the criminal fraternity from London to Yorkshire and beyond that anything worthy of an attack on my credibility would be newsworthy,

One day, in 1982, I was at the Royal Courts of Justice in the Strand, arranging to see a judge in chambers with a view to applying for the release from prison of two Sheffield criminals who were, in my opinion, wrongly convicted. Standing in the Grand Hall that day, a prostitute known to ply her trade in the Park Lane area of London approached me and with a smile, said, 'You ain't been sleeping with me and I ain't saying that you have, Mr. Sagar. You put up with a lot of stick looking after my brother and them lads after that Hull Prison riot thing, so nobody is going to stab you in the back now them journalists are after you.' She wandered off almost as quickly as she appeared. She was quite smart and elegant and few would believe her to be a prostitute. No doubt she had some other purpose in the Royal Courts of Justice that day. I was quietly amused and then horrified by her comment and wanted to know more of what she said but she was gone. But the message was clear enough. Thankfully, as far as I know, no one ever came up with allegations of a sexual nature against me. The allegations about my handling of the investigation I could handle, but a personal intrusion affecting my family life would have been extremely difficult to cope with.

During Christmas 1983, just two weeks after the *Sunday Times* publicly rejected the judges' call to apologise, I decided that, come hell or high water, the only way to rectify the situation was to take action for libel. I did not accept the view some people expressed months earlier that the newspaper would probably have a defence of justification. I knew that the Superintendents Association, unlike the Police Federation (which looks after police ranks up to and including Chief Inspector), did not have the funds to support a libel action. I accepted that, should I lose, I would indeed lose everything I had and I would be ruined. Having given the whole process a great deal of thought, I chose to rely on justice being my saviour and take action. The allegations were false.

I began to collect statements from people I knew had been taken in by the *Sunday Times*. I was surprised by what I discovered. For example, on one occasion, in September 1982, Detective Constable Martin Sylvester was dealing with a charge against a juvenile at Priory Road Police Station in West Hull, when an adult, attending the police station with the juvenile, asked the Detective Constable, 'What's your Ronald Sagar doing these days. He seems to be out of the news lately?' He went on, 'Silly man. He could have been a Chief Constable but he'll lose all that now. He's been very silly, he's gone over the top with this Bruce Lee episode. He's gone too far really.' Detective Constable Sylvester replied, 'I can't really comment. I was not on the Lee enquiry, but he was convicted.' The man replied, 'Of course, he was, Sagar made sure of that. Haven't you ever heard of auto-suggestion.'

A man then working at the Hull Salvation Army Hostel in Great Passage Street provided me with a statement saying that the *Sunday Times* reporter told him that Lee had been 'fitted up' for the Wensley Lodge fire. The reporter 'was anti-police and certainly anti-Detective Superintendent Ron Sagar,' the man claimed.

Ros Fenton told me that about April 1981, when I was deeply involved seeking out the truth about allegations of police corruption in Sheffield, a reporter visited her and told her that 'there was more than Lee responsible for the fire at my house'. He had asked her if she would allow him to hide microphones in her home in order that they could tape record a conversation between herself and me. She stated that he wanted her to ask me some questions so that I would admit that others were responsible with Lee for causing the fire at her home. She was told that the reason behind this was to produce a re-trial of Lee in order that, if others were responsible, then it would be brought out into the open. I knew of no one else involved with Lee. According to Ros Fenton, the journalist appeared to know that I was working in Sheffield and later abandoned the idea of bugging her house as someone with the listening devices could not keep himself available until I was back in Hull.

Later Ros Fenton and the journalist went with Ros to the office of solicitor, Max Gold, to ask him to write to the police to request the statements Ros had made regarding the fire at her home which would then be available for the journalist's scrutiny. Max Gold, with his much admired street-wise and legal knowledge, soon realised what was happening and told the journalist that I was straight. Ros Fenton, too, began to smell a rat. Max Gold later gave me a statement confirming the visit by Ros Fenton and the journalist.

Statements in my support were a pleasure to read. A woman who had heard that a journalist was saying that Lee could not ride a bicycle promptly gave me statement saying that she knew Lee and had seen him ride a bicycle as well as anyone else in the district. The three men sentenced to imprisonment, whose convictions I was asked to enquire into by the Home Office and the Director of Public Prosecutions, and who were then found to be the subject of wrongful convictions, also gave me statements in support of my honesty of purpose.

Most people would accept my name was cleared by the Court of Appeal. However, the *Sunday Times* stood by its damaging allegations and in my view the pollution of my character had not been completely dispelled. I was the only one who could put the record straight and the only way to do it was to continue to seek expensive legal advice from an expert in the laws of libel with a view to issuing a writ for libel. The ideal firm of solicitors to handle the matter were Russell Jones and Walker, the well-known London firm, at 324 Grays Inn Road.

Libel is a dreadfully complicated business. I knew that it was for me, the plaintiff, to establish that the matter I was complaining about had been published; that it referred to me and that it was defamatory. I was, of course, able to do so and therefore establish a *prima facie* case. However, I was told that Andrew Neil, the editor, the journalist and Times Newspapers Limited would escape liability if they could show they had a good defence, such as: justification and fair comment. I also knew English law does not protect the reputation that a person either does not or should not possess. Stating the truth, therefore, does not incur liability and the plea of justification, namely, that what is complained of is true in substance and in fact, is a complete answer to an action for libel. The *Sunday Times* would go all out for that answer. In respect of 'fair comment' the *Sunday Times* would need to prove that what I complained of was nothing more than fair comment made in good faith and without malice on a matter of public interest. In my view, 'fair' means honest. 'Fair comment' means, therefore, the expression of the newspaper's genuinely held opinion. It does not necessarily mean opinion with which a jury agree. Comment could therefore be quite extreme and still be fair in the legal sense.

My discussions with legal advisers made it perfectly clear that a libel action is by no means an easy road to travel. Much evidence was prepared for Lee's prosecution and subsequent appearance before the Court of Appeal, but now, due to the unyielding attitude of the *Sunday Times*, evidence of a civil kind was needed. Every moment of each facet of my thinking and every avenue of the arson enquiry now demanded complete exploration. Appreciating that my action could be financially ruinous, the strong tendency I had for wanting to record the truth overwhelmed the known problems of litigation.

Every word published in the newspaper was discussed and thoroughly analysed by my solicitors. In due course it was agreed to take action and I soon appreciated the great care which Hugh Williams at Russell Jones and Walker showed in respect of the problems I was likely to encounter as the action went ahead. He knew well that Times Newspapers and the *Sunday Times* editor would fight the action tooth and nail. And not having financial backing, I quickly learned, was a huge stumbling block.

My advisers noted that neither Lee nor his solicitors ever made any claim about pressure from the police until after the *Sunday Times* decided to publish their allegations.

Many letters and telephone discussions took place in the months that followed, but it was not until 2 February 1984, after receiving more legal advice, and over a year since the Court of Appeal hearing, that I succeeded in obtaining a Writ of Summons in the High Court of Justice, Queens Bench Division against: Andrew Neil, who was still the editor of the *Sunday Times*; the journalist responsible for the series of articles which defamed me; and Times Newspapers Limited, the publishers of the articles concerned. I also obtained an Injunction restraining the newspaper from defaming me further.

At this time I was in danger of becoming depressed, an attitude not at all typical of myself. I had to do something and the only way I knew was by litigation.

Many bundles of paper were needed to support my action, and most of the statements I needed were also part of the Hastie arson and subsequent Bruce Lee enquiry. I could not just use those statements without my Chief Constable's permission, even though his agreement with producer Clive Entwhistle of Yorkshire TV had revealed all the producer wanted to know.

The process of civil law was ultra careful but very slow. In June 1984, I wrote to my Chief Constable requesting his permission to formally release a number of statements I required in furtherance of my action. On 27 June, I received a memorandum from one of my senior officers stating that, if I were to obtain the statements I required, I was to 'delete all references showing use of Humberside Police documentation'. I couldn't believe it. I considered that to delete anything in a statement, for criminal or civil process, would be looked upon as an attempt to pervert the course of justice. In any case, what was the point in deleting any references to Humberside Police? Although I believed I knew the answer, in order to get more backing, I quickly sought my own legal advice on the contents of the memo. As expected, I was advised that I should not alter any of the documents as they were subject to legal process.

Meantime we were in the process of discovery of documents on both sides, and now Detective Sergeant John Martin decided to join me in my action as a client of Russell Jones and Walker. He was supported financially by his Police Federation. He accepted that the defamation was mainly directed against me, although in the one article where he was mentioned it was stated that 'Detective Sergeant John Martin was a key member of Sagar's team.' I was pleased he was now joining me again.

It was ironic that the Police Federation were able to underwrite the less serious allegations against a junior officer, whilst the Superintendents' Association were unable (due to the relatively small number of superintending ranks and lack of funds) to underwrite a claim in respect of much more serious allegations against a senior officer. I was comforted by the libel specialists' legal advice but there was always the knowledge that I was holding out a begging cap.

Many letters passed between me and my legal advisers in 1984, with the solicitors doing everything to cover all that was relevant. *The Sunday Times'* solicitors were quite properly exploring their clients' articles in every possible detail and I could not help but feel that some tactful, and quite legal, delays were being employed. All the time I was pleased by the way the advisers were handling the matter. I also found myself thankful that the criminal law process does not take so long.

I was appointed Coordinator of the Regional Crime Squad in October 1984 and promoted to the rank of Detective Chief Superintendent. Some people obviously thought my reputation was unblemished!

Early in 1985 I received a letter from the Superintendents' Association Secretary enquiring about the present position in my action and saying that 'the whole of the Police Service is watching anxiously at this case which you are fighting, not only for yourself but on behalf of all senior investigators throughout the country. Great concern is being expressed, particularly by senior detective officers who could so easily find themselves in your predicament. Some have expressed an unease and uncertainty in carrying out their already difficult tasks.' The letter ended: 'The Police Service does not easily succumb to outside pressures but it is fact that we are now into the third year of this action and whilst for you, personally, it must be very worrying, for the remainder of the Police Service it is undermining morale. For this reason we must give you every possible support in this action which has repercussions affecting the whole of the British Police Service.'

I appreciated the Secretary's words of support but I needed financial support too, and I did not have any. I still did not have support for using the statements I wanted, either, without agreeing to the nonsensical suggestion that I delete all references to Humberside Police.

About the same time I received an unsolicited note from the Home Office in regard to financial assistance to police officers in legal proceedings: 'It has long been recognised, as a basic principle, that police officers should not be entitled to more privileged treatment than their fellow citizens. On the other hand, their duties may place them in a vulnerable position, and it may be in the public interest for their police authorities to offer some protection.' It wasn't much, but the note did tend to point towards some form of help. I needed to put pen to paper and write to my Chief Constable with a view to seeking financial backing from the Chairman and members of the Police Authority.

Unfortunately, Police Authority Chairman, Councillor Charles Brady, had suggested I be suspended from duty after he read some of the *Sunday Times* articles three years earlier. Several weeks went by before I received a reply from Humberside County Council and my costs were spiralling. On 20 September 1985, the Director of Humberside County Council wrote to inform me that the Committee agreed to indemnify me against my own costs as plaintiff, adding that the indemnity should not exceed the sum of £50,000. It was also pointed out that 'the indemnity would cease to apply' if I discontinued the action.

I was soon to realise that £50,000 was nowhere near enough to cover all my legal costs. I had no intention of discontinuing the action, but, even if I had, I was in an impossible situation as my costs were now well beyond my means. Being an optimist I carried on. As the months went by more and more details continued to be asked for by the *Times'* solicitors. Naturally all this was adding greatly to my costs.

On 7 March 1986, the *Hull Daily Mail* reported that 'the fight to free Hull arsonist Bruce Lee has failed to win him a Royal Pardon. And there is to be no review of the catalogue of fires and deaths for which he was sent to a mental hospital for life. Home Secretary Mr. Douglas Hurd has refused to exercise the Royal Prerogative of Mercy, despite claims that Lee was convicted on inadmissible evidence.'

During 1986, the legal correspondence continued almost daily as a result of the many queries from the *Sunday Times'* solicitors. I began to look at each of the letters I received as additional debt instead of legal help.

In September 1986, I decided to speak to Charles Brady myself without going through the formality of speaking to my Chief Constable first. Mr. Brady told me that in his view he and his fellow councillors spoke for the public of Humberside in agreeing to support me by underwriting my action for £50,000 and he did not consider it appropriate to increase it further at the present. I replied that it is not unknown for wealthy defamers, such as newspaper groups, to manipulate the already intricate machinery of defamation litigation in an effort to exhaust the resources and moral of a defamed plaintiff. There was nothing improper in this ploy, I told him, since if unsuccessful, the additional burden of costs involved fell ultimately on the defendants.

I got the impression that he would possibly consider my plea further in due course. But the delay was causing me a lot of worry and Times Newspapers appeared to know that I was supported financially to a sum now exhausted, which was a mere fraction the whole of my costs. But we were gradually nearing the end of 1986, and still there was no indication of a court date for the hearing.

My solicitors and my libel specialist counsel were pressing ahead as much as they could but the intricacy of defamation litigation in general, compounded by the complexity of the evidence in Bruce Lee's case, apparently demanded time and patience. As we moved into 1987, I found that the *Times*' solicitors were still seeking out witnesses to support their cause. One of these was former Detective Sergeant Peter Nesbitt, who received a letter from them in April 1987. He was one of my officers on the original enquiry but had since left the police service to set up his own business. Peter Nesbitt did not acknowledge the letter but handed it to me for the information of my legal advisers.

As time went on, and knowing the lengths they were going to, I thought perhaps they might call Bruce Lee to support their case. Then, giving it more thought, I knew that they would not do that because they would know that when he appeared before the Court of Appeal he told the judges that I 'had treated him alright'.

In July 1987, the defendants' solicitors obtained a summons applying for leave to amend the Particulars of Justification in their case. This amendment related to approximately 60 additional enquiries which my advisers sent to me for further examination and comment. Theodore Goddard was indeed doing a grand job for Times Newspapers Limited. In a way I welcomed Theodore Goddard's thorough and persistent inquisitiveness about the case, for at least I knew that at the end of it all no one could possibly find something else to allege against me. One of many incorrect matters claimed was that after Lee's arrest I had visited a witness to one of the fires who had moved from Hull to Chatham in Kent. I had last visited Chatham in 1952, 30 years before!

Shortly after I returned the answers to the latest amended defence particulars, someone sent me a copy of an item in a magazine about suing for libel. It read: 'If you have been defamed by the press and you feel like suing, take a long walk and then go and lie down, especially if you are not used to games of chance. A libel law suit today is the most desperate of all confrontations with the law of England, short of strangling the Lord Chancellor.' It was too late for me to take a long walk or lie down. I was in it up to my neck with no possibility of withdrawing my action without becoming bankrupt.

Fortunately, during the summer of 1987, I was fully engaged in an undercover operation, penetrating a major South American cocaine supplying gang in Amsterdam. It involved undercover work on the Continent and in Israel and America, so the natural adrenalin-flowing type of work and the travel involved kept my mind occupied. As the gang members were caught, in a cynical fashion I wanted to thank them for giving my mind a welcome break. I did receive a letter from one of the gang's girl friends in Bolivia. She expressed her thanks for the kindness my colleagues and I had shown her boyfriend, now imprisoned. It was a pleasant change from those about libel.

Why carry on with it? It was a fairly regular question from some people, as time moved on without any sign of a date for a hearing. The answer was twofold: firstly I had a powerful need to clear my name; then, and some may find this odd, I wanted to prove, in the only way I could, in the interests of Bruce Lee and those closely involved in the fires, that all we had done throughout our enquiries was done with the most honourable intentions and integrity. The purpose was to show just that: it was not a gold-digging action.

In August 1987, I was delighted when I was told that the trial for my libel action was listed to start on 5 October. I could at last see the beginning of the end of the matter, but the anxiety about my funding gradually became a heavier burden. My legal advisers wrote to inform me that my libel specialist Leading Counsel, Mr. David Eady Q.C., would have the full brief for my action on 15 September 1987, and my solicitors must have either formal confirmation of my full funding from my police authority by then or my own collateral security. I was told that the trial would take up a period of about ten weeks, that costs were, and would continue to build up to, hundreds of thousands of pounds. I was also told I would go through hell during the trial and I should get myself away from work, fax machines and telephones for a good break and period of contemplation before the trial.

My solicitors were still being presented with difficulties seeking authority for the release of various reports and other documents which they were still advised were the property of the Humberside Chief Constable. Copies of all the papers I needed were in fact by law given to solicitors who originally represented Bruce Lee.

My wife knew that I was taking the libel action, but we were never the kind of people to spend our time discussing my duty problems at home. It was always my belief that my home was a sanctuary from the rough and tumble of my professional life. I certainly did not worry my wife about the financial burden I was now facing either, although I have to say it was becoming heavier by the day. My fundamental optimism was that all would be well in time. I suggested to my wife that it might be nice to get away from my Regional Crime Squad work for a week or so, and, if she would like to have a break, perhaps she could contact a travel agent and arrange a week away somewhere in the sun.

Before that I had to do something about my financial plight, and do it soon. I decided that I would cut through the red tape again and approach Councillor Charles Brady direct. My opportunity came quite quickly when I saw him at a Regional Crime Squad committee in a hotel one lunch time. I told him that the trial date was now set for just a few weeks time, 5 October, and that without his help the effort to clear my name was facing disaster as the costs of the case were reaching hundreds of thousands of pounds. Bless him, he agreed to help. Charles Brady telephoned me two days later to say that he had arranged for the Police Committee to hold a special meeting on 10 September to discuss my request.

Meanwhile, my wife arranged the proposed holiday. She booked a week in the Greek Islands for the week commencing 7 September! I quickly telephoned Charles Brady and told him that I would not be available for the meeting on 10 September. Due to the short notice my wife had already paid for the holiday. Two days later Mr. Brady telephoned me again. 'Just you send me a few pages giving me as much detail as you can about your problem and put as much detail in as you can about the need to resolve the financial situation before 15 September. I'll do my best. I know a good bit about the case because I once discussed it with the Deputy Chief Constable.'

I told my deputy in the Regional Crime Squad, Detective Superintendent John Hope, about the predicament I now faced. I gave him the telephone number for the hotel where I would be in on the day of the Police Committee's Special Meeting and explained that Charles Brady had promised to telephone the Regional Crime Squad office in Wakefield as soon as he had any news from the meeting. John Hope promised to contact me as soon as the result of the meeting was known. We flew out from Manchester for the advised break.

The day after I left England someone leaked my request to the Police Authority to the media. The *Hull Daily Mail* banner headline on 8 September read: 'SAGAR SEEKS AID FOR LIBEL ACTION'. The story detailed my request and told the readers that the committee would be having private talks the following Thursday. The item quoted Charles Brady as saying, 'I will not make any statement until the committee has met.'

In another *Mail* article the heading was, 'LIBEL CASE: WE FACE THE BILL. Ratepayers could end up paying up to £250,000 to finance CID Chief's libel action'. Charles Brady was quoted as saying, 'We will pay whatever costs are necessary to back this officer.' That comment was indeed encouraging, for £250,000 was well below the mark should the trial last ten weeks. Two days later, according to the *Hull Star*, my request was under fire. They reported that a councillor, 'who cannot be named', said, 'I think Mr. Sagar's request is an amazing lottery. If he loses we pay up and if he wins he gets the damages.'

The *Hull Daily Mail* also published a letter from someone with a North Hull address who asked if I would share the damages with the ratepayers if I won. It seemed that some people were much more interested in the damages award than clearing my reputation. No doubt many more would have made their comments known if they had realised that at that time I was trying to relax in the Greek Islands' sunshine.

On Thursday, 10 September 1987, I had an ear for the telephone all day, but it didn't ring. My dear wife did not know, of course, and I did not know at what time Charles Brady's Special Meeting was to take place, but I assumed that, as with most meetings it would be in the morning.

Lunch time came and went, but there was no call from my deputy, John Hope. I began to think that he had heard that my request had been refused and that he did not want to ring me with the bad news. In my anxiety, I did not appreciate either that we were an hour ahead of UK time. But by 7 p.m. that day I gave up and decided that I had in fact been refused help and John Hope would tell me upon my return to England. My wife and I were just about to go out to dinner later that evening when the telephone rang. I grabbed the handset and heard John's voice. 'Charles Brady has just telephoned and he has told me to tell you not to worry because they have agreed to fund your case fully.' I suddenly felt a huge surge of anxiety disappear from my mind. I was completely and utterly relieved. I couldn't wait to see Charles Brady and thank him. 'Roll on,' I said. 'What a relief.'

'What was that all about?' asked my wife when I replaced the telephone handset.

'Well, you may not believe this, darling, but I was facing a debt amounting to well over £250,000 for my *Sunday Times* libel action. But don't worry. Charles Brady and his committee have just agreed to indemnify me.'

'Why didn't you tell me? I thought that we shared everything in this marriage of ours,' she replied. We went out to dinner that night. I don't think I have ever been cross-examined about anything so well in any court as I was by my wife that evening.

Upon my return to my office a few days later, I found that, although the Special Meeting had recommended that I should be fully indemnified, the recommendation had to go before a full meeting of the Humberside County Council. The next meeting was not due until 14 October 1987, which, of course, was too late for my purposes, so I was not yet covered.

Mr. P. R. Wellings, the Director of Administration at Beverley, wrote to my solicitors and told them, that, due to the urgency of the matter, he would make use of the Council's urgency procedure whereby a decision is made on behalf of the Council by the Chief Executive in consultation with the Chairman of the Policy Committee and a leader of one of the other party groups. This meeting was arranged for 1 October, still too late for my solicitors' deadline of 15 September, but it was all encouraging. Eventually my solicitors accepted the situation and waived the deadline to the 1 October. That day could not come soon enough.

The date of the trial now became known by the media and, much to my surprise and pleasure, I found, that, apart from many colleagues and friends, members of the legal profession and several well-known members of the criminal fraternity telephoned to wish me well. I felt quite humble when, one morning, I received a letter from Richard Pooley, a former London criminal and the Founder of Liberty Trust set up in the 1960s. Originally known as PROP (the Proper Rehabilitation of Prisoners), it was organised with a view to seek to care for and rehabilitate mostly long-term prisoners. In his letter. Richard Pooley went to considerable lengths to give me a completely unsolicited and rather sparkling character reference for the benefit of my solicitors at the forthcoming trial. He said he spoke for a great many long-term criminals whom I knew.

I also received a most helpful letter from Dr. Hugo Milne, who had examined Lee in Leeds Prison. His letter was highly supportive of my view of Lee's mental state. Three people who had valuable evidence to give were the Coroner, Dr. Philip Science, Chief Prison Medical Officer Dr. Daphne Sasiene, and Solicitor's Managing Clerk, Mr. Eric Pearce, but by now all three were dead. In particular, the inconvenient timing of Dr. Sasiene's death robbed me of additional corroboration of Lee's admissions as she had also heard what he had to say.

Of course, everyone who helped on the original Lee enquiry gave their support throughout. Detective Sergeant John Martin, free of any financial restraint with Police Federation backing, and Detective Inspector Alan Holmes were particularly helpful with their good cheer and their ability to recall detail.

Meanwhile there was an increasing flurry of activity emanating from the solicitors on both sides. The trial would take about ten weeks I was told once again. 'Be prepared for a real battle!' 'They (the defendants) have now got the formidable Anthony Scrivenor Q.C., you know. It's going to be a hard fought case. I hope you are ready for it.' These were but some of the comments from my advisers.

On 15 September, I received a telephone call from my solicitors who told me that the *Sunday Times* had paid £15,000 into court which I could take and, as a result, drop my action. I refused. Much to the consternation of some, my main concern was the question of putting the record straight. Dangling £15,000 before my eyes, would not include any kind of apology or withdrawal of the allegations.

On 1 October, the Director of Humberside County Council confirmed that the meeting about my full funding had taken place that day and that I was now fully supported financially by the Police Authority. What a relief! The trial was now less than a week away.

On Monday morning, 5 October 1987, various lawyers, court officials, witnesses, jurors, members of the public, and the defendants gathered in the Royal Courts of Justice before Mr. Justice Simon Brown in Court 13, in the High Court, at half past ten. The man at the heart of the matter, Bruce Lee, was not there, nor was he needed.

Mr. Anthony Scrivenor, for the defence, addressed the Judge and asked for an adjournment, as he had a number of matters to attend to before proceeding with the trial. Surely no more delays, I thought. But Mr. Justice Simon Brown agreed to a one-day adjournment only, so I was not too disappointed. I then went to my leading Counsel's Chambers, just off the Strand, and discussed a variety of matters now pending, including a long opening speech which David Eady had ready. We had not been in Chambers very long when a call came through from the defendants' advisers saying that they were considering a settlement to my action. There then followed many long hours of deliberation and to and fro-ing of a variety of forms of written apology between my side and the *Sunday Times* advisers. Our view of the written words of apology apparently proved difficult for the other side to accept.

Returning to court the following morning the defence asked for another short adjournment until 2 p.m. This was agreed by all concerned as time was still needed to reach a settlement, the exact words of apology being the stumbling block.

At 11.30 a.m. that day final settlement was agreed. The *Sunday Times* would withdraw their allegations, pay my costs in full, publish a complete apology and pay Detective Sergeant John Martin and myself substantial damages. Damages, incidentally, that did not amount to the hundreds of thousands of pounds some members of the public suggested.

Finally at 2 p.m. on Tuesday, 6 October 1987, almost eight years after the fire at Edith Hastie's home in Selby Street, leading Counsel David Eady Q.C., stood in Court 13 of the High Court and told Mr. Justice Simon Brown that the actions before him arose from a series of six articles published in the *Sunday Times* between March 1982 and December 1983 which concerned the police investigation into a series of fatal fires in and around Hull. Mr.

Eady then addressed the Judge on the details of the fires, subsequent deaths, the police investigation and the fact that Bruce Lee had pleaded guilty and was ordered to be detained in a special hospital without limit of time. He also detailed the allegations and general coverage given in the many columns of the *Sunday Times*. Mr. Eady also told the Court about the Court of Appeal hearing and the result of that hearing.

Counsel continued, 'The very serious charges against Detective Chief Superintendent Sagar and Sergeant Martin made in the *Sunday Times* were, as the defendants now recognise, entirely baseless. The defendants now accept that Lee's confessions were properly obtained and that Mr. Sagar in no way sought either for himself or by those under his command to tamper or otherwise interfere with or improperly influence the evidence of witnesses. The articles predictably caused the two officers the greatest distress and anxiety which has continued until today.

'However, since the defendants are now prepared to acknowledge both in the *Sunday Times* and in open court today that these allegations are without foundation, to apologise for having published them, and to pay both officers substantial damages and their legal costs in full, they are now prepared to let the matter rest.'

Mr. Anthony Scrivenor, for the *Sunday Times*, said it was now recognised that the criticisms made of myself and Sergeant Martin could not be sustained now that they had an opportunity to examine in detail all the evidence available. The defendants welcomed the opportunity to apologise for the distress the articles caused, he said.

It was now almost eight years since I volunteered to be 'on call.'

According to the media, the day after the libel hearing Councillor Terry Geraghty, then leader of Humberside County Council, said, 'The settlement of the libel case was a vindication of the Authority's decision to stand by Mr. Sagar, now the Regional Crime Squad Co-ordinator. We are very pleased that the *Sunday Times* has been persuaded it was all wrong.'

Throughout the years since Lee was convicted I could not help but feel unhappy for him whenever those, who, for one reason or another, decided to campaign for him. Did they not appreciate that, without any honest-to-goodness evidence, they were simply building up his hopes and tormenting him?

Strangely, when it was all over I did not feel the surge of anger I had harboured against the *Sunday Times* journalist over the past seven years. Instead, I found I could, to a point, understand his endeavour, for who would want to believe that Bruce Lee did all he claimed? Why the journalist did not ask to speak to me about his thoughts before publication I shall never know.

Many times in the past I have been asked if Lee did do all he claimed. Bruce Lee, and Bruce Lee alone is the only one who knows why he allowed me and John Martin into his apparently secret world to tell us all he did. He is also the only one who knows why he chose to plead guilty before Mr. Justice Tudor Evans on that cold, unpleasant January morning in Leeds in 1981.

I would only hope that, in due course, those in the medical world and elsewhere who are responsible for his future will be able to believe what he said to me on Wednesday 15 October, 1980. 'I'll never ever set fire to another dwelling house as long as I live.'